THE LATE GREAT USA

THE COMING MERGER WITH MEXICO AND CANADA

JEROME R. CORSI, Ph.D.

WND Books

THE LATE GREAT USA
A WND Book
Published by World Ahead Media
Los Angeles, CA

Copyright © 2007 by Jerome R. Corsi, Ph.D.

Cover Design by Concord Editorial & Design

WND Books are distributed to the trade by:

Midpoint Trade Books
27 West 20th Street, Suite 1102
New York, NY 10011

WND Books are available at special discounts for bulk purchases. World Ahead Media also publishes books in electronic formats. For more information call (310) 961-4170 or visit www.worldahead.com.

First Edition
ISBN: 9780979045141
Library of Congress Control Number: 2007925850
Printed in the United States of America

10 9 8 7 6 5 4 3

For the millions who,
now for more than two centuries,
have given their last true measure of devotion
to preserve, protect, and defend
a sovereign United States of America.

CONTENTS

ILLUSTRATIONS

FIGURES

TABLES

FOREWORD

THIS BOOK BEGAN when I coauthored *Minutemen: The Battle to Secure America's Borders*.

My research revealed the true extent of the illegal immigrant invasion occurring across America's wide-open border with Mexico. I wrote extensively of the criminal gangs and drug cartels exploiting our open borders and examined statistics and quoted experts, arguing that allowing Mexico's impoverished millions to cross our borders illegally creates an economic threat to our lower-skilled workers and places a severe strain on America's middle class. One chapter was devoted to Los Angeles County Deputy David March—killed in cold blood by Armando Arroyo Garcia, an illegal alien with a criminal record who had been deported three times before the shooting. I documented that Hezbollah terrorists who entered the United States through Mexico are in federal prison today, prosecuted for sending money back to Hezbollah terrorists in Lebanon.

I realized something was terribly wrong when the Bush administration took no action against the thousands of illegal immigrant protestors and their supporters who marched on May Day 2006 in American streets under the Mexican flag. The only conclusion I could reach was that the Bush administration was leaving our border with Mexico and Canada wide open because that was the way the Bush administration *wanted* the borders.

As I worked on *Minutemen*, I came to suspect that President Bush had made a fundamental policy commitment when he agreed to the Security and Prosperity Partnership of North America at a summit meeting with Mexico and Canada on March 23, 2005. More than a declaration of friendship by neighboring countries, the agreements made at the Waco summit were perhaps the reason our borders with Mexico and Canada have remained so porous.

The argument made in *The Late Great USA* is that policy makers in the three nations and multinational corporations have placed the United States, Mexico, and Canada on a fast track to merge together economically and politically.

The goal of this book is to bring the North American integration argument into the arena of full public discourse, where the evidence can be examined, while the pros and cons are debated. A public debate is the only way to avoid seeing a North American Union created through a stealthy, incremental process in which our public policy makers are intentionally less than candid about their true intentions.

I believe that an informed American public will fight to retain American sovereignty, rejecting the globalist determination to merge the United States, Mexico, and Canada on the way to a borderless "free trade" world. Publishing this book will test whether American patriots remain who will resist the movement toward a North American Union.

Jerome R. Corsi

INTRODUCTION

ON NOVEMBER 19, 1863, Abraham Lincoln strode forward onto the field of Gettysburg, some four months after the great battle. The short speech he delivered that day is one of the most enduring statements of American freedom ever uttered.

In that speech, Lincoln observed that the Civil War was a test of how long a nation "conceived in Liberty, and dedicated to the proposition that all men are created equal" could endure.

In these few words, Lincoln captured the historic significance of America. The United States was the first nation ever brought forth to preserve the God-given rights endowed to all people. He also recognized the preciousness of any human institution designed to preserve those rights, especially one created "under God" to be a government "of the people, by the people, and for the people." Before, governments had been created of the elite, by the elite, and for the elite.

That day, Lincoln prayed that the United States of America, so created and so dedicated, should "not perish from the earth."

Today, we again face the possibility that the United States of America may not long endure. Our national sovereignty is in danger of being compromised in favor of an emerging regional government, designed of the elite, by the elite, and for the elite, who are working to achieve global ambitions in the pursuit of wealth and power for themselves.

There are movements afoot in Mexico, Canada, and the United States, similar to those in Europe that led to the formation of the European Union that, if left unchecked, will erode U.S. sovereignty and lead to a North American Union.

But how exactly did the Europe of World Wars I and II—a Europe that was fiercely nationalistic—become the Europe of today? In order to understand the significance of contemporary developments in the United States, it is imperative to compare them to those that occurred in Europe over half a century ago.

The Formation of the European Union

The European Union was formed by people determined to destroy the nation-states that had dominated European politics for centuries. Many European intellectuals, especially in Germany, blamed the two world wars on the rise of nationalism. Those planning to undercut national sovereignty in Europe knew they would succeed only if they kept their true intentions concealed. Any direct proposal to eliminate nation-states—most with proud histories extending across centuries—would have been overwhelmingly rejected by citizens loath to see their national identities absorbed into a "European" consciousness.

Despite these odds, the backers of a European Union succeeded, due in large part to the efforts of Jean Monnet, widely regarded as the father of the European Union. Monnet was born on November 9, 1888, to a French cognac merchant. Discharged from the military for health reasons, Monnet spent much of World War I forging an international alliance between the French and British-led effort to defeat Germany. Monnet emerged from this experience a true globalist who believed that nation-states were ultimately destructive. Monnet believed more European wars were inevitable as long as Europeans saw themselves first as British, French, Italian, or German, and only secondarily as European.[1]

On August 5, 1943, as a member of the National Liberation Committee of the free French Government in Algiers, Monnet addressed the committee, stating:

> There will be no peace in Europe if the States rebuild themselves on the basis of national sovereignty, with its implications of prestige politics and economic protection...The countries of Europe are not strong enough to be able to guarantee prosperity and social development for their peoples. The States of Europe must therefore form a federation

or a European entity that would make them into a common economic unit.[2]

Monnet was instrumental in forging this federation, and he did so by prioritizing economic unity over political unity.

On May 9, 1950, French Foreign Minister Robert Shuman, in a speech inspired by Monnet, announced what became known as "The Shuman Declaration," a plan to pool French and German coal and steel production.[3] Shuman argued that this solidarity would make war between France and Germany "not merely unthinkable, but materially impossible."[4] On December 18, 1951, "the Six"—a group of European nations consisting of Belgium, France, Germany, Italy, Luxembourg, and the Netherlands—signed the Treaty of Paris, formally establishing the European Coal and Steel Community (ECSC).[5] Then, on March 25, 1957, the Six signed the Treaty of Rome establishing the European Economic Community (EEC), commonly referred to in the United Kingdom as the European Common Market.[6]

From here, a series of incremental steps can be traced that moved a European common market into a European regional government. Once Europe started taking steps toward economic unity, political unity followed.

On March 25, 1957, the European Atomic Energy Commission was created by a second treaty of Rome, signed the same day that the more famous Treaty of Rome created the EEC. On October 17, 1957, a European Court of Justice was established in order to settle regional trade disputes. In 1960, Austria, Denmark, Norway, Portugal, Sweden, Switzerland, and the UK set up the European Free Trade Association (EFTA). In 1965, the three already-established European communities—the European Economic Community, the European Coal and Steel Community, and the European Atomic Energy Community—merged under the European Economic Community (EEC) moniker. In 1968, in a move toward abolishing duties at internal borders and establishing a uniform system for taxing imports among EEC countries, the European Customs Union was formed.

Brussels and Luxembourg were selected as the executive sites of the EEC almost by accident. In 1951, Luxembourg's foreign minister had insisted that the European Coal and Steel Community set up headquarters in Luxembourg, but refused to accept any more "Eurocrats." When the Treaty of Rome established the EEC in 1957, Brussels became a "provisional site" that eventually grew into a permanent fixture. In Luxembourg, ECSC committees were established, just as EEC committees were established in Brussels. Over time, these committees evolved into the bureaucratic "working groups" that even today run the executive functions of the European Union.[7]

In 1978, the European Council met in Brussels and established a European monetary system based on a European currency unit (ECU) and an exchange rate mechanism (ERM). Initially the ECU was just used for travelers' checks and interbank deposits. However, the agreement set the stage for the emergence of a common European currency. In 1986, the Single European Act modified the Treaty of Rome and set up a framework for a completely unified European market. Gradually, what began as a limited coal and steel agreement transformed into a common market and a European customs union, with the underpinnings for a European currency.

The Treaty of the European Union, signed in Maastricht, the Netherlands, on February 7, 1992, formed a full-fledged regional government.[8] The flag of twelve yellow stars in a circle against a blue background, first seen as the EEC flag in 1985, became the official flag of the European Union—just as the EU passport supplemented and then supplanted national passports from the various European nations participating in the union. Over a period of fifty years, the internal borders between EU countries were largely erased so European Union citizens could live and work in the EU country of their choice. Over this same period of time, a professional bureaucracy sprouted and grew in Brussels and Luxembourg. On January 1, 2002, the euro was introduced and the traditional national currencies of the participating EU countries were phased out.[9]

Today, some 70 to 80 percent of the laws passed in Europe involve nothing more than rubber stamping regulations already written by nameless "working group" bureaucrats in Brussels or

Luxembourg. Virtually gone is the ability of European countries to set their own policy direction and the ultimate arbiter of justice is the European Court of Justice in Luxembourg, not the highest national court in each country.

In short, Monnet's vision of a future where the nations of Europe would gradually surrender their sovereignty to participate in a regional government had been largely achieved.

The Incremental Approach and the Stealth Plan

The European Union succeeded because its supporters took an incremental approach. While advancing step by step toward a united Europe, they studiously avoided suggesting their goal was to create a "supra-government." What began as a coal and steel agreement advanced to a common market and ended as a regional government—exactly as Jean Monnet had always wanted as expressed in the closing words of his *Memoirs*:

> The sovereign nations of the past could no longer solve the problems of the present; they cannot ensure their own progress or control their own future. And the Community itself is only a stage on the way to the organized world of tomorrow.[10]

In *The Great Deception*, perhaps the most comprehensive examination of the emergence of the EU yet written, authors Christopher Booker and Richard North conclude:

> Even though he had long since been honored as "the Father of Europe," Jean Monnet had always preferred to work behind the scenes, away from the limelight. He knew that, only by operating in the shadows, behind a cloak of obscurity, could he one day realize his dream. What he pulled off…was to amount to a slow-motion coup d'etat: the most spectacular coup d'etat in history.[11]

Although he died in 1979 before seeing his plan for establishing an EU fully realized, Monnet lived to see many events unfold as he had recommended. The original nation-states, including the governments, courts, and parliaments of France, England, and Germany remained, but "only so they could gradually become subordinated to a new supranational government which was above them all."[12]

From this brief history of the European Union, several defining characteristics emerge from which parallels can be drawn to the movement to merge the United States, Mexico, and Canada:

- A highly motivated and passionate organizer
- Economic union as a means to economic growth, which was later followed by political union;
- A desire to foster security and eradicate war;
- A desire to establish a collective consciousness that superseded national consciousness;
- A *de facto* political union that resulted from economic treaties followed by formal ratification;
- The blurring of borders and the transfer of passports from the countries to the "supra-government";
- A reticence to acknowledge the real goals of the movement;
- The creation of a common currency.

Had Germany, France, or Italy realized in 1957 that the Treaty of Rome would lead to a loss of self-government, the European Union movement would have been dead before it started. By 2002, however, most European states made the decision to abandon their national currencies in favor of the euro with little hesitation, despite the loss of national sovereignty entailed in the decision.

Will the same be said of the United States twenty or thirty years from today? If we don't heed the handwriting on the wall, it might very well be.

The Late, Great USA

Abraham Lincoln understood that liberty is precious, so he stood on the field of Gettysburg and reminded people that it was their duty to continue "the great task remaining before us...that this nation, under God, shall have a new birth of freedom." Eternal vigilance, it has been said, is the price of freedom, and just as it was the duty of Americans in Lincoln's day to fight to preserve that freedom, so it is the duty of Americans in our day.

The government established by our forefathers, a government "of the people, by the people, and for the people," was not established quietly. Unlike Jean Monnet, the Founding Fathers were upfront about their goals for the new government they formed. The democratic process and the liberty it brings depend upon such openness. Elites are as susceptible to corruption as ordinary citizens. In a constitutional republic, the power of correction rests with all the people; but the people can only correct that of which they are aware. As the EU experience shows us, secrecy is the great friend of tyranny.

Unfortunately, steps similar to those that resulted in the European Union are being taken in America, Mexico, and Canada. If we do not wish to follow the EU into regional government, it's the duty of each of us to hold our leaders accountable for placing our country's sovereignty in danger. While it would be presumptuous to claim that a North American Union is inevitable, it is equally presumptuous to insist that it is impossible. This book will demonstrate that disturbing parallels exist between the stealth process that resulted in the EU, and the incremental actions being taken by the governments of the United States, Mexico, and Canada to unite our nations into an emerging regional configuration. Preserving U.S. sovereignty is up to those of us who still care about freedom and the nation our forefathers bestowed upon us.

PART I

NAFTA PLUS

CHAPTER ONE

FORMING THE NORTH AMERICAN UNION

"Sovereignty is an anachronistic concept; it has been inherited from an age when kings ruled over their subjects."

George Soros[1]

INCREMENTALISM has proved to be a highly effective way of implementing social and political change. Europe, for example, experienced what might be termed a "quiet revolution" between the 1940s and the 1990s, as European leaders slowly and almost imperceptibly sacrificed national sovereignty for the concept of a European union. The process began with a formal agreement between six countries that established the European Coal and Steel Community (ECSC). As Europe integrated economically, judicial and political integration followed.

North America has its own version of the ECSC in NAFTA and in the SPP (Security and Prosperity Partnership), put into place by an informal agreement between Mexico, Canada, and the United States in 2005. A North American Union is even advocated by America's own Jean Monnet—Professor Robert Pastor, who has proposed a North American currency called the "amero," and who has played a significant role in a number of meetings and conferences, closed to the public, between top American, Canadian, and Mexican officials. Who is Robert Pastor? What would the amero mean for America's economy? What exactly is the SPP and where did it begin? The first part of this book is devoted to answering these questions.

First Steps with Mexico: The "Partnership for Prosperity"

On July 4, 2000, two days after winning the presidency of Mexico, Vicente Fox called for a twenty-year timetable for the creation of a North American common market. Termed his "20/20 vision," which Fox hoped would be realized by 2020, his plan for North American integration was ambitious. Fox called for the creation of a North American customs union, a common external tariff, greater coordination of policies, common monetary policies, free flow of labor, and fiscal transfers for the development of poor Mexican regions within twenty years.[2] Referring to the model of the European Fund, Fox suggested that $10–30 billion should be invested in NAFTA to support underdeveloped regions. An international financial institution such as the Inter-American Development ment Bank would administer the fund. Wasting no time after his election, Fox pushed ahead with North American integration on the model of the European Union.

On February 16, 2001, President George W. Bush and Vicente Fox met at Fox's home, Rancho San Cristobal, in the state of Guanajuanto, Mexico.[3] This was President Bush's first official state visit with a foreign leader, less than one month after taking office to begin his first term. During the joint press conference that followed their meeting, both presidents spoke in general terms about a prosperity partnership between Mexico, the United States, and Canada. President Fox commented that, "We have identified a renewed will for cooperation to design, together with our Canadian partners, a region guided by the search for shared prosperity." President Bush, speaking in Spanish, called Fox a "friend," and noted he felt like he was "among family" when visiting Fox's home and meeting his mother. Then, President Bush said, "I came here today to seek President Fox's views on how we can go about building on our partnership."

Although the Rancho San Cristobal press conference made no mention of any signed agreement, the White House website published a joint statement by the two presidents. The statement referenced a "Guanajuanto Proposal," and an official White House press release claimed we were moving "Toward a Partnership for Prosperity."[4] The last paragraph of the joint statement stressed,

"We believe our two nations can now build an authentic partnership for prosperity, based on shared democratic values and open dialogue that bring great benefits to our people."

President Bush was not the only one who caught Fox's 20/20 vision. Robert L. Bartley, the editor of the *Wall Street Journal*, also decided to lend his voice to the move for North American integration. In a *Wall Street Journal* editorial published July 21, 2001, Bartley wrote: "Reformist Mexican President Vincente Fox raises eyebrows with his suggestion that over a decade or two NAFTA should evolve into something like the European Union, with open borders for not only goods and investment but also people. He can rest assured that there is one voice north of the Rio Grand that supports his vision. To wit, this newspaper."[5]

Bartley concluded by noting that, "President Fox is nothing if not a visionary. Many scoffed at his ambition to unseat the machine that had run Mexico for generations; now they scoff at his proposals on immigration. But over the decade or two he mentioned, a NAFTA with open borders may yet prove not so wild a dream."

At the time, these declarations of support seemed innocuous enough—not much more than an expression of friendship between two neighboring nations. In retrospect, however, the language "partnership for prosperity" should have lit a signal that a move toward more formal economic and political integration was afoot. The phrase, somewhat modified, was to reappear in an expanded form after the tragic 9/11 terrorist attacks later that year.

On September 5 and 6, 2001, just a few days before the 9/11 terrorist attacks, President Fox traveled to Washington, D.C., for a state visit at the White House.[6] This visit got off to a rocky start, however, when President Fox issued a challenge to President Bush to develop a plan for legalizing all Mexicans in the United States by the year's end. In making this suggestion, Fox was pushing an amnesty, a politically unpopular idea that no American president could openly support. In private meetings, the two leaders hit on prosperity as the theme to present as a public summary of their discussions. The idea was that generating prosperity in Mexico might reduce the need for Mexico's impoverished millions to cross the American border in search of jobs. The United States could also stress that Mexican labor was needed for advancing American prosperity. During their discussions at the White House, President Bush proposed an idea he wished to advance: namely, that public-private alliances would be needed to involve private investment capital in the effort to spur private sector growth to develop Mexico economically.

The two leaders decided to term the outcome of their discussions as the Partnership for Prosperity Initiative. The final joint press release called on "senior-level" coordinators on both sides to "draw on the best expertise among Mexican and U.S. economists, businesspeople, and civil society" to develop a concrete plan of action to be presented to the presidents by March 1, 2002.[7] The goal was to identify investments that would stimulate job growth in Mexico, thereby creating an environment where Mexicans could economically survive in their own country rather than illegally entering the United States for work.

Over one hundred experts from the public and private sector attended two conferences held later that year—one in Merida, Mexico and the other in Washington, D.C. According to a State Department "fact sheet" published on March 22, 2002, Deputy Treasury Secretary Kenneth Dam and Under Secretary of State Alan Larson led the U.S. effort.[8] The Partnership for Prosperity action plan identified specific economic investments that could stimulate housing, commerce, and small business in Mexico.

These two conferences assumed that North American integration was for the good of all involved and that defining a path for Mexican immigrants to obtain American citizenship was politically preferable to outright amnesty for the millions of Mexican immigrants already illegally in the United States.

The Council on Foreign Relations Takes Center Stage

The terrorist attacks on 9/11 added the issue of security to the then-emerging Partnership for Prosperity with Mexico. Interestingly, this development even more closely parallels the initial stages of the European Union. World Wars I and II drove the formation of the European Coal and Steel Community—an organization that is commonly viewed as one of the first significant precursors to the EU. Twice in the first half of the twentieth cen-tury, Germany had wreaked havoc on neighboring countries by trying to dominate Europe. Proponents of economic integration— and ultimately political integration—wanted to make Germany's economic welfare interdependent on other nations, specifically France, in hopes that this union would prevent further warfare. That was, at least, the proximate cause. Developments in a re-gional direction led to the diminishing of national sovereignty of all parties involved.

On October 17, 2001, the Council on Foreign Relations (CFR) held a roundtable meeting in Atlanta, Georgia, under the title "The Future of North American Integration in the Wake of the Terrorist Attacks."[9] This was the beginning of including "security" in what had previously been only identified as a partnership for prosperity between Mexico and the United States. Also, the CFR language redefined the partnership to be "North American," thus including Canada for the first time. The meeting proceeded under the as-sumption that NAFTA's "limits have been reached" and that what is now needed is an "institution that thinks about these problems in a continental role."[10]

Since its formation in 1921 from the group of academics who advised President Wilson about post-war Europe, the CFR has seen the formation of international organizations as essential to world peace. The failure of the League of Nations to prevent World War II did not dissuade the CFR about the effectiveness of interna-tional organizations. Instead, the failure of the League of Nations elicited renewed resolve from within the CFR to establish the United Nations after World War II as a "new and improved" ver-sion of the League of Nations. Under the sponsorship of David Rockefeller, the CFR continues today to press for the United States to accept international solutions, including the promotion in the Western Hemisphere of North American regional integration as a necessary successor to NAFTA. Consistently, the CFR has an im-pact on the language and thought around which U.S. foreign pol-icy is formed.

The CFR roundtable held in Atlanta stressed the importance of a transportation infrastructure in advancing the integration of North America:

> The deepening of NAFTA means greater coordination or harmonization of policies. Thinking continentally for transportation and infrastructure would facilitate economic cooperation and integration.[11]

The group recommended establishing an advisory North American Commission to set the agenda for future summit meetings between the leaders of the United States, Mexico, and Canada.

A Task Force on North America's Future

On October 15, 2004, the CFR created an independent task force on the future of North America.[12] The task force was headed by former Canadian Deputy Prime Minister and Minister of Finance John P. Manley; former Minister of Mexico Pedro C. Aspe; and former governor of Massachusetts and Assistant Attorney General William F. Weld. The task force consisted of prominent government officials and business leaders from the three countries, each of whom had an established history of supporting North American integration. The three vice chairs of the task force were all strong proponents of North American integration: Thomas d'Aquino, chief executive of the Canadian Council of Chief Executives; Andres Rozental, president of the Mexican Council on Foreign Relations; and Robert A. Pastor, then identified as president of international affairs at American University.

In March 2005, the CFR task force issued its first report, a chairmen's summary entitled "Creating a North American Community."[13] The Consejo Mexicano de Asuntos Internacionales (COMEXI) and the Canadian Council of Chief Executives (CCCE), two groups also on record as supporting North American integration, issued the report together with the CFR. The CFR intentionally published the report before the trilateral summit planned for later that month in Waco, Texas. The CFR expected the Waco summit to be a defining moment in U.S.-Mexican-Canadian relations and the intent was to issue prior to the meeting the CFR's recommendations of what the summit should accomplish.

The report reflected the consensus of the task force's three chairs and three vice chairs:

> To build on the advances of the past decade and to craft an agenda for the future, we propose the creation by 2010 of a community to enhance security, prosperity, and opportunity for all North Americans.[14]

This was the first time that a specific date was set for North American integration: 2010, only five years forward from the publication of the task force report. Also, the word "security" was added to the prosperity formula. What President Bush and President Fox previously specified in San Cristobal as a "partnership for prosperity" became, after 9/11, a "security and prosperity" partnership.

Building on the theme of a terrorist security threat to North America, the CFR task force called for the creation of a security border around the continent. This was a fundamental shift away from defining national borders as key to protecting against terrorism. In other words, from a North American perspective, the CFR was suggesting that the three North American nations would primarily screen foreigners entering North America. This shift implied that the United States, even in the face of a foreign threat of terrorism, would not rely primarily on a secure border with Mexico and Canada—even to keep terrorists out of America herself.

Simultaneously, the CFR task force suggested that the borders between the United States and Mexico and between the United States and Canada be largely opened in the pursuit of regional economic prosperity. The task force clearly pushed for a North American common market:

> We focus our recommendations on the creation of a single economic space that expands the economic opportunities for all people in the region, and the establishment of a security zone that protects the region from external threats while facilitating the legitimate passage of goods, people, and capital.[15]

Open borders with Mexico and Canada would allow "migration" of "North Americans" (the citizens of the United States, Mexico, and Canada), relatively free passage across North American borders, provided the travelers presented the proper "North American" documents.

The task force supported their North American focus with the following three specific recommendations:

- To adopt a common North American external tariff by "harmonizing" tariffs to the lowest possible rate between Mexico, Canada, and the United States;

- To develop a North American Border Pass with biometric identifiers to expedite passage through customs, immigration, and airport security throughout North America;

- To establish a North American Investment Fund to stimulate infrastructure development in Mexico.

The goal was to transform NAFTA into a European Union–type customs union, to redefine the border as continental rather than national, and to develop Mexico economically as a precondition for integration with the larger, more developed economies of the United States and Canada.

This CFR "Chairmen's Statement" noted that a full report would be issued by the task force, following the March 2005 trilateral summit in Waco, Texas, "to take full stock of the results of the Texas summit and reflect the views of the full task force membership."[16]

The Waco Declaration

On March 23, 2005, at the conclusion of their Waco summit, the three North American leaders declared their participation in the Security and Prosperity Partnership of North America.[17]

With this announcement, the United States, Mexico, and Canada entered into a new era, even if the public of the three countries did not fully comprehend the importance of the declaration. To implement the Security and Prosperity Partnership (SPP), the three leaders decided that bureaucrats from the three nations would create "working groups" tasked with "integrating" and "harmonizing" the administrative law and regulatory structures of the three nations in a broad range of public policy areas. "Working groups" is a term commonly used in the European Union to describe the bureaucratic entities that run the EU from behind closed doors in

Brussels and Luxembourg. Working groups were constituted at the Waco summit to put in motion the creation of a continental set of administrative rules and regulations the bureaucrats in the three nations would use to set continental public policy within the legal structure of their three countries, a feat to be achieved by "memoranda of understanding," not laws or treaties.

The Waco Declaration also included several additional language conventions common in the European Union. When the working groups were constituted, cabinet-level officers in each government were assigned to oversee their work. In the United States, the cabinet members were Secretary of State Condoleezza Rice, Secretary of Homeland Security Michael Chertoff, and Secretary of Commerce Carlos Gutierrez. Yet the Waco Declaration referred to these cabinet level officers not as "secretaries," but as "ministers," a term commonly used in Europe. Similarly, the Waco Declaration said the working groups would report to "the leaders," a generic specification that avoided referring to the president of the United States, the president of Mexico, or the prime minister of Canada.

The White House website archived several photographs of the three leaders, generally with President Bush positioned in the middle, with a backdrop of their three national flags.[18] Three nations working together as one was the subtext of the entire press conference. Mosaics of the three flags were even on display, further emphasizing the three country theme. Also showcased for the first time was a new logo—a stylized map of North America against a blue background with the words "Security and Prosperity Partnership of North America" written across the center. The logo displayed no distinct borders between the United States and Mexico or between the United States and Canada. The logo emphasized a circle drawn around North America, calling attention to a continental vision. This new logo quickly became the official logo of the Security and Prosperity Partnership of North America.

This Security and Prosperity Partnership of North America (SPP) was never submitted to Congress for debate and decision. There was no law passed by Congress, no law signed by the president, and no treaty ratified by the Senate. Evidently, the three leaders never signed anything. So, at most, the legal status of the SPP was that of a press conference. The major accomplishment of the Waco Declaration was to mandate the creation of trilateral working groups, in effect creating a new trilateral government structure of U.S. bureaucrats working behind closed doors with their bureaucratic counterparts in Mexico and Canada.

This trilateral working group structure was never expected to show up on the formal organizational chart of the three governments. This way, if the public or the press questioned what the working groups were doing, the answer was simple—the working groups were just engaging in a dialogue between three countries who are friendly neighbors. The substance of the working group work would be produced in countless boring documents too technical or too legal for the average person to comprehend.

Curiously absent in the Waco Declaration was any distinct mention of the United States of America. Very subtly, the USA was transformed into an SPP partner on a level basis with their two partners in North America. Even in the press conference following the summit, the three leaders emphasized "North America" and stressed their goals as "advancing our common security and our common prosperity." In a twist of semantics, the focus shifted to North America. Gone were distinct references to the three sovereign and distinct nations of the United States of America, Mexico, or Canada.

The Waco Declaration called for the working groups to report to "the leaders" in ninety days:

> Within 90 days, Ministers will report back to us with their initial report. Following this, the groups will report on a semi-annual basis. Because the Partnership will be an ongoing process of cooperation, new items will be added to the work agenda by mutual agreement as circumstances warrant.[19]

This March 23, 2005, Waco, Texas, joint statement ended with a Bobby McFerrin–like, "Don't Worry, Be Happy" directive:

> Through this Partnership, we will ensure that North America remains the most economically dynamic region of the world and a secure home for our people in this and future generations.[20]

The unchallenged assumption was that North American integration was the solution to continental security and prosperity.

The Council on Foreign Relations Advises SPP— "Toward a North American Community"

As promised, the Council on Foreign Relations (CFR) Independent Task Force on the Future of North America issued its full report in May 2005, only two months after the Waco summit meeting.

The CFR report was entitled "Building a North American Community."[21] From virtually the first page, the CFR report declared itself the blueprint for the plan behind the Security and Prosperity Partnership. The final CFR task force report began by referencing the Waco meeting:

> At their meeting in Waco, Texas, at the end of March 2005, U.S. President George W. Bush, Mexican President Vicente Fox, and Canadian Prime Minister Paul Martin committed their governments to a path of cooperation and joint action. We welcome this important development and offer this report to add urgency and specific recommendations to strengthen their efforts.[22]

The CFR task force then openly volunteered their willingness to advise SPP:

> In March 2005, the leaders of Canada, Mexico, and the United States adopted a Security and Prosperity Partnership of North America (SPP), establishing ministerial-level working groups to address key security and economic issues facing North America and setting a short deadline for reporting progress back to their governments. President Bush described the significance of the SPP as putting forward a common commitment "to markets and democracy, freedom and trade, and mutual prosperity and security." The policy framework articulated by the three leaders is a significant commitment that will benefit from broad discussion and advice. The Task Force is pleased to provide specific advice on how the partnership can be pursued and realized.[23]

The CFR Independent Task Force on the Future of North America repeated the earlier statement of the CFR Chairman's Statement that 2010 was an important date:

> The Task Force's central recommendation is the establish-
> ment by 2010 of a North American economic and security
> community, the boundaries of which would be defined by a
> common external tariff and an outer security perimeter.[24]

So, by 2010 the only borders or tariffs remaining in North America would be those around the continent, not those between the countries within:

> Its [the North American Community's] boundaries will be
> defined by a common external tariff and an outer security
> perimeter within which the movement of people, prod-
> ucts, and capital will be legal, orderly, and safe. Its goal
> will be to guarantee a free, secure, just, and prosperous
> North America.[25]

The rationale behind the Waco Declaration parallels the reasons given for creating the EU. Just as economic and security concerns were the ostensible rationale behind the EU, so are economic and security concerns behind the push to create the SPP. Just as venerable nationalist identities were subsumed under the new "European consciousness," so the SPP agreement risks our uniquely American identity in favor of a North American consciousness. While the end result of the SPP is not yet known, much suggests that it may take the first step toward formalizing a union between the United States, Canada, and Mexico. We can gain additional insight into the purpose of SPP by examining the thinking of Robert Pastor, one of the primary architects of what he envisions as a "North American community."

CHAPTER TWO

MEET ROBERT PASTOR

"Instead of stopping North Americans on the borders, we ought to provide them with a secure, biometric Border Pass that would ease transit across the border like an E-Z pass permits our cars to speed through toll booths."

Robert A. Pastor, testifying to U.S. Congress, 2005[1]

JEAN MONNET'S organizational abilities were not the only reason he was regarded as the "Father of the European Union." He was also a gifted intellectual who could argue persuasively for his cause, and a savvy political operator who knew to stay out of the limelight. America has its own such organizer, intellectual, and political operative who has taken it upon himself to foster a North American community: Robert Pastor.

Like Monnet, Pastor is a productive thinker and a highly capable organizer. He has spent time in the trenches of leftist political think tanks, and his name has been on the short list of valued advisors to most every major Democratic leader and presidential hopeful since Jimmy Carter. In the Carter administration, he played an important role in developing public policy toward Latin America. He has now assumed a prominent role in the movement to create a North American community. To further his goals, he has adopted Monnet's strategy of incrementalism—knowing that he must, at all costs, avoid a direct call for the creation of a North American Union. Though he adamantly insists that his proposals will not lead to a North American Union, it's difficult to see where else his efforts could be going.

Pastor and the Panama Canal Give Away

Robert Pastor has a long and established career as a left-wing policy advisor. In what appears to be his first job after getting his Ph.D. from Harvard, Pastor served as the executive director of the Linowitz Commission. Formally named the Rockefeller Foundation's Commission on U.S.-Latin American Relations, the commission got its unofficial name from its chairman, Sol Linowitz, who was a registered foreign agent of the communist regime of Salvadore Allende in Chile.[2] Today, the commission is primarily remembered for recommending that the United States return the Panama Canal to Panama.

Prior to joining the Linowitz Commission, Pastor contributed to a report entitled "The Southern Connection," issued by the Institute for Policy Studies (IPS). The report foreshadowed the Linowitz Commission's argument that the United States should be more accepting of the leftist revolutionary governments then forming in Latin America. Author David Horowitz's *DiscoverTheNetworks.org* called the IPS "America's oldest left-wing think tank" that "has long supported communist and anti-American causes around the world." By its own admission, the Institute for Policy Studies is "an avowedly radical organization"[3] created to influence public policy in a leftward direction. Interestingly, Pastor neglects to mention his history with IPS in his *curriculum vitae*.[4]

In the Carter White House, Pastor directed the Office of Latin American and Caribbean Affairs in the National Security Council. There, he served as President Carter's "point man"[5] in getting the Senate to narrowly vote in favor of the Carter-Torrijos Treaty on April 18, 1978—the treaty that gave control of the Panama Canal to Panama in 1999.[6]

Toward a North American Community

Pastor's political vision is clearly driven by the anti-American strain of thought that is so common in extreme leftist politics—especially the leftist distaste for American nationalism. His vision for the future of North America is very much in line with the vision of Jean Monnet.

Like Monnet, Pastor rejects traditional notions of American sovereignty. In a 2004 article in CFR's *Foreign Affairs* entitled "North America's Second Decade," Pastor argued that the United States would gain by ceding U.S. national sovereignty. "Countries are benefited," he wrote, "when they change these [national sovereignty] policies, and evidence suggests that North Americans are ready for a new relationship that renders this old definition of sovereignty obsolete."[7]

In place of traditional notions of sovereignty, Pastor has advocated the establishment of a "North American community." Such a community would entail "an inclusive identity that would inspire citizens of all three countries to think of themselves also as North Americans."[8] In his 2001 book *Toward a North American Community*, Pastor never used the phrase "North American Union," but he devoted an entire chapter to asking: "Is a North American Community Feasible? Can Sovereignty Be Transcended?" Here Pastor argued that trilateral thinking is "contrary to habit, but essential."[9] Carefully, Pastor follows the lead of Jean Monnet, who learned to suppress any reference to his desire to create a "European union." Monnet realized he could get further by promoting the more politically acceptable suggestion that Europe should form a "European community" that was centered upon a "common market"[10] Like Monnet, Pastor argued that sovereignty is an anachronism,[11] citing public opinion polls that show that the people of Mexico, the United States, and Canada would form a single country if the result was a higher quality of life.[12] What is needed, he concluded, to establish this community "is the nurturing of a regional identity and small steps that would help the peoples of the three countries understand the need for deeper integration."[13]

The Push to Transcend National Sovereignty

Pastor's vision for the North American community is already taking shape, bit by bit. True to Monnet's example, he intends for integration to proceed incrementally.

Booker and North describe Monnet's strategy as *"engrenage,"* or "gearing." His method was to implement a series of small steps, each calculated to advance an underlying agenda best defined as a "steady, relentless pressure" to extend the European Commission's supranational powers. Each small step was seen as a means of gearing up for the next. Each new step was designed to begin with a "small, innocuous-seeming proposal to which nobody could object." The ultimate goal was to assemble a great European supranational structure, even if it had to be done "brick by brick."[14] As early as 1952, Monnet argued that "Europe's nations should be guided toward their super-state without their people understanding what is happening. This can be accomplished by successive steps each disguised as having an economic purpose, but which will eventually and irreversibly lead to federation."[15]

In *Toward a North American Community* Pastor developed his ideas about how North America could benefit from lessons learned from the European Union.[16] Pastor wrote the book to develop an agenda that "would permit the three governments of North America to lift their relationship to a new level."[17] He argued that free trade alone was not enough to integrate the three NAFTA countries into his view of a North American community. Institutional structures that could translate the vision of integration into policies that would modify the patterns of interaction among the three governments were also needed.[18]

In his book, Pastor openly acknowledged that the goal in Europe was to eliminate the sovereignty of the nations participating in the EU.

Pastor's book faulted the EU for creating too many supranational institutions and argued that NAFTA "made the opposite mistake of establishing almost none that are serious."[19]

To remedy this deficiency, Pastor proposed the creation of the following three institutions to move NAFTA toward North American integration. Interestingly, even the names of these proposed North American institutions copy almost exactly the names of their EU counterparts.

1   Create a **North American Commission (NAC)**. This executive group would be composed of fifteen "distinguished individuals," five appointed by each of the leaders of the three countries, for a fixed term. A chair would be elected for two years.

The leaders of the three countries would meet every six months to implement NAC recommendations.[20]

2   Create a **North American Parliamentary Group (NAPG)** composed of legislators from the Canadian Parliament, the Mexican Congress, and the U.S. Congress.[21] The NAPG would replace the bilateral U.S.-Mexican and U.S.-Canadian inter-parliamentary groups created by the U.S. Congress in 1960. The NAPG would propose North American policies. If it concluded, for instance, that a "North American Transportation Plan" is necessary, then each country would need to establish uniform transportation laws and regulations.

3   Create a **Permanent North American Court on Trade and Investment**. This would involve upgrading the current NAFTA Chapter 11 tribunals to a permanent court with appointed judges serving extended terms.

The structures that Pastor recommended in his writings and speeches resurfaced in the task force recommendations of the Council on Foreign Relations' May 2005 report, "Building a North American Community." The relationship between the two documents is not surprising: Pastor was vice chair of the task force and a principal editor of the CFR's final report.[22] SPP working groups today pursue most of these structures, in somewhat modified form.

Pastor openly admits that the report was a "blueprint" for articulating the goals of the Security and Prosperity Partnership of North America (SPP). In his June 2005 testimony to the U.S. Senate, Dr. Pastor informed the Foreign Relations Committee of the link:

> Entitled "Building a North American Community," the report offered a blueprint of the goals that the three countries of North America should pursue and the steps needed to achieve these goals.[23]

These institutions do stop short of being a full-fledged regional government, but there is clear movement in that direction. In defining these institutions, Pastor proposed an executive branch, a legislative branch, and a judicial branch that could easily evolve into supranational institutions.

In order to integrate the countries more effectively, Pastor has also devoted extensive attention to creating "a North American Plan for Infrastructure and Transportation."[24] His focus on this subject set the stage for a NAFTA superhighway system in which intermodal transportation structures will be put in place across the continent.

Pastor has also argued that we should expand the NAFTA visa program into a North American passport,[25] an idea SPP advanced as biometric "trusted traveler" border passes. He recommended the formation of a single North American Customs and Immigration Force, an idea the CFR task force report in May 2005 advanced as developing a North American security perimeter.[26]

In addition, Pastor supported the development of a North American Energy Plan, a proposal that was to be taken up by the SPP energy working group.[27] He proposed a North American Education Plan that would establish regional community colleges in order to solve Mexico's rampant problem of illiteracy and provide funding to support scholarships and research at university centers for North American studies.[28] He advocated advancing NAFTA to a European-style customs union in five years, following another step implemented in Europe along the path to the EU.[29]

Even if these developments are not in themselves a regional supra-government, they form the foundation for what might someday become such a government. Free transportation between the countries of North America, a unified visa, a single energy plan, and other such integrative policies will no doubt create disagreements amongst the member countries. As happened in Europe, it is likely that more comprehensive legal and political regional organizations will arise to resolve future regional disputes. Thus, the Monnet process of "gearing" can be expected to proceed here in North America.

A North American Development Fund

Pastor's writings clearly indicate that there exist at present serious roadblocks to the development of a North American community. In particular, the poverty in Mexico is the chief hindrance to integration, since it is unlikely the United States and Canada will want to integrate with Mexico's struggling economy. To overcome that obstacle, Pastor recommended the creation of a North American Development Fund that would invest $20 billion a year for twenty years, $400 billion in total, to the economic development of Mexico. Again, this idea surfaced in the CFR report.

Pastor argued for the improvement of road infrastructure from the U.S. border to stimulate economic development in the heart of Mexico. Since the signing of NAFTA in 1994, approximately one million Mexicans have moved from central and southern Mexico to work in the sweatshop *maquiladora* factories just south of the border. Rather than seeing this as a serious failure of NAFTA, Pastor pointed out that even at $4-per-day wages, these assembly factories still pay three times the Mexican minimum wage.[30] Pastor felt that if roads were built within Mexico, U.S. manufacturers would relocate to the interior of the country where the Mexican wages were still cheap. "Build the roads, and the investors will come," he wrote, echoing a theme of the baseball fantasy novel *Field of Dreams*.[31] He reasoned that, as a result, Mexico would develop more evenly and the economic motivation to immigrate illegally to the United States would be reduced.

Pastor has written many monographs and studies about this idea, even editing a comprehensive fifty-seven-page study sponsored by the North American Development Bank (NADB), another NAFTA creation.[32] Entitled "The Paramount Challenge for North America: Closing the Development Gap," this study openly admits the failure of NAFTA:

> Mexicans who expected NAFTA to lift their country to a first-world economy were disappointed. Americans who expected NAFTA to reduce undocumented migration have been disillusioned. Canadians who expected that the United States would not shut the border either for security or health-related reasons were disenchanted.[33]

Instead of abandoning NAFTA, Pastor recommended advancing it by pouring billions more dollars into Mexico.

Pastor's plan presents some problems, however. He did not calculate how many jobs Mexico would lose to cheaper labor in China and the Far East. Nor did he consider that Mexico as well as the United States would be swamped with Chinese goods produced by some of the cheapest labor available in the world. Additionally, Pastor failed to realize that the $400 billion needed to build a transportation infrastructure in Mexico might benefit the drug cartels whose bribes dominate Mexico's widespread system of political graft. Moreover, Mexico has a traditional disparity in economic levels—a few privileged families control the vast majority of the country's wealth, while the masses live in abject poverty. The income gap in Mexico is a structural feature of Mexico's economy and society that is extremely resistant to change, regardless of how much development money is poured into the country.

Pastor's dream remains that "North America will illuminate a path for all middle-income developing countries to reach a modern economy through global trade."[34] A globalist at heart, Pastor does not understand that Mexico is doomed to remain poor because it is dominated by a few wealthy families that have no intention of sharing their oligopoly with the masses. The United States and other developed nations have already poured billions into Mexico with no apparent amelioration of Mexico's massive poverty. It is unreasonable to expect a North American Development Fund focused on developing transportation infrastructure in Mexico to work, especially when so many previous equally well-intentioned efforts have failed.

Pastor Calls for a New 9/11 Crisis to Create the NAC

There are other problems with the implementation of the North American community. Monnet had the backdrop of two world wars to make his argument for a supranational governing body. Pastor has no such "advantage." While 9/11 brought security to the forefront of the American consciousness, the effect on American politics was not enough to make Americans seriously consider a supranational government as a means to keep us secure. Pastor has argued that it may take another 9/11-type event to overcome governmental lethargy and establish a North American community.

On October 24, 2006, a Spanish-language magazine published an interview with Pastor. This Spanish-language interview made some positions more clear than did the more carefully crafted English statements. Pastor made it clear that many conservative critics were mistaken in their criticisms. He correctly distinguished that he had never called for the creation of a North American Union, and that those who claim such are in error. When pressed, Pastor made it clear that his main objections to a North American Union were pragmatic. He explained, "For now, none of the three governments has the political capability, the willingness, or the imagination for undertaking important North American initiatives."[35]

Pastor went on to explain that at the time of the interview, late 2006, he was frustrated at the lack of progress the North American leaders had made toward regional integration. He was concerned that little progress toward his goal would be accomplished as long as Canada had a minority government, Mexico had a government involved with confronting what amounts to a leftist insurgency, and the United States had a "lame duck" president on the way out whose principal preoccupation is the war in Iraq and the instability in the Middle East. "Because of this," Pastor told the magazine, "my proposals are not viable in the short term." Still, he did not seem ready to give up. "I believe that the question should better be if the proposals are desirable in the long run and how we begin to construct a coalition that backs them if, in the end, they are desirable."

Pastor went one step further. When asked how such a coalition could be created, Pastor suggested a new crisis on the magnitude of 9/11 might advance his North American agenda. Crises, Pastor explained, can force decisions that otherwise would not be made. "The 9/11 crisis made Canada and the United States redefine the protection of their borders," he stated. "The debt crisis in Mexico forced the government to adopt a new economic model. The crises oblige the governments to make difficult decisions."[36]

World Net Daily called Pastor in his office at American University and conducted a telephone interview to make sure his statements published in the Spanish-language publication accurately reflected his views. He affirmed that the Spanish interview did represent his thinking.

"What I'm saying is that a crisis is an event which can force democratic governments to make difficult decisions like those that will be required to create a North American community," Pastor told *WND*. "It's not that I want another 9/11 crisis, but having a crisis would force decisions that otherwise might not get made."[37]

"When there's a crisis, people accept proposals they wouldn't have otherwise accepted," Pastor explained to *WND*. "The Europeans facing the crisis of two world wars turned to the European community as a means to prevent war and advance their economic interests. The United States turned to the Marshall Plan when faced with the crisis of Western Europe falling into the hands of communism. So, I'm not advocating, or encouraging, or wanting a crisis, I'm only saying that in order to take important initiatives sometimes one manner in which this occurs is when there is a crisis to which leaders need to respond."

Pastor's position that a crisis may be needed to move plans forward seems inconsistent with his other stated plan for integration. In the same interview, he made it clear that he sees the process to integration as incremental. "What I am recommending is a series of functional steps that are more than incremental," Pastor admitted. "Each of the proposals I have laid out represent more than just small steps. But it doesn't represent a leap toward a North American Union, or even to some confederation of any kind. I don't think either is plausible, necessary, or even helpful to contemplate at this stage."[38]

Pastor made it clear, however, that full political integration is only a bad idea *right now* because "people…immediately begin to fear that their sense of America would disappear. Somehow if you're fearful that America's sovereignty will disappear, you won't even take small steps forward."

The interview brought to light some interesting parallels between Jean Monnet and Robert Pastor. Pastor wants integration without political union, but only because some people aren't ready to have the sovereignty of their nation undercut by a supra-regional government. At the same time, he appears to be working toward a *de facto* North American body. Once a North American Union is created, further governmental structures would be necessary in order to protect and preserve such a body. The development of such a community places American sovereignty at risk.

North American Students Trained for Merger

Pastor is not sitting idly waiting for disaster to hit. In order to fight the idea of "America" that makes people "fearful of losing American sovereignty," he has moved beyond political action into education. At American University in Washington, D.C., he teaches a class entitled "North America: A Union, Community, or Just Three Nations?" in the Center for North American Studies, which he directs. Among the center's four stated goals are to "instill in a new generation of leaders and the public a novel way of thinking about themselves and their neighbors, not just as citizens of their countries but also as residents of North America."[39]

Additionally, the Center for North American Studies sponsors a summer institute. The brochure for the program includes a photograph of Dr. Pastor and the students posing before a lawn marker with the words "The American University" inscribed in the stone. Above the stone monument the students hold a printed sign that reads "North," so that the modified inscription reads "The North American University."

Finally, Pastor is on the board of the North American Forum on Integration (NAFI), a nonprofit organization that annually holds a mock trilateral parliament for one hundred selected students drawn from ten universities in the United States, Canada, and Mexico. According to the NAFI website, the exercise is designed "to raise awareness among future North American leaders regarding regional integration issues" and to allow the students "to develop their sense of a North American identity."[40] Rotated each year between the three countries, NAFI bills the mock parliament as "Triumvirate—the only North American model parliament." The participating students role-play as parliamentary legislators and newspaper and television journalists. A variety of issues pertinent to the formation and operation of a North American community are debated by the mock parliament, including expanding immigration, stimulating investment in Mexico, and revising NAFTA. Pastor is committed to engendering a "North American identity" in the lives of American young people.

The Influence of Pastor

At first glance it is tempting to dismiss Dr. Pastor as one of many frustrated academics with no influence on the real world. Such a dismissal would, however, fail to do justice to his impressive credentials. Pastor is no ivory tower academic. He has had the ear of presidents, ranking Mexican government officials, and at least one Republican senator.

Consider Pastor's credentials from early in his career. Not only did he sit as executive director on the Linowitz Commission, which recommended returning the Panama Canal to Panama, but he was Carter's representative in making the treaty that actually returned it.

This position and his role in giving away the Panama Canal would eventually come back to haunt Pastor. In December 1993, President Clinton nominated Pastor U.S. ambassador to Panama. While Pastor's nomination had been approved by a 16-3 vote in the Senate Foreign Relations Committee, the nomination failed and he was withdrawn by the administration in February 1995, after Senator Jesse Helms swore to prevent a Senate vote on Pastor's nomination. Helms, who had vehemently opposed handing over the Panama Canal, placed much of the blame squarely on Pastor. Helms declared that Pastor "presided over one of the most disastrous and humiliating periods in the history of U.S. involvement in Latin America."[41] In addition, Helms claimed that Pastor bore responsibility for "a Carter administration cover-up of alleged involvement by Nicaragua's Sandinista government in arms shipments to leftist rebels in El Salvador."[42]

Pastor's Communist Coauthor

In 1989, Pastor coauthored a book entitled *Limits to Friendship* with his long-time friend, Jorge G. Castañeda, who began his career as a member of the Mexican Communist Party.[43]

Castañeda, a lifelong admirer of the radical left, published a 1998 biography complimentary of the revolutionary "hero" Che Guevara.[44] Castañeda, like Pastor, has sought to work in government positions to implement his theories. Not satisfied to be a political scientist who writes books and teaches at universities, Castañeda has had a varied career as a government employee, author of more than a dozen books, and a university professor at various times on the faculties of the University of California at Berkeley, Princeton University, New York University, as well as El Colegio de México, where he taught international relations.

Castañeda and Pastor traded homes while writing their book. They wrote separate chapters on the North American situation, coauthoring only the final chapter. Aside from its format, however, the content is typical integrationist fare, arguing that economic integration is good for everyone. "The United States...should demonstrate to the left in the region that it can live with genuine social change or revolutionary regimes,"[45] etc.

More important even than the book are Castañeda's political connections. For instance, he served as President Vicente Fox's foreign minister when Fox and President George W. Bush met at Rancho San Cristobal on February 16, 2001. As mentioned in the previous chapter, at that meeting Fox and Castañeda discussed the EU and got from Bush a statement conceding the need to "consolidate a North American economic community whose benefits reach the lesser-developed areas of the region and extend to the most vulnerable groups in our countries." At this meeting, Fox pressed for open borders and for the creation of a compensation fund to help the poor of Mexico.[46]

The Guanajuato meeting marked the crossing of a threshold on the way to developing the Security and Prosperity Partnership of North America. It is not surprising that Robert Pastor's good friend was present at that meeting. Castañeda also traveled with President Fox on his three-day state visit to pre-9/11 Washington.[47] While it is unclear what Castañeda's role in this second meeting was, it is intriguing that he was present in both the conversations that laid the basic framework for the emergence of the SPP. While it is impossible to tell how much of these decisions derive from Pastor's influence, the link between coauthors Pastor and Castañeda is at least suggestive.

Pastor Impacts Presidential Politics

Dr. Pastor's nineteen-page *curriculum vitae* on the website of American University documents his service as an advisor to every Democratic Party presidential candidate for three decades, since he first supported Jimmy Carter in 1976.[48]

In 2004, Pastor declared his support for presidential candidate John Kerry.[49] At the National Press Club on October 6, 2004, Pastor commented, "I have traveled in many parts of the world in the last few years. I don't recall a time when so many friendly people told me that they don't like the United States anymore."

Citing public opinion polls as his proof, Pastor claimed that this attitude was President George W. Bush's fault. "Our friends are distressed with President Bush's arrogance and unilateralism," he explained. Pastor, who had served as a Peace Corps volunteer in Malaysia, worried that four more years of a Bush presidency would "irrevocably stain the image and the influence of the United States in the world," so that "we will never again be safe—no matter how strong."

Had John Kerry won the 2004 presidential election, Robert Pastor would likely have emerged with a government position from which he could have pursued his agenda. Kerry might even have restored him to the National Security Council, where he could have directed the activities of the Security and Prosperity Partnership of North America.

Senator Cornyn Advances Pastor's Plan

Pastor's influence extends even to the office of an otherwise conservative Republican senator from Texas. Though the move attracted little public attention at the time, on October 7, 2004, Senator John Cornyn (R-TX) introduced a bill in the U.S. Senate (S. 2491) that authorized the president "to negotiate the creation of a North American Investment Fund that was distinct from the North American Development Bank."

The move did not escape Pastor's attention. He called S. 2491 "a far-reaching bill that incorporates lessons from Europe and proposes to channel funds from all three governments toward infrastructure and education in Mexico."[50] He was pleased to see his pet project introduced to Congress, especially since a conservative Republican Party senator from a state adjoining Mexico introduced the bill. The language of Cornyn's bill was so close to Pastor's own writings that many suspected Pastor had worked directly with Senator Cornyn in developing the proposed legislation. "The senator is aware," Pastor commented in a published paper, "that few of his colleagues understand the necessity and urgency of such a fund, but he introduced the bill to begin the debate."[51]

Pastor was so excited that Senator Cornyn had introduced this cornerstone proposal to Congress that he commented on the move extensively when he testified before a subcommittee of the U.S. Senate Foreign Relations Committee on June 9, 2005. Pastor's comment quoted here also connects the CFR task force he co-chaired in May 2005:

> The Council Task Force proposed serious reforms by Mexico coupled with a North American Investment Fund, which was also proposed by Senator John Cornyn. This is a far-sighted initiative that deserves the support of this Committee and Congress. I have written a report [for the North American Development Bank] explaining the need for such a Fund and the way it would work.[52]

Senator Cornyn reintroduced S. 3622, titled the "North American Investment Fund Act," to the 109th Congress on June 29, 2006.

In July 2006, *World Net Daily* began to investigate S. 3622, pointing out to Senator Cornyn's staff that the passing of this legislation put a key piece of Robert Pastor's North American community in place. On Friday, July 21, 2006, *WND* informed Senator Cornyn's office that a content analysis of S. 3622 and the various writings of Dr. Robert Pastor showed similarities in content and wording to Dr. Pastor's writing. *WND* told the senator's office that the correlation was so strong that a conclusion could be reliably drawn that the person drafting and proposing the legislation drew from Dr. Pastor's writings and intended to advance Dr. Pastor's political agenda.

For instance, in addressing the Standing Committee on Foreign Affairs and International Trade of the House of Commons in Ottawa, Canada, on February 7, 2002, Dr. Pastor presented his recommendation that a North American Development Bank be created:

> The three leaders [of Canada, Mexico, and the U.S.] should establish a North American Development fund, whose priority would be to connect the U.S.-Mexican border region to central and southern Mexico. If roads were built, investors would come, immigration would decline, and income disparities would narrow. If Mexico's growth rate leaped to twice that of its neighbors, the psychology of the relationship would be changed.[53]

World Net Daily compared this to S. 3622, which in Section 4, "Projects Funded," stated as the first purpose of the fund "to construct roads in Mexico to facilitate trade between Mexico and Canada, and Mexico and the United States." Section 4, part (b)(2) of S. 3622 further specified: "PRIORITY—in selecting grantees to carry out projects in subsection (a)(1), priority should be given to projects in the interior and southern regions of Mexico that connect to more developed markets in the United States and Canada."

When Pastor's proposal surfaced in the May 2005 CFR task force report, the name had evolved to the "North American Investment Fund," identical to the title of S. 3622. On page fourteen, the CFR report stated:

> The United States and Canada should establish a North American Investment Fund to encourage private capital flow into Mexico. The fund would focus on increasing and improving physical infrastructure linking the less developed parts of Mexico to markets in the north, improving primary and secondary education, and technical training in states and municipalities committed to transparency and institutional development.[54]

Section 4(a)(2) of S. 3622 identified a secondary purpose of the fund proposed by Senator Cornyn: "to encourage the development and improve the quality of primary, secondary, and post-secondary education throughout Mexico," a purpose consistent with the intent and language of the CFR task force report.

On Monday, July 24, 2006, Senator Cornyn's office notified *WND* that the senator had decided to back away from the bill he had submitted. Rather than withdraw the bill, he sought assurance from the Senate Foreign Relations Committee that no action would be taken on S. 3622 in the 109th Congress. The bill expired at the end of the 109th Congress.

"Senator Cornyn has no intention of filing the bill again," a spokesman for Cornyn told *WND*, "until after we have conducted an internal review and inquiry." The spokesperson further clarified that "Senator Cornyn is adamantly opposed to any North American Union being formed like the EU has been formed in Europe."[55]

While the response by Cornyn's office is clearly an attempt to distance the senator from Pastor, the connection may be stronger than the senator cares to admit. The brochure for Robert Pastor's Center for North American Studies 2005 summer institute featured a photograph of Senator John Cornyn delivering a speech to the students on the North American Development Fund.[56] Such evidence indicates that Cornyn's bill was at least influenced by Pastor's ideas.

Pastor is clearly at the forefront of the push to integrate Mexico, the United States, and Canada. His ideas and proposals, formed in leftist political think tanks, have an impact on major policy proponents. Not only was his work on the CFR task force report responsible for guiding the decisions of the SPP, but he cowrote a book with the advisor to President Vicente Fox, who worked toward the creation of the SPP. He is actively involved in educating young people to view themselves as "North Americans," in order to eliminate the distasteful "American nationalism" that makes people hesitant about taking steps to give away American sovereignty. The anti-American streak that influenced Pastor's early politics under girds his later politics, only in different form.

Pastor might as well be taking his cues directly from Jean Monnet, father of the European Union. He openly advocates an incremental approach to a North American community, but will not call it a North American Union. At the same time, he exerts what influence he has (and doubtlessly works to gain more!) to move America forward with integration as its chief North American policy. If Bill Clinton thought highly enough of him to appoint him ambassador to Panama, what will happen if the

Clinton family wins their second presidency? Will Barack Obama turn to him for advice?

If Pastor has his way, the economic, legal, and executive capacities of Mexico, the United States, and Canada will fuse in such a way that a North American community develops. Such a community depends upon the diminishing of national identities even though it will preserve the sovereignty of each nation. It is an open question, however, whether it will preserve the sovereignty of each nation as it currently is, or as Pastor sees it. Either way, it is clear that if a communal union is established, the barriers to establishing a full political union will be few. If that occurs, it is clear that citizens of the resulting union will hail Pastor as its father.

Among Pastor's key recommendations is that we establish the amero. The amero is a regional currency designed to replace the U.S. dollar, the Canadian dollar, and the Mexican peso, much as the euro has replaced the currencies of the participating European Union nations. Is the amero a viable idea or simply an academic musing? This is a key question in determining whether Pastor's ideas are best seen as harmless speculation or as the precursors to public policy that has a real chance of being implemented. To answer this question, we are next going to turn our attention to understanding what the amero proposal is all about and to asking the likelihood that the amero could ever become North America's regional currency.

CHAPTER THREE

THE AMERO

"On the day the North American Monetary Union is created—perhaps on January 1, 2010—Canada, the United States, and Mexico will replace their national currencies with the amero."

Herbert G. Grubel, "The Case for the Amero," 1999[1]

THE QUESTION OF A UNIFIED CURRENCY is one of the more contentious aspects of a prospective North American Union. Whether such a currency will ever be adopted, and how, is a matter of some speculation. But it is clear that those who favor a supranational government along the lines of the EU see a unified currency as essential. Not only do they believe that it would facilitate everyday financial transactions, but they argue it would help foster the "North American consciousness" so valued amongst NAU enthusiasts.

However, rather than embrace "dollarization"—the practice already occurring in many Latin American nations of adopting the U.S. dollar as a country's currency—globalist scholars argue that a new currency, the amero, must be created. Even before 2002, when the euro was finally adopted by a number of the European Union countries, academics in the United States and Canada were actively discussing the need to create a North American Monetary Union.

These academics are not the ivory tower type, either. One, we are already well-acquainted with. The other is well known in Canada, where he was elected to Parliament. Both have influenced national and international policy in the past, and will likely do so in the future.

Herbert Grubel's Arguments for the Amero

Economist Herbert G. Grubel of the Simon Fraser Institute in Vancouver, British Columbia, Canada, coined the term "amero" and has led economic thinking about the advantages of a unified North American currency. Grubel is an eminently qualified economist; he holds a Ph.D. in economics from Yale University. He has taught at Stanford, the University of Chicago, and the University of Pennsylvania. He was a Reform Party Member of Parliament in Ottawa for Capilano-Howe Sound from 1993 to 1997. From 1995 to 1997, he served as finance critic in Parliament. He has published twenty-seven books and more than 130 professional articles in economics, international trade, and finance.[2] He is a professor of economics (emeritus) at Simon Fraser University in Vancouver. If nothing else, Grubel has had a successful career both in academics and government. His thinking should be expected to affect public policy in economics and international trade.

In a 1999 paper entitled, "The Case for the Amero: The Economics and Politics of a North American Monetary Union,"[3] Gruber explained his plans for creating the amero. He took pains to argue that the innovation would not necessarily erode national sovereignty. He suggested printing the new currency with the amero symbols on one side and the national emblems on the other side. The amero, however, would have its own value on foreign exchange markets, after the three countries converted their currencies into the amero "at rates that leave unchanged each country's real income, wealth, and international competitiveness at the time of conversion."[4]

Grubel proposed, as an example, a plan to convert to the amero in 2010.

> On the day the North American Monetary Union is created—perhaps on January 1, 2010—Canada, the United States, and Mexico will replace their national currencies with the amero. On that day, all American dollar notes and coins will be exchanged at the rate of one U.S. dollar for one amero. Canadian and Mexican currencies will be exchanged at rates that leave unchanged their nations' competitiveness and wealth. In all three countries, the prices of goods and services, wages, assets, and liabilities

will be simultaneously converted into ameros at the rates
at which currency notes are exchanged.[5]

Ironically, this coincides with the Council on Foreign Relations
task force's report "Building a North American Community,"
which suggests that same date as a target for putting in place the
basic institutions required for a new regional government.[6]

At the same time, Grubel proposed a North American central
bank that would replace the national central banks of the three
countries and a board of governors that would be chosen to reflect
the economic importance and the population of the three countries.
Almost as an aside, Grubel mentions an important rule: "As in Europe, membership in the union will require that countries do not
incur persistent budget deficits."[7] While the United States should
reduce federal budget deficits, this provision presupposes that the
board of governors of that regional bank would have supremacy
over the U.S. Treasury, such that the North American Central Bank
could dictate specific U.S. budget deficit reductions as a condition
of continuing to participate in the continental banking and currency structure. In other words, this suggestion would clearly im-
pinge on the U.S. Treasury's sovereignty.

Grubel argued that creating the amero would yield several
important benefits, including a reduction in the "size and risk of
foreign-exchange operations engaged in by banks, firms, and
travelers as part of their routine economic activities."[8] In a highly
technical analysis, he argued that the U.S., Canada, and Mexico
constitute an "optimal currency area," which economists feel jus-
tifies the creation of a common currency across the region. That
common currency would then fluctuate in value on world currency exchanges, establishing a currency value for the amero
across North America. The argument is similar to reasoning that
each individual state in the United States is too small an entity
and not sufficiently distinct, such that each individual state
should not have its own currency. Instead, the "optimal currency
area" has been the United States as a whole. Thus, Grubel's basic
argument is that North America is now the optimal currency
area, and as such the common currency should be a North

American currency designed to replace the U.S. dollar, the Canadian dollar, and the Mexican peso.

Robert Pastor Promotes the Amero

While Grubel is the leading proponent on the Canadian side of the border, not surprisingly, Robert Pastor is leading the charge in America. In his 2001 book *Toward a North American Community*, Robert Pastor endorses the concept of the amero. Along the way, Pastor rejects "dollarization" as the method for obtaining a North American Monetary Union. Under dollarization, Mexico and Canada would simply link or replace their currencies with the U.S. dollar, as several Central and South American countries have already done.

Pastor openly acknowledges that the idea of abandoning the dollar will be unpopular in the United States. He also understands that the United States economy dominates the North American market and, as such, the United States has less to gain by abandoning the dollar to a new currency that would incorporate Canada and Mexico in a monetary union. Still, Pastor argues that in the long run the concept is "fair" in that the introduction of the amero "does not alter the relative power equation in North America, but it provides space for our neighbors to participate in decision making."[9] Pastor compares "the essence of the idea" with how Woodrow Wilson and Franklin D. Roosevelt envisioned international organizations that allowed decision-making space for all participating nations on an equal basis, regardless of their relative strength or size. For this reason, Pastor urged readers not to dismiss the idea, but to consider that "in the long term, the amero is in the best interests of all three countries."[10]

As early as 2002, in a speech given to the Trilateral Commission, Dr. Pastor recommended the amero. In that speech he argued that Mexicans and Canadians were ambivalent about adopting the American dollar, "but they are more willing to become part of a single country of North America and of a unified currency like the amero, proposed by Herbert Grubel."[11] Pastor argued that "at the outset, the wealth of all three countries would be unchanged, and the power to manage the currency would be roughly proportional to the existing wealth." He then continued in uncharacteristically unguarded fashion, expressing hostility toward the concept of national sovereignty. Pastor argued that the peoples of the three nations would be more willing to accept a new unified currency than to enter into a new regional government. "The three governments remain zealous defenders of an aging concept of sovereignty," Pastor told the Trilateral Commission, "whereas the people seem ready to entertain new approaches."[12]

A Coming Dollar Collapse?

The arguments to implement the amero gain strength as the dollar continues to weaken. With our large trade and federal budget deficits, a fiscal crisis is building for the dollar. Other nations are increasingly diversifying their foreign exchange holdings into the euro. In late 2006, the dollar hit a twenty-month low against the euro. For the year, the dollar fell approximately 11.5 percent versus the euro, 13.6 percent versus the British pound, and 7.3 percent versus the Swiss franc.[13]

Even as the stock market hit new record highs almost every day during the end of 2006 and the beginning of 2007, the Federal Reserve and Treasury Department were quietly coordinating a devaluation of the dollar that the Bush administration hoped would make its value decline slowly, rather than collapse.

On November 10, 2005, the Federal Reserve announced that it planned to stop publishing M3 data. Professional economists consider M3 the broadest measure of the U.S. money supply, including checking and savings accounts, cash, time deposits, and money market funds. In a technically worded March 2006 announcement, the Federal Reserve stated simply that "M3 does not appear to convey any additional information about economic activity that is not already embodied in M2 and has not played a role in monetary policy for many years." The Federal Reserve decided that M3 data would no longer be published because "the costs of collecting the underlying data and publishing M3 outweigh the benefits."[14]

The Fed's decision shocked many professional economists. Milton Friedman, one of the key economists contributing to the conservative theories that led to the development of "Reaganomics," argued that money supply is a key measure correlated both with economic growth and inflation. Many economists felt that, by not releasing M3 data, the Fed was giving itself even greater license to print money. The Fed has the ability to increase liquidity by manipulating the supply of money available in the United States and around the world. Surplus liquidity is virtually assured when interest rates are kept artificially low by the Fed, allowing credit to be readily available such that borrowing flows freely under relaxed rules of credit worthiness.

Many economists feared that a sustained liquidity surge might be the Fed's formula for prolonging economic expansion in the United States and for floating our growing trade and budget deficits. By not publishing M3, the Fed could more easily increase the money supply under the radar of public scrutiny.

John Williams, an economist who writes a popular blog, "Shadow Government Statistics,"[15] decided to reconstruct M3 data by working to compile the measure from statistics the Fed and others continued to publish.

Williams is a consulting economist in Whitehouse Station, New Jersey. For more than twenty years, Williams has provided highly accurate forecasts and analyses on U.S. economic activity and interest rates to private investors and Fortune 500 companies. Early in his career, Williams found it necessary to become a specialist on the quality of government statistics and alternative measures, in order to provide meaningful and reliable information for his clients. Williams holds an MBA from Dartmouth College, where he was the Edward Tuck Scholar.[16]

At the end of 2006, Williams reported that M3 was growing at close to 9.6 percent and trending higher, compared with an 8 percent rate early in 2006, when the Fed quit reporting the measure. According to Williams, "The Fed is pumping liquidity into the U.S. economy and the Fed evidently did not want the markets to follow too closely what the Fed was doing with the money supply."[17]

Is the American dollar collapsing? "Not yet," according to Williams. "I believe we're going to have a dollar collapse, but the Fed is going to do its best to slow play the dollar's decline in value, so that it takes a year or two for the dollar value to reach its low point." Williams explained the risk the dollar faces:

> There will be a central bank, most probably in Asia, who will start the move away from the dollar and when it happens, you're going to see other central bankers covertly trying to follow. The move will magnify very quickly and it could become a full-fledged panic and a dollar collapse.
>
> The Fed is struggling right now to contain inflation and stimulate economic growth. All the Fed is doing right now with all their grand policy shifts is using a lot of propaganda and market massaging to try to prevent a financial panic.[18]

Reports at the end of 2006 indicated that U.S. gross domestic product (GDP) growth slowed to 1.6 percent in the third quarter, the lowest in more than three years.[19] A Fed decision to increase interest rates to control "stag-flation," the unusual situation of inflation experienced in an economic downturn, could trigger a stock market sell-off of major proportions. The housing market bubble of the post-9/11 recovery is also vulnerable to an increase in interest rates. This is the hub of the dilemma. The Fed needs to raise rates to prop up the dollar, but any move the Fed does make to raise interest rates could send the U.S. economy into a tailspin.

"The Fed is faced with an impossible circumstance with the trade and budget deficits being run by the Bush administration," Williams maintained, "and they are just playing games with the markets and the public by not publishing M3, the broadest measure of money supply and the best indicator we have of long-term activity."[20]

Is a U.S. Recession Inevitable?

Bob Chapman, who publishes *The International Forecaster*,[21] also agreed. "The world is awash in money and credit," Chapman said. "My numbers show M3 increasing at about a 10 percent rate right now."

Chapman knows his stuff. He has spent forty-five years in the finance and investment business, twenty-eight years of which were spent as a stockbroker. He is a graduate of Northwestern University. His newsletter has some one hundred thousand subscribers worldwide, and while it covers a wide range of financial and political developments, he has a well-established reputation as a reporter of economic data with a surprisingly accurate history of financial and political predictions. Chapman typically provides analyses of economic development that run counter to mainstream media economic reporting, which often amounts to little more than Wall Street cheerleading. Yet, consistently, Chapman's predictions have an uncanny knack of coming true.

Chapman explained that he believes the U.S. economy entered a recession in February 2006. In his December 9, 2006, newsletter, Chapman predicted that the Fed would hold interest rates at 5.25 percent. "The Fed is in a very tough spot here," Chapman wrote, "If they raise rates, the real estate market will collapse, and if they lower rates, the dollar will collapse." On Tuesday, December 12, 2006, the Federal Reserve Open Market Committee voted, as Chapman had predicted, to hold the overnight lending rates between banks steady at 5.25 percent. This was the fourth straight meeting the Fed had voted not to change rates. In their rate announcement, the Fed affirmed that the economy had slowed.

Almost immediately after the announcement of the Fed's decision, the dollar weakened to a new twenty-month low against the euro, with currency markets reportedly expecting that the Fed will be forced to lower rates to bolster the economy.[22] Following the announcement by the Fed, the U.S. dollar on foreign exchange currency markets (USDX) also dropped, with the dollar going below 83. The dollar, which began January 2006 at 88.86 on the USDX, ended the year at 83.67, a drop of approximately 6 percent.

Chapman continues to insist that a dollar collapse is imminent. "Technicians studying the USDX think there is a support level for the dollar at 75, but I don't think so." How low could the dollar go? "If the dollar breaks through 78.33 on the USDX," Chapman answered, "my guess is the dollar will go through a 35 percent correction, which would put it at 55."

Will the Amero Rescue a Collapsing Dollar?

A U.S. dollar collapse, if and when it occurs, will have been caused by mismanagement of the U.S. economy by presidents and congresses over decades, both Democrats and Republicans alike.

Our federal budget deficits reflect decades of passing overly generous entitlement programs, beginning with the formation of the Social Security Administration by Franklin D. Roosevelt during the Depression of the 1930s. Now with the baby boomers retiring and with a declining U.S. birthrate, funding future Social Security liabilities is a serious problem. Similarly, Medicare liabilities are intensifying as the government adds new programs like the prescription drug programs.

Free trade agreements such as NAFTA, CAFTA, and the WTO benefit many U.S. multinational corporations, but only at the expense of shipping a large and growing percentage of U.S. manufacturing overseas. Our growing trade deficits reflect a flow of manufacturing and assembly jobs from the United States.

Put simply, the economic reality today is that the U.S. dollar is losing value and will most likely continue losing value. Whether a dollar collapse occurs depends upon the Federal Reserve and the Treasury's ability to engineer a gradual decline. But some sort of decline in the value of the dollar is almost inevitable.

As that happens, proponents of the amero will most likely advocate its introduction with increasing vigor.

They will presumably contend that America needs a larger North American market to compete with regional marketplaces such as the European Union. In order to fulfill this potential, the argument will go, a unified North American currency is necessary.

A North American Monetary Union would seek to value this new currency with the combined resources of North America. These resources would include the largest retail market in the world, ample oil resources in the tar sands of Alberta, Canada, and Gulf of Mexico, and fresh water and mineral resources from Canada. Free migration within a continentally defined North America would provide employers throughout the continent a constant stream of relatively cheap, untrained, and uneducated Mexican workers to fill a host of low-paying jobs.

The implementation of Robert Pastor's North American Investment Fund would arguably increase the value of the continental union. In addition, government leaders could continue to attract foreign capital by promoting public-private partnerships and leasing existing infrastructure, including highways.

This regional currency would be difficult to sell, especially in the U.S. and Canada. Most Americans and Canadians would think the idea is preposterous, and rightly so. Still, the emergence of a unified North American currency is likely if we continue down the free trade path. The winners in free trade have been multinational corporations, who already operate across countries to such an extent that they view borders as anachronistic, if not an impediment to their business expansion and profit potential.

Still, professional economists can see why a unitary currency promotes the efficiency and size advantages of regional markets. A regional currency would eliminate currency fluctuations as a business risk for those corporations operating in North America. A regional currency would create a larger North American market, which in turn should promote the growth and development of corporations that operate throughout North America, regardless in which country they establish headquarters. Economists such as Grubel argue that larger capital markets should promote economic development throughout North America, to the benefit of all.

But potential regional economic advantages are unlikely to be sufficient to persuade the United States population to drop the dollar in favor of the amero. Like it or not, we have an emotional attachment to the dollar, as it is one of the most prominent and effective unifiers of the strongest nation in the world since World War II. But even this view of an economically predominant United States can be expected to change as the dollar continues to decline.

The introduction of the amero would entail the same loss of sovereignty that the introduction of the euro has caused in Europe. Today, the central banks of the European Union countries using the euro are no longer in charge of their own national destinies. The central banks of the participating countries are represented only as directors on the ECB's board. Monetary policy for the euro is set by the ECB Executive Board, which consists of six individuals who are nominated by a unanimous decision of member states. Four of these six members come from Europe's four largest central banks—France, Germany, Italy, and Spain.

Even though interest rates set by the ECB, for instance, will affect the value of the euro on international currency markets, the individual European Union states have no recourse but to accept decisions made by the ECB's Executive Board. If the economy of a particular state suffers as a result, that country has no recourse but to accept the hardship.

A move to the amero as a unitary North American currency would entail a similar move to a North American Central Bank, which would have similar supremacy over the U.S. Treasury and the Federal Reserve. Loss of sovereignty over our own currency would clearly indicate that the United States had surrendered financial sovereignty.

While the immediate reaction of most Americans would be that the idea is preposterous, as we learned in 9/11, unanticipated crises can cause otherwise unimaginable changes in national policy. A severe financial crisis, such as the impending devaluation of the dollar, could serve as a catalyst to make the amero a more acceptable idea. If the alternative were to continue with a dramatically declining dollar or to move to a new currency that would compete strongly in world markets, Americans may be surprisingly ready to accept the amero.

If the dollar were today displaying historical strength, the argument for the amero would go nowhere with the U.S. public. The prospect for the amero changes, however, in the current world of a diminishing dollar. Crises, as Robert Pastor has already suggested, have a nasty habit of making solutions appear reasonable that otherwise would never have been considered. Although the U.S. stock market has hit historical highs in 2007, the decreasing value of the dollar should not be dismissed as unimportant. Today, we cannot expect to benefit from a decreasing dollar because the export of our goods will increase as the dollar weakens. Today, our economy is increasingly a service economy. As a consequence, we have far fewer goods to export.

Globalists typically argue for regional currencies over national currencies because they see multinational corporations as our future. The next section of this book discusses a secret globalist conference that I helped expose to the public. The North American agenda is being advanced by international elite who prefer to meet behind closed doors, out of view of the reporting press.

When the Security and Prosperity Partnership of North America does form a public council, the council is composed almost entirely of multinational business leaders, not the public or their elected representatives.

CHAPTER FOUR

SECRET MEETINGS, FORMAL COUNCILS

"We want to begin by imagining a different North America."

Dr. Robert A. Pastor, North American Forum Conference
Banff, Canada, 2006

IT'S THE ECONOMY, STUPID. Or so they say. In post–World War II Europe, Germany's economic dependence upon France was considered the key to keeping Germany within its borders and to reviving Europe as a whole. The idea that such economic inter-dependence could breed stability, peace, and prosperity made the potential loss of national sovereignty palatable to a war-ravaged Europe. As a result, the first steps toward the European Union were economic steps. The 1957 Treaty of Rome is widely regarded as the first such step toward creating a European Union, though all the Treaty of Rome established was a common steel and coal economic agreement between six European countries.

There's a crucial difference between what happened in Europe and what is happening in North America. No matter how incremental and underhanded the steps, at least the European elites argued for European integration in public. In North America, the merger is happening apart from public scrutiny, driven by multinational corporations who prefer to make their decisions in the boardroom, closed to the watchful eye of the public.

If a North American Union emerges, multinational corporations will have played a major role. Such corporations already transcend borders in their search for talent, low-cost labor, and market access. Multinational corporations feel they have the right to set the rules, since their economic activity produces the wealth and employment individual nation-states rely upon for taxation and revenue. Without multinational corporations, the United States, Canada, and Mexico would become economic basket cases. Or so leaders of such companies claim.

If the North American nation-states exist merely to promote the interests of multinational corporations, why shouldn't these same international executives integrate entire regions as they like? Given this logic, a North American business executive advisory council would be the perfect group to architect a North American Union.

That's exactly what's happening. The North American Forum in Banff, Canada, was a meeting of elite businesspeople, government officials, and academics held without announcement or press reports of their proceedings. They gathered in secret behind closed doors to examine and promote North American economic and political integration.

The North American Competitiveness Council, a public group consisting of businesspeople and formed under the SPP, has been created to allow multinational corporations to advise the three governments on the future progress and direction of SPP. These big business–influenced working groups are hard at work attempting to integrate North America.

The North American Forum—the 2006 Meeting in Banff

World Net Daily was among the first news organizations to obtain and publish the agenda and list of attendees for the North American Forum meeting. Held at the Fairmont Banff Springs Hotel in Banff, Alberta, Canada, from September 12–14, 2006,[1] the meeting was closed to the press. Documents obtained by *WND* were marked "Internal Document, Not for Public Release."

Mel Hurtig, a noted Canadian author and publisher who was the elected leader of the National Party of Canada, was responsible for providing *WND* with the agenda and attendee list.[2] Hurtig told *WND* that the meeting was designed to undermine the democratic process:

> What is sinister about this meeting is that it involved high-level government officials and some of the top and most powerful business leaders of the three countries and the North American Forum in organizing the meeting intentionally did not inform the press in any of the three countries. It was clear that the intention was to keep this important meeting about integrating the three countries out of the public eye.[3]

Hurtig further explained that a goal of the United States was "to gain access and control of Canada's extensive natural resources, including oil and water." Hurtig argued that the Canadian Council of Chief Executives "wants to make sure that the 150 Canadian top companies who are their members gain access to the American market and to American capital."[4]

The office of Thomas d'Aquino, the president and CEO of the Canadian Council of Chief Executives and a vice chair of the CFR task force on the Americas, confirmed that Mr. d'Aquino did attend the September meeting.

Three individuals cochaired the North American Forum: George Schultz, former secretary of state under President Reagan; Canadian Peter Lougheed, former Alberta premier and former leader of the Progressive Conservative Party of Alberta; and Mexico's Pedro Aspe, former secretary of the Treasury of Mexico.

The North American Forum itself is a shadow organization, difficult to research or learn about. The North American Forum has no business office and no business address. Basically, the North American Forum is nothing more than the three cochairs and their extensive network of international contacts.

Attendees at the Banff meeting contributed funds to cover the organizational expenses. Attendees, including government attendees, were responsible for the travel, lodging, and *per diem* expenses they incurred to attend the meeting. These arrangements contribute to keeping the North American Forum below the radar of public view.

The Banff Meeting Exposed

Word about the meeting first surfaced in the Canadian press when the Council of Canadians,[5] a citizens' organization opposed to free trade, began leaking word that the Banff meeting was taking place. Immediately, the Canadian Council of Chief Executives, a business group comparable to the U.S. Chamber of Commerce, retaliated by charging that the Council of Canadians was nothing more than a "far left-wing radical group" that was determined to damage legitimate Canadian business interests.

Meera Karunananthan, a spokesperson for the Council of Canadians, confirmed to *WND* that their group was responsible for obtaining and releasing the meeting agenda and attendee list to the Canadian press. She took exception with the Canadian Council of Chief Executives, preferring to characterize her group instead as "a citizens' advocacy group." When asked why the Council of Canadians released the North American Forum information, Ms. Karunananthan responded:

> We question the privacy of a meeting that involves senior ministers of our government meeting with senior government officials in the United States and Mexico. The Canadian public has not been adequately informed about the ongoing North American integration process and we believe it is wrong for a meeting that involves top North American business executives and government officials to be held in secret behind closed doors.[6]

Jean-Yzes LeFort, also a spokesperson for the Council of Canadians, told *WND* that the group opposes the effort to create a North American Union because "the NAU represents an elite corporate agenda and to us what is being planned would be an unacceptable loss of sovereignty."

Attending the Banff meeting was the ubiquitous Dr. Pastor; Dr. Thomas A. Shannon, the U.S. assistant secretary of state for Western Hemisphere affairs; Roger Gibbons, the president and CEO of Canada West Foundation, a nonprofit organization founded to promote business development in western Canada;[7] and Andrés Rozenthal, president of the Consejo Mexicano de Asuntos Internacionales, a Mexican counterpart to the CFR.[8]

Considerable overlap exists between the CFR task force and the Banff meeting, with approximately one-third of those listed as CFR task force members also attending the Banff conference. Andrés Rozenthal was the Mexican vice chair of the CFR task force that wrote the May 2005 report, "Building a North American Community." Another prominent participant in both was Carla A. Hills, who served as U.S. trade representative from 1989 to 1993 and was the primary U.S. negotiator for NAFTA.

Other members of that CFR task force who attended the Banff secret confab include:

- Pedro Aspe, a cochair of the CFR task force and a Mexican investment banker who shows up frequently on international panels and boards, including those put together by the United Nations;

- Thomas d'Aquino, whom we have already named as the chief executive of the Canadian Council of Chief Executives;

- Wendy Dobson, professor of international business at the University of Toronto;

- Pierre Marc Johnson, a Canadian attorney who was the former premier of Quebec;

- John Manley, another Canadian attorney who is a former deputy prime minister of Canada;

- Carlos Heredia, a senior advisor on International Affairs to Governor Lázaro Cárdenas-Bartel of the Mexican state of Michoacán;

- Luis Rubio, president of the private Centro de Investigació Para el Desarrollo (Center of Research for Development);

- The Hon. Perrin Beatty, president and CEO of Canadian Manufacturers and Exporters,[9] Canada's largest trade and industry association. Beatty confirmed to *WND* that he attended the Banff North American Forum meeting. Mr. Beatty described the meeting as "an opportunity for a small group of people from our three North American countries to get together informally and discuss issues of common interest."[10]

When asked why the meeting was closed to the press, Mr. Beatty responded that the meeting was not a "decision forum" but a "discussion forum."[11] Mr. Beatty claimed that not all attendees shared Dr. Pastor's views. "My interest in attending the meeting was economic," he told *WND*. "How do we insure we keep pace with the explosion in competition in the North American industry? It's absolutely critical to the economic growth of our three countries that we stay competitive and successful."

Secretary of Defense Donald Rumsfeld was listed as a participant, though *WND* reported that Rumsfeld did not attend. Still, the Department of Defense was represented at a senior level. Lt. Gen. Gene Renuart, U.S. Air Force military assistant to Secretary Rumsfeld attended. Also listed was Major Gen. Mark A. Volcheff, director of plans, policy, and strategy for NORAD-NORTHCAM.

Many other U.S. government officials were among those that attended:

- From the State Department: Dr. Thomas A. Shannon, assistant secretary of state for the Western Hemisphere, and Ryan Henry, deputy under secretary of defense for policy;

- John Dickson, the deputy chief of mission at the U.S. Embassy in Ottawa represented the U.S. ambassador to Canada;

- Clay Sell, the deputy secretary of energy, attended from the U.S. Department of Energy;

- Admiral Tim Keating, the commander of the U.S. Northern Command, and Major General Mark A. Volcheff attended for NORAD-NORTHCOM, along with Deborah Bolton, the political advisor to the commander of U.S. NORTHCOM;

- Dan Fisk, the senior director for the Western Hemisphere, attended representing the National Security Council, from within the White House.[12]

The entire attendee list is published as an appendix to this book.

Clearly, the Bush administration took the Banff meeting very seriously. Top government officials from both Mexico and Canada were on the attendee list. The sole journalist listed was Mary Anastasia O'Grady of the *Wall Street Journal*. No articles on the Banff meeting appeared in the *Wall Street Journal* and Ms. O'Grady declined public comment, even after *WND* published that she had attended the meeting. In what is apparently intended to be an annual event, the first North American Forum meeting was held in September 2005 in Sonoma, California, and a meeting for September 2007 is planned for Mexico.

The agenda for the Banff conference was organized into the following sessions:

- Session I: Opening comments by Messrs. Aspe, Lougheed, and Schultz;

- Session II: A Vision for North America: Issues and Options;

- Session III: Toward a North American Energy Strategy;

- Session IV: Opportunities for Security Cooperation in North America;

- Session V: Demographic and Social Dimensions of North American Integration;

- Session VI: Border Infrastructure & Continental Prosperity;

- Session VII: Roundtable Conversation with the Cochairs.

The conference focused on North American demographics, social integration, economic development, and energy utilization. Rather than considering U.S. national defense or the protection of U.S. borders with Mexico and Canada, sessions covered continental defense and border security.

The meeting may have been secret, but once the Council of Canadians got their hands on the documents, the attendee list and the agenda of the North American Forum meeting were widely published and discussed on the Internet. The complete agenda for the Banff meeting is published as an appendix to this book.[13]

State Department Refuses Comment on Banff Meeting

Session III of the Banff meeting was moderated by Thomas A. Shannon, the assistant secretary of state for the Western Hemisphere. Robert Pastor served as one of the panelists at this session.

WND contacted Eric Watnik of the State Department to see if a copy of Pastor's presentation with Thomas Shannon could be obtained.[14] Mr. Watnik confirmed to *World Net Daily* that Mr. Shannon did attend the Banff meeting and that Mr. Shannon's expenses for attending the meeting were paid for by U.S. taxpayers. The State Department, however, refused to discuss anything about Mr. Shannon's attending the conference or the content of the panel, including any paper Dr. Pastor may have presented.

When *WND* pressed Mr. Watnik, the State Department objected. Watnik argued that Shannon may have chaired the panel to allow Pastor to present his views, even though Shannon may have disagreed with Pastor. Watnik argued that Shannon may have chaired the panel to stimulate a debate over views he found objectionable. Reading Shannon's subsequent articles, we doubt Mr. Watnik's response was valid.

The State Department website documents that Shannon addressed a group of Canadian diplomats, academics, and Fulbright scholars in Ottawa on September 14, 2006, where he specifically discussed the North American Forum conference in Banff.[15]

In the speech entitled "Why the Americas Matter," Shannon characterized the North American Forum as "a parallel structure to the Security and Prosperity Partnership of North America." Shannon described SPP as designed to "enhance NAFTA" and again as "an add-on to NAFTA." He added that the three co-conveners of the group were senior officials with considerable public experience: former American Secretary of State George Schultz, Mexican Finance Minister Pedro Aspe, and former Canadian premier of Alberta Peter Lougheed. The purpose of the meeting, according to Shannon, was "to bring opinion-makers, private-sector leaders, university professors and presidents, and leaders of nongovernmental organizations together with government officials from the three countries of North America to begin to talk about North American security" and "to create a vision for North America and an understanding of what North America is as an entity."[16]

Couched in the reaction to 9/11, Shannon said, the North American Forum aimed to get the three governments working together "to fashion more productive cooperation and address the kinds of problems we saw in the immediate aftermath of September 11." Shannon acknowledged that the three countries had identities that are "as different as we are in our national sovereignty." Still, his emphasis was that "Canada, the United States, and Mexico do share a common place, do share a common market, and increasingly are connected demographically and culturally."

Shannon stressed his goal was to look for ways "to enhance that degree of connectedness" in order to "remain competitive in the world" as well as protecting "our open societies against threats which aren't going away." According to Shannon, 9/11 provided the security justification for greater North American cooperation, while the need to remain competitive in an emerging world market provides economic justification. The inevitable "security and prosperity" partnership involves a North American vision or a North American community in which we learn to think and act as North Americans, not simply as Americans, Mexicans, and Canadians.

Implicitly rejected is the possibility that the United States, Mexico, and Canada could either be secure or prosperous unless we integrate. Note how Shannon answered the question of "why the Americas matter."

> What we are doing in North America today is consolidating democratic states, integrating them economically but then providing a security overlay and a level of cooperation and dialogue that will strengthen the economic institutions, strengthen our ability to protect and promote our prosperity, and enhance our ability to create the opportunity that people can...take advantage of.[17]

This statement embraced the CFR argument that U.S. national security and prosperity can best be served by forming a security perimeter around North America and by establishing a North American common market. The speech strongly suggested that the State Department endorsed both the CFR views about North American integration and Pastor's vision of a North American community.

Judicial Watch Releases Pentagon Notes on Banff Meeting

Pursuant to a Freedom of Information Act (FOIA) request, Judicial Watch obtained a set of notes from the Pentagon attendees at the Banff meeting.[18] The notes permitted Judicial Watch to conclude that the presentations at the North American Forum included discussion of U.S. immigration policy and border enforcement, as well as revisiting one of Dr. Pastor's favorite ideas, the creation of a North American investment fund. Judicial Watch noted that references to the SPP occur repeatedly throughout the notes of the Pentagon attendees.

One particularly disturbing comment was noted in the official conference record of the speeches given, as recorded in the "Rapporteur Notes" obtained by the Judicial Watch FOIA request.[19] In Section VI of the conference, entitled "Border Infrastructure and Continental Prosperity," the reporter summarized as follows:

- To what degree does the concept of North America help/hinder solving problems between the three countries?

- Vision is helpful

- A secure perimeter would bring enormous benefit

- While a vision is appealing working on the infrastructure might yield more benefit and bring more people on board ("evolution by stealth")

Reflecting on the "evolution by stealth" comment, Judicial Watch President Tom Fitton said:

> It is not encouraging to see the phrase "evolution by stealth" in reference to important policy debates such as North American integration and cooperation. These documents provide more information to Americans concerned about the Security and Prosperity Partnership. The more transparency the better.[20]

The comment is particularly disturbing, though not necessarily surprising given the trajectory that Europe followed from the coal and steel free trade agreement to a full-fledged regional government with a common currency in the euro. Remember that Monnet wanted to keep his dream of a European Union from the general public, as it would have been rejected.

Dr. Pastor's Secret Paper at the Banff Conference

The notes on the Banff conference obtained by Judicial Watch included a copy of the paper Dr. Robert Pastor delivered.[21] In this paper, Pastor wrote openly about his desire "to define and build a North American community, a new and different relationship among the peoples and governments of Canada, Mexico, and the United States." He continued, "Our purpose is to build a greater sense of being a part of North America."

As previously noted, Pastor is careful to articulate his view of a North American community as a further transitional step in the political and economic integration of North America, advancing beyond SPP. Pastor lamented that North American integration has been slowed by the weakness of the executives of the three countries and the reluctance of the legislatures to embrace bold proposals. He commented: "The lack of progress even on an incremental approach suggests that a compelling vision is needed for any change in the relationship."

Pastor urged the conference to decide whether the North American Forum wanted to articulate modest or bold proposals. He cautioned that "the political climate in all three countries may not be conducive to the immediate realization of either an incremental or bold objective." Pastor carefully included the word "immediate" in his phrasing, suggesting that the barriers to more complete North American integration are only temporary.

Pastor recommended that several institutional steps be taken to advance North American integration. He touched on the need to establish a North American development fund, to develop Mexico economically in a way that NAFTA had failed to accomplish. He urged the formation of a defense and security perimeter around the continent, especially as U.S. borders with Mexico and Canada are relaxed to reduce border-crossing time. Finally, he pushed for a North America customs union, another transitional step Europe had used to move from a common market to a full-fledged regional government.

Pastor's comments on North American trade corridors were particularly interesting. He noted that in "imagining a different North America," we had to have new trade corridors built from northern Canada to southern Mexico. He encouraged that goods and services needed to "traverse the borders smoothly," such that trucks "do not have to off-load their cargoes at the border." Pastor expanded on these thoughts as follows:

> Trade has tripled in North America, and more than two-thirds of that trade is carried by trucks, and yet trucks still cannot cross the U.S.-Mexican border despite a Supreme Court decision, and trucks are subject to about fifty-four different sets of regulations on the continent. Moreover, no new transportation corridor has been built to connect the three markets, and infrastructure at the border is woefully inadequate. This explains why some manufacturers

> believe it is cheaper to ship goods from Shanghai to Los
> Angeles than from Monterrey to Los Angeles.

Pastor encouraged the conference to decide whether a new transportation corridor should be designed and built between Canada and Mexico, and how such a corridor should be financed and managed.

Pastor ended by asking the conference to consider recommending the creation of a North American passport similar to the European Union passport that has opened up travel between European countries.

The North American Competitiveness Council (NACC): Multinational Corporations Form SPP Executive Group

The North American Forum is not the only body of economically interested individuals gathering to discuss the North American Union. On June 15, 2006, Secretary of Commerce Carlos M. Gutierrez convened the first meeting of the North American Competitiveness Council (NACC). The NACC was presented as an advisory group organized by the Department of Commerce (DOC) under the auspices of the SPP.

A March 31, 2006, press release on the White House website, under the title "Security and Prosperity Partnership of North America: Progress," announced the formation of the NACC.[22] The press release noted that the NACC would meet annually "with security and prosperity Ministers and will engage with senior government officials on an ongoing basis."[23]

The White House press release referenced no U.S. law or treaty under which the NACC was organized. Nor did it specify the advisory role this council of business leaders would have. The White House commented only that the council "will provide us with recommendations on North American competitiveness, including, among others, areas such as automotive and transportation, steel, manufacturing, and services."[24]

With the organization of the NACC, multinational business leaders were placed in a key position to direct the decision making and policy outcomes of the SPP working groups. With the formation of NACC, the Bush administration signaled that the

SPP would primarily serve the interests of the multinational corporations. The three governments formed no advisory group of citizens or interest group activists to advise their SPP efforts.

The International Trade Administration of the Department of Commerce noted that the NACC membership consisted of ten "high-level business leaders" from Mexico, Canada, and the United States.[25] An April 2006 report in the Mexican media quoted Angel Villalobos, undersecretary of international trade negotiations for Mexico's secretariat of economy, as saying that nothing like NACC had ever before been created in NAFTA. Mr. Villalobos described NACC as "an umbrella organization within the SPP," claiming further that SPP was created in 2005 to operate parallel to NAFTA.[26]

A DOC press release[27] on the day of the first NACC meeting confirmed that the "SPP ministers" are the various cabinet-level secretaries in the three countries to whom the SPP working groups report. The press release also referenced the March 23, 2005, Waco, Texas, meeting as the origin of SPP:

> On March 23, 2005, leaders of North America launched the SPP. This initiative is meant to reduce trade barriers and facilitate economic growth, while improving the security and competitiveness of the continent. The leaders of North America confirmed their commitment to SPP when they met on March 31, 2006 in Cancun, Mexico.

The press release quotes Secretary Gutierrez as affirming the importance of NACC within SPP: "Today is a continuation of President Bush's strong commitment to our North American partners to focus on North America's security and prosperity. The private sector is the driving force behind innovation and growth, and the private sector's involvement in the SPP is key to enhancing North America's competitive position in global markets."

The Council of the Americas, which "include[s] some of the largest blue chip corporations domiciled in the United States, who, collectively, represent the vast bulk of U.S. investment in and trade with the rest of the Americas,"[28] provided detail regarding the June 15, 2006, meeting of the NACC. An NACC membership list found on the Council of the Americas' website[29] lists the U.S.

members as coming from the following corporations (listed in alphabetic order):

- Campbell Soup Company

- Chevron

- Ford

- FedEx

- General Electric

- General Motors

- Kansas City Southern Industries

- Lockheed Martin Corporation

- Merck

- Mittal Steel USA

- New York Life

- United Parcel Service

- Wal-Mart

- Whirlpool

Some of these companies were chosen because of the closeness of their executives to the Bush administration and the Council on Foreign Relations. Others have direct ties to SPP projects. Kansas City Southern Industries includes Kansas City Southern, which has described itself as a NAFTA railroad. Wal-Mart is one of the major forces driving U.S. manufacturing to the Chinese underground market.

A separate document on the Council of the Americas website presents a summarized transcript, which claims that U.S. Representatives in the June 15 meeting explained the composition of the U.S. delegation as follows:

> "The U.S. section of the NACC has organized itself through a Secretariat—composed of the U.S. Chamber of Commerce and the Council of the Americas—to maximize its efficiency and better communicate with its members." Secretary Gutierrez was also paraphrased as stating, "The

> purpose of this meeting was to institutionalize the North American Security and Prosperity Partnership (SPP) and the NACC, so that the work will continue through changes in administrations."

The NACC places a significant amount of influence in the hands of the business community. Nine of the ten appointees of the Canadian NACC delegation were drawn from the Canadian Council of Chief Executives, an organization of business leaders that ardently supports the SPP. Maude Barlow, the national chairperson for the Council of Canadians objected, stating, "This latest development clearly puts business leaders in the driver's seat and gives them the green light to press forward for a North American model for business security and prosperity...How truly accountable is the Harper government to the Canadian people, when it gives preferential treatment to the big-business community in the design of its policies?" The same question, of course, is applicable to both the governments of the United States and Mexico.

NACC Implements Robert Pastor's North American Advisory Council

The NACC signifies an important step in Robert Pastor's incremental approach to building a North American community. At a press conference presenting the CFR report, "Building a North American Community," Pastor said the following:

> The North American summit that occurred in Texas on March 23rd is a very important statement. But if it's to be more than a photo opportunity, we felt that a second institution was essential, and that would be a North American advisory council made up of eminent individuals, appointed for terms that are longer than those of the governments, and staggered over time. This council would propose ideas for dealing with North American challenges, whether they be regulatory or transportation or infrastructure or education, and put forth options to the three leaders to consider ways to adopt a North American approach.[30]

Pastor described this advisory council as playing an active policy role in the formation of his hoped-for North American community.

> And hopefully, the three leaders would turn to this North
> American council and say, "Look we're getting wonderful
> advice on what we should do about North America as a
> whole. Why don't you prepare a plan for us on education,
> on agriculture, on the environment, and we would consider
> that even as we consider the advice of our government."

A White House website shows photographs of President
Bush, President Vicente Fox, and Prime Minister Harper at their
March 31, 2006, joint news conference in Cancun, Mexico, shak-
ing hands in front of a backdrop proclaiming "Cancun 2006—
Security and Prosperity Partnership of North America."[31] At the
Cancun press conference,[32] Prime Minister Harper confirmed that
the decision had been reached to advance SPP by forming NACC,
a business council designed to advise SPP much as Pastor had
recommended:

> During my meetings with Presidents Bush and Fox, we
> reviewed the progress of our Security and Prosperity
> Partnership, which provides a framework to advance the
> common interests in the areas of security, prosperity, and
> quality of life.
>
> We committed to further engage the private sector. We've
> agreed to set up a North American Competitiveness Coun-
> cil, made up of business leaders from all three countries, to
> advise us on ways to improve the competitiveness of our
> economies. They will meet with our ministers, identify pri-
> orities, and make sure we follow up and implement them.

In his comments at the Cancun press conference, President Bush
also affirmed the presence of unnamed business leaders who had
attended the trilateral summit meeting. "I want to thank the CEOs
and the business leaders from the three countries who are here."

On June 15, 2006, NACC held its first meeting, following Pastor's recommendation in detail, even describing the NACC members as an "advisory council."

The DOC SPP website announcing the formation of NACC
provides no information about the membership requirements, the
selection process, or the terms of the members appointed to the
NACC.[33] Nor is there any discussion of who pays for the travel
expenses and the time of the participants. No charter has been pub-

lished for the NACC, nor any other specific delineation of roles and responsibilities, or reporting authority (except for a mention of the "SPP Ministers"). Equally lacking is a description of the enabling legislation or treaty under which the NACC operates.

What is clear is that the formation of the NACC supports the contention that the SPP agenda is increasingly set by multinational companies, without any direct input from voters in the three countries.

NAFTA Chapter 11 Tribunals Trump U.S. Supreme Court

The European Court of Justice was established just six years after the Treaty of Paris was signed. As Europe entered into new economic treaties, a court with jurisdiction over such areas became necessary to settle trade disputes. A similar process has already occurred in America. Chapter 11 of the NAFTA agreement allows a private NAFTA foreign investor to sue the U.S. government if the investor believes a state or federal law damages the investor's NAFTA business.[34]

Under Chapter 11, NAFTA established a tribunal that may conduct a trial to decide the case according to the legal principals established by either the World Bank's International Centre for the Settlement of Investment Disputes or the UN's Commission for International Trade Law. If the decision is adverse to the United States., the NAFTA tribunal can impose its decision as final, trumping U.S. law, even as decided by the U.S. Supreme Court. U.S. laws can be effectively overturned and the NAFTA Chapter 11 tribunal can impose millions or billions of dollars in fines on the U.S. government, to be paid ultimately by the U.S. taxpayer.

On August 9, 2005, a three-member NAFTA tribunal dismissed a $970 million claim filed by Methanex Corp., a Canadian methanol producer challenging California laws that regulate against the gasoline additive MTBE.[35]

The additive MTBE was introduced into gasoline to reduce air pollution from motor vehicle emissions. California regulations restricted the use of MTBE after the additive was found to contaminate drinking water and produce a health hazard. Had the case been decided differently, California's MTBE regulations would have been overturned and U.S. taxpayers forced to pay Methanex millions in damages.

While this case was decided in favor of U.S. laws, there is no guarantee that the NAFTA Chapter 11 court will always decide in favor of the United States. Eventually, a U.S. law may be overruled by the NAFTA Chapter 11 adjudicative procedure, as long as the determinant law adjudicated by the NAFTA Chapter 11 tribunals continues to derive from World Court or UN law. As the SPP advances, will the U.S. Bill of Rights be among the laws that have to be "integrated" and "harmonized" with Mexico's and Canada's? Citizens of Canada already cannot speak freely without worrying about hate crimes legislation or other political restrictions on what they say. The United States remains the only country among the three where citizens can claim a right to own firearms.

NAFTA Chapter 11 tribunals already empower foreign NAFTA investors and corporations to challenge the sovereignty of U.S. law in the United States. Senator John Kerry (D-MA) has said, "When we debated NAFTA, not a single word was uttered in discussing Chapter 11. Why? Because we didn't know how this provision would play out. No one really knew just how high the stakes would get."[36] Congress's hesitation to understand and address this complex issue is distressing.

While the NAFTA court has disturbing implications for U.S. sovereignty, even those who advocate integration recognize its imperfections. Rather than abandoning it, however, they wish to replace it. The CFR plan clearly calls for the establishment of a "permanent tribunal for North American dispute resolution." As the CFR report details:

> The current NAFTA dispute-resolution process is founded on ad hoc panels that are not capable of building institutional memory or establishing precedent, may be subject to conflicts of interest, and are appointed by authorities who may have an incentive to delay a given proceeding. As demonstrated by the efficiency of the World Trade Organization (WTO) appeal process, a permanent tribunal would likely encourage faster, more consistent, and more predictable resolution of disputes. In addition, there is a need to review the workings of NAFTA's dispute-

settlement mechanism to make it more efficient, transparent, and effective.[37]

Robert Pastor has repeatedly argued for the creation of a North American Union "Permanent Tribunal on Trade and Investment." He understands that a "permanent court would permit the accumulation of precedent and lay the groundwork for North American business law."[38] Pastor says nothing about U.S. business law or the U.S. Supreme Court.

The executive branch under the Bush administration is quietly putting in place an unprecedented bureaucratic infrastructure without any direct Congressional input. This infrastructure will provide the rules to which any NAFTA or NAU court would refer when adjudicating NAU trade disputes. The SPP *2005 Report to Leaders* clearly states the goal: "We will develop a trilateral Regulatory Cooperative Framework by 2007 to support and enhance existing, as well as encourage new cooperation among regulators, including at the outset of the regulatory process."[39]

The expansion of Chapter 11 NAFTA tribunals is an important concern since proponents of regional integration have long recognized that expanded free trade engenders trade disputes, which require expanded regional court structures to resolve differences, as clearly happened in Europe. Chapter 11 tribunals are an example of a regional political dispute institution that arises as a logical consequence of economic integration. NAFTA has already moved incrementally from a free trade agreement to a legal dispute mechanism in which the supremacy of our own Supreme Court is necessarily compromised. If a NAFTA Chapter 11 tribunal can overturn even Supreme Court decisions, we have already entered the era where a regional judicial structure created under a trade law has power over the highest court in the land.

The movement toward a North American Union begins with the economy, moves to the courts, and ends with political union. It's a simple story, and one that's taking shape right under our noses. At the North American Forum, business and political leaders from Mexico, the United States, and Canada gathered to discuss economic integration. Meanwhile, the formation of the NACC established a business-class advisory council to the SPP, which

Pastor proposed as a necessary step toward creating his dream of a North American community.

While discussions that could lead to the undermining of U.S. sovereignty between top U.S. officials and their Mexican and Canadian counterparts are concerning enough, there is a certain comfort that comes from knowing that these discussions remain just that—talk. Unfortunately, as will be seen, the movement to form a North American Union has moved from talk to action in a number of areas—not the least of which is in the areas of regional government and transportation.

PART II

BUILDING THE NORTH AMERICAN COMMUNITY

CHAPTER FIVE

THE SPP SHADOW GOVERNMENT

"In short, the case-by-case approach can produce some remarkable concessions of 'sovereignty' that could not be achieved on an across-the-board basis."

Richard N. Gardner, writing in the Council of Foreign Relations Magazine *Foreign Affairs*, April 1974[1]

AT FIRST GLANCE the movement to integrate the North American economy might appear amorphous, unorganized, and isolated, the dream of a few extremists. Unfortunately, that's not the case.

The speed at which North America is being integrated is astonishing, and there is little reason to think it will slow any time soon. The SPP has already assumed a definite structure and is enacting changes within the governments of Mexico, Canada, and the United States. Clear steps are being taken to integrate transportation systems and ease border crossing in order to facilitate more trade and movement of people between the three nations. The only "working group" that hasn't been consulted is that of the working people of the United States.

SPP.Gov

Shortly after the summit meeting in Waco, Texas, a new website, www.spp.gov, was created by the Department of Commerce to disperse information about the Security and Prosperity Partnership.

The *2005 Report to Leaders* on the SPP website was the first indication of how the SPP had been organized.[2] In this document, some twenty different working groups were described in a wide range of areas, including manufactured goods, movement of goods, energy, environment, e-commerce, financial services, business facilitation, food and agriculture, transportation, and health. This report was completed within the first ninety days after the summit meeting at Waco, Texas, as promised.

The *2005 Report to Leaders* revealed the names of the "ministers" charged with directing the working groups. Basically, the SPP reports to three top cabinet-level officers from each country.

Representing the United States are:

- Secretary of Commerce Carlos Gutierrez,

- Secretary of Homeland Security Michael Chertoff,

- Secretary of State Condoleezza Rice.

Representing Mexico are:

- Secretario de Economía Fernando Canales,

- Secretario de Gobernación Carlos Abascal,

- Secretario de Relaciones Exteriores Luis Ernesto Derbéz.

Representing Canada are:

- Minister of Industry David L. Emerson,

- Deputy Prime Minister and Minister of Public Safety, Anne McLellan,

- Minister of Foreign Affairs Pierre Stewart Pettigrew.

The report emphasized the extensive working group structure that had been established to pursue an ambitious agenda:

> In carrying out your instructions, we established working groups under both agendas of the Partnership—Security and Prosperity. We held roundtables with stakeholders, meetings with business groups and briefing sessions with Legislatures, as well as with other relevant political jurisdic-

> tions. The result is a detailed series of actions and recom-
> mendations designed to increase the competitiveness of
> North America and the security of our people.

Clearly, the SPP was intent on producing policies that each country agreed upon, which were to be implemented directly without
Congressional oversight.

> Upon your review and approval, we will once again meet
> with stakeholders and work with them to implement the
> work plans that we have developed.

The report stressed:

> The success of our efforts will be defined less by the con-
> tents of the work plans than by the actual implementation
> of initiatives and strategies that will make North America
> more prosperous and more secure.

Nearly every work plan revealed in the *2005 Report to Leaders* included action steps described variously as "our three countries
signed a Framework of Common Principles..." or "we have
signed a Memorandum of Understanding..." or "we have signed
a declaration of intent..." etc.

Canada has established an SPP webpage within their Department of Foreign Affairs and International Trade Canada.[3] Mexico
has placed the SPP within the office of the secretaria de economia
and created an extensive website for the Alianza Para La Securidad
y La Prosperidad de América del Norte (ASPAN).[4] The Mexican
website describes ASPAN as "a permanent, trilateral process to
create a major integration of North America."

Myths vs. Facts

In response to increased public attention, the SPP created a "Myths
v. Facts" page on their website aimed at debunking theories that
they are creating a new regional government along the model of
the European Union.[5] The first myth/fact exchange addresses the
legal status of the SPP:

*Myth: The SPP was an agreement signed by Presidents [sic] Bush
and his Mexican and Canadian counterparts in Waco, TX, on March
23, 2005.*

Fact: The SPP is a dialogue to increase security and enhance prosperity among the three countries. The SPP is not an agreement nor is it a treaty. In fact, no agreement was ever signed.

This sort of language downplays the importance of what is happening within the many cabinet-level working groups constituted within the executive branches of the three countries. The Bush administration claims that the SPP activity is nothing more than a dialogue, but constraints upon the Executive Branch demand such a labeling. If written agreements resulted from the SPP, they would need to be submitted to Congress as legislation, or to the Senate as treaties for ratification, or published in the Federal Register as proposed rule changes. A "dialogue among bureaucrats" sounds like an innocuous discussion designed to improve communication but make no fundamental changes in U.S. laws or administrative regulations.

The claim that the SPP is simply a dialogue is at worst spurious, and at best dubious. The first five public policy areas listed in the *2005 Report to Leaders* illustrate the nature of the formal written agreements, decisions, and actions proceeding from the dialogue. These are not the result of a harmless bureaucratic dialogue, but of a planned agenda. Terms suggesting more than a neighborly conversation are in italics:

- **Electronic Commerce**. "In June 2005, our three countries signed *a Framework of Common Principles for Electronic Commerce* that will encourage the development of trans-border online business in North America."

- **Liberalization of Rules of Origin.** "We have *completed the implementation of modifications of rules of origin,* covering goods such as household appliances, precious metals, and various machinery and equipment parts."

- **Consumer Products.** "Canada and the United States have *signed a Memorandum of Understanding* to enhance and strengthen the exchange of information and cooperative activities on public health and safety protection related to the safety of consumer products, and encourage compatibility of standards-related measures to the greatest extent practicable. Likewise, Mexico and the United States are *holding* *negotiations to reach an agreement on a similar Memorandum of Understanding."*

- **Textiles and Apparel Labeling.** "We have *reached an arrangement* on the Use of Care symbols on Textile and Apparel Goods Labels that will facilitate market access of textile and apparel goods by the uniform acceptance of harmonized care symbols in North America. *We plan to sign this agreement in July."*

- **Temporary Work Entry.** "The three countries have *forwarded a trilateral* document setting out each country's domestic procedures to modify NAFTA's temporary entry appendix on professionals to the NAFTA Free Trade Commission for approval. This will clarify procedures in each country, thereby providing a mechanism for more North American professionals to be given temporary entry."

The many trilateral agreements discussed in the report are not published on the website. There is no evidence that Congressional oversight hearings have examined these agreements.

Much More than a Dialogue

The dozens of government websites devoted to the SPP indicate that the SPP is engaged in more than a simple dialogue. The Mexican government SPP website refers to the SPP as an "alliance," a word suggestive of a treaty or formal status of international relations. Consider this White House press release from the time of the Cancun summit describing the extensive trilateral administrative work underway in the many executive branch agencies of the three governments:

> This Partnership [SPP] has increased our institutional contacts to respond to our vision of a stronger, more secure, and more prosperous region. In June 2005, our three governments released detailed work-plans identifying key initiatives that form an ambitious agenda of collaboration. Since June, we have worked to implement these initiatives. Many will take months or years to be completed, but we already note significant results. We ask our Ministers to build on this momentum.[6]

On September 13, 2005, Deputy Secretary of Commerce David A. Sampson called the SPP a "blueprint" in a speech given to the Canadian-American Border Trade Alliance:

> The SPP announced last March by President Bush, Prime Minister Martin, and Mexican President Vicente Fox, unveiled a blueprint for a safer and more prosperous North America for the 21st century.[7]

One wonders what the SPP blueprint is intended to build.

The second myth/fact exchange on SPP.gov forcefully denies that the Bush administration intends to create a North American Union:

Myth: The SPP is a movement to merge the United States, Mexico, and Canada into a North American Union and establish a common currency.

Fact: The cooperative efforts under SPP, which can be found in detail at www.spp.gov, seek to make the United States, Canada, and Mexico open to legitimate trade and closed to terrorism and crime. It does not change our courts or legislative processes and respects the sovereignty of the United States, Mexico, and Canada. The SPP in no way, shape, or form considers the creation of a European Union–like structure or a common currency. The SPP does not attempt to modify our sovereignty or currency or change the American system of government designed by our Founding Fathers.[8]

Unfortunately, presidential protestations of innocence cannot always be taken at face value. Should we accept on faith White House press secretary Tony Snow's denial[9] that the Bush administration intends to create a North American Union?[10] Or should we believe the ample evidence already published on the SPP Web page documenting the extensive rewrite of U.S. administrative law?

FOIA Documents Disclose "Shadow Government"

After filing a Freedom of Information Act (FOIA) request, I obtained approximately one thousand pages from the SPP office in the U.S. Department of Commerce.[11] These documents are archived on The Minuteman Project website.[12] Judicial Watch also obtained a set of documents from the SPP office under a separate FOIA request.[13] These documents prove that the Bush administration has cooperated with Mexico and Canada on a broad range of policy issues. It is clear that the SPP is creating a new regional infrastructure that includes Mexico and Canada and is aggressively rewriting U.S. administrative law, all without congressional oversight or public disclosure.

The following is a formal organization chart. This chart depicts thirteen working groups on a reporting structure diagram. Working groups within the U.S. government report through the National Security Council (NSC) and the Homeland Security Council (HSC),[14] which in turn report directly to the Office of the President.

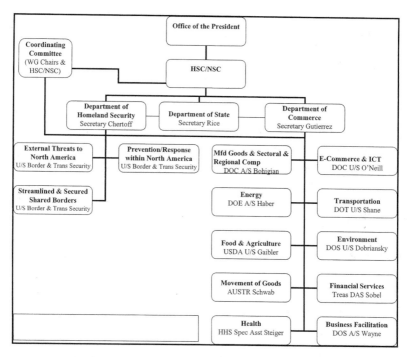

Figure 1. Organizational chart of the Security and Prosperity Partnership of North America, obtained by a Freedom of Information Act request, 2006

Three working groups report to U.S. Department of Homeland Security Secretary Chertoff:

- External Threats to North America
- Prevention/Response within North America
- Streamlined and Secured Shared Borders

Ten working groups report to U.S. Department of Commerce Secretary Gutierrez:

- Manufactured Goods and Sectoral and Regional Comp
- Energy
- Food and Agriculture
- Movement of Goods
- Health
- E-Commerce and ICT (Information and Communication Technology)
- Transportation
- Environment
- Financial Services
- Business Facilitation

At the cabinet secretary level of the organizational chart, Secretary of State Condoleezza Rice is listed between Secretary Chertoff and Secretary Gutierrez, with no working groups directly reporting to her. Secretary Rice is immediately below the HSC/NSC reporting structure at the next highest level of the chart, suggesting that she is the cabinet-level coordinator chosen to coordinate directly with the HSC/NSC.

It is not known how many working groups exist within the SPP. The *2005 Report to Leaders* references twenty or so groups. One organizational chart depicts thirteen working groups (cf. figure 1) and the Canadian SPP website lists nineteen, ten addressed to the "Security Agenda" and nine addressed to the "Prosperity Agenda."[15] Another document lists thirty-six working groups. Many documents referencing these working groups are still inaccessible.[16]

As far as can be determined, SPP working group participants came from the following Bush administration departments:

- U.S. Department of State

- U.S. Department of Commerce

- U.S. Department of Homeland Security

- U.S. Department of Treasury

- U.S. Department of Agriculture

- U.S. Department of Transportation

- U.S. Department of Energy

- U.S. Department of Health and Human Services

- U.S. Trade Representative

Hundreds of pages of internal emails and memoranda document that dozens more administrators were involved in the various levels of working group activity.

This level of activity within the Bush administration points to far more than a mere dialogue with two foreign nations. Documents released through the FOIA and information posted on government websites, prove that a wide range of U.S. administrators and departments are involved in functioning working groups within the three governments. The working groups are assigned specific, detailed tasks. The reports published by the SPP indicate that the working groups are signing a large number of new memoranda of understanding, mutual agreements, and other forms of cooperation. There is ample evidence to suggest that a newly formed administrative structure is active within the three North American governments. Those working from within the SPP are actively integrating and harmonizing U.S. administrative law and regulations, including those involving national security, with administrative law and regulations in Mexico and Canada.

None of this has been made clear to the American people. Those who want to learn more about the SPP must resort to FOIA requests and comb through hundreds of government Web sites written in language best suited to lawyers and bureaucrats.

SPP Gains Momentum

In late 2006, the Department of Commerce published the 2005 and 2006 editions of *Report to Leaders*. The books carried the three-flag

SPP symbol and were published in English, Spanish, and French. The copyright page of the 2005 report indicates that the report was copublished by the governments of the United States and Mexico, and is also copyrighted in Canada.

Over two hundred and fifty "memorandums of understanding," "modifications of rules," "frameworks of principles," and other agreements are listed in the 2005 and 2006 *Reports to Leaders*. The reports discuss the modification of administrative rules and regulations under the rubric of "integrating" and "harmonizing" into a North American structure what had previously pertained to the United States, Canada, and Mexico.

For instance, the energy working group announced in the 2005 report that their goal was "creating a sustainable energy economy for North America." To seasoned readers of international documents, the word "sustainable" used in this context is a code word to globalist thinking embedded in UN doctrines intended to limit the growth of developed nations such as the United States.

SPP working groups are active within the traditional departments of the U.S. government. The North American Energy Working Group (NAEWG), for instance, has a Web page on the U.S. Department of Energy website.[17] A January 2006 report entitled "North America—The Energy Picture II" documents that the NAEWG first met on June 27–28, 2001, in Washington, D.C. There have since been eight more NAEWG working group meetings "convened in various locations of the three countries, with many more meetings of the various expert groups convened under the NAEWG agenda."[18]

SPP working groups have ranged across virtually every area of public policy. The *2006 Report to Leaders* documents the following working group activity in the Prosperity Agenda:

- Manufactured Goods and Sectoral and Regional Competitiveness
- Movement of Goods
- E-Commerce and ICT
- Financial Services

- Transportation

- Energy

- Environment

- Food and Agriculture

- Health

The *2006 Report to Leaders* identifies the following Security Agenda initiatives, milestones, and status of completion in the following areas:

1. Secure North America from External Threats
   - Traveler Security
   - Cargo Security
   - Bio-protection

2. Prevent and Respond to Threats within North America
   - Aviation Security
   - Maritime Security
   - Law Enforcement Cooperation
   - Intelligence Cooperation
   - Protection, Prevention, and Response

3. Further Streamline the Secure Movement of Low-Risk Traffic Across Our Shared Borders
   - Border Facilitation
   - Science and Technology Cooperation

Despite the advanced stage of activity, many U.S. congressmen and senators have no idea that SPP working groups are producing a North American regulatory structure. SPP remains one of the best-kept secrets in Washington, though it is disclosed on dozens of U.S. government websites and has now published full-color books in three languages.

SPP "Trusted Travelers" and "Trusted Traders"

The *2005 Report to Leaders* made clear that a "continental perimeter" has been defined as the primary line of defense against terrorists. In a section entitled, "Securing North America from External Threats," SPP discloses:

> We have established plans to develop and implement comparable processes which produce consistent outcomes for screening individuals prior to departure and at first point of entry into North America, as well as to develop and implement compatible screening methods for goods and cargo prior to departure from a foreign port and at the first point of entry to North America.

Among the strategies identified to implement this commitment is the issuing of biometrics to facilitate "legitimate travel" within North America. "We will devise a single, integrated global enrollment program for North American trusted traveler programs within the next thirty-six months."

This statement suggests that Mexican "trusted travelers" might be able to go to the SPP office in Mexico and obtain a biometrics border pass that would allow them to cross our borders at will. The SPP is silent about reconciling this program with current U.S. visa or work-permit programs. The SPP has pledged to "develop standards for lower-cost secure proof of status and nationality documents to facilitate cross-border travel" before January 1, 2008. This suggests that the first steps may be in place to create a North American passport.

For "trusted traders," the SPP *2005 Report to Leaders* recommended the use of electronics to speed border crossings. The report indicated that trusted traders would be able to pass the border quickly by streamlining Free and Secure Trade System (FAST) processing at ports of entry and expanding the Secure Electronic Network for the Travelers' Rapid Inspection (SENTRI) program to priority ports of entry within twelve months.

SENTRI Electronics, FAST Lanes, and RFID Chips

The United States, Canada, and Mexico have implemented various programs to enable rapid border crossings using electronic identification. The NEXUS program in Canada gives preapproval to citizens or permanent residents of Canada or the United States who have registered and been accepted as "preapproved travelers" through either the Canadian government[19] or the U.S. government.[20] NEXUS is a trusted traveler ID program jointly operated by Canada Border Services Agency and the U.S. Customs and

Border Protection. Additionally, all three nations have agreed to participate in the FAST program, which allows commercial truck carriers and drivers, manufacturers, or other import/export companies and professionals to register with the appropriate government offices in the three countries to obtain preapproval as "trusted traders" of North America.[21]

At border crossing points, FAST lanes are created as express lanes, designed to reduce border-crossing time to a minimum. Generally involving an electronic check equivalent to the E-ZPasses used on U.S. toll roads, the NEXUS and FAST electronic ID allows those "trusted travelers" and "trusted traders" to enter restricted lanes where border crossing is expedited. While those without electronic IDs are often forced to wait for hours at border crossing checkpoints, the trusted travelers and trusted traders zip right by. Border guards do not inspect the cargo of trusted travelers and trusted traders. These programs could conceivably be expanded to the point where virtually any citizen of the three countries could register as a trusted traveler and any business operation could become a trusted trader.

A recent innovation, the SENTRI program, allows applicants to apply to U.S. Customs and Border Protection be preapproved as a "low-risk traveler."[22] After conducting a thorough international criminal records search, "low-risk travelers" are issued a Radio Frequency Identification Card (RFID) that records the person's status in the CBP database. SENTRI electronic decals are also issued for the vehicles of low-risk travelers. Under the SPP, the United States and Mexico have begun establishing SENTRI electronic border-pass checks at multiple locations across the Mexican border, with the ultimate goal of expanding the program to all border crossing locations on the U.S. borders with both Canada and Mexico.

NEXUS, FAST, and SENTRI are controlled by all three nations. While our borders with Mexico and Canada will not be erased any more than the borders between EU countries have been erased, those equipped with the right electronic equipment will soon be able to cross borders at will if they qualify as trusted travelers and traders. The SPP documents do not envision that many trusted travelers will be screened individually at border crossing points, nor will the commercial vehicles driven by SPP trusted traders be inspected at the border. This strategy places unwarranted confidence in Mexico, a drug cartel dominated country where a culture of political corruption yet prevails.

It is very possible that terrorists will attempt to enter the United States through the auspices of the trusted traveler program and that drugs will enter the United States in the vehicles of trusted traders.

Hezbollah terrorists have already bought their way into the United States through our open border with Mexico. On March 1, 2005, Mahmoud Youssef Kourani pleaded guilty to federal charges of using meetings at his home in Dearborn, Michigan, to raise money for Hezbollah's terrorist activities in Lebanon.[23] Kourani was an illegal alien who had been smuggled across our border with Mexico after he bribed a Mexican consular official in Beirut to get him a visa to travel to Mexico. Kourani and a Middle Eastern traveling partner then paid *coyotes* to get them into the United States. Each year thousands of OTMs (Other Than Mexicans) enter the United States from Mexico, including hundreds from "suspect" Middle Eastern countries. Unfortunately, U.S. Border Patrol agents never apprehend the vast majority of these OTMs.

A drug war waged by the Mexican drug cartels is spilling across the U.S. border. In March 2007, a Mexican truck that was stopped in Laredo, Texas, carried 4,723 pounds of marijuana in a false compartment.[24] How much more easily will drug trucks pass into the United States once the drug cartels have SPP trusted trader electronics installed on their trucks?

Despite these dangers, the SPP continues to work to increase free trade by simplifying the border crossing process.

SPP Reduces Time at Border Crossings

NAFTA trade has, then, become the final standard for the SPP, not sovereignty. The SPP boasts that transit times have been reduced at the border-crossing gateway, knowing fully that the efficiency was created via electronics. This raises serious security concerns. Once a system is created, criminals will find ways to bypass the required security checks. In addition, the SPP is not concerned about the invasion to privacy or loss of freedom involved for citizens who will be required to submit to background checks in order to qualify for, acquire, and use the electronic systems. Dr. Pastor's dream that border crossings would be as easy as using an E-ZPass on a U.S. highway may soon be realized by SPP trusted traveler and trusted trader planning.

CHAPTER SIX

THE TRANS-TEXAS CORRIDOR

"Bienvenidos a Kansas City, centro de Norteamérica."
("Welcome to Kansas City, the center of North America")

Susan Segal, President and CEO, Council of the Americas[1]

THE BEGINNING OF A REGIONAL GOVERNMENT is not the only thing taking shape. Private, government, and international interests have already begun work on integrating North America's transportation system. In order to facilitate the integration of the Mexican, American, and Canadian economies, a transportation system allowing for easy access between the three countries is necessary. While the beginnings of regional government are being put in place by the SPP, governmental, private, and international interests are also beginning work on the integration of a North American transportation system.

While the SPP has worked to ease border restrictions by implementing trusted traveler and trusted trader programs, the Bush administration through the Federal Highway Administration (FHWA) has supported plans in the state of Texas to build a huge NAFTA superhighway, four football fields wide, from the Mexican border at Laredo, Texas, to the Canadian border north of Duluth, Minnesota. The moment the Texas Legislature suggested imposing a two-year moratorium on the construction of TTC-35 parallel to Interstate 35, the chief counsel for FHWA sent a letter to the executive director of the Texas Department of Transportation (TxDOT) threatening a loss of federal highway funds should the legislature move ahead.[2] This massive project, which will include separate lanes for trucks, trains, and utility lines, will not only tie together the three countries, but will also allow containers from the Far East and China to access the lucrative American market from Mexico.

While Mexican trucking companies carry goods into America's heartland, Mexican trains acquired by Kansas City Southern Railway Company will operate as a "NAFTA railroad" to carry containers from the Far East and China to the Laredo border.

The first customs stop in the United States will be a Mexican customs office in the Kansas City SmartPort complex, a facility being built for Mexico at a cost of $3 million to the U.S. taxpayer. Internal emails obtained under a Missouri Sunshine Law request show that KC SmartPort officials have been told by the State Department that the facility will most likely be considered Mexican soil, though it is located in the heart of the United States.

The first Trans-Texas Corridor segment of the NAFTA superhighway is already under construction. Many U.S. government agencies, dozens of state agencies, and scores of private nongovernmental organizations (NGOs) are working behind the scenes to create the NAFTA superhighway along a route parallel to Interstate 35.

The pieces are almost in place to facilitate an ever-increasing influx of Chinese goods into the American economy, while lining the pockets of the foreign investors who finance the superhighways and the multinational corporations that manufacture goods overseas for retail sale in the U.S. marketplace.

Spanish Investors Fund Trans-Texas Corridor Construction

Construction began on the Trans-Texas Corridor (TTC) following the reelection of Governor Perry in November 2006. In a four-way race in which a plurality of the vote was sufficient to win, Perry was reelected with less than 40 percent of the vote. All three of his opponents campaigned against the Trans-Texas Corridor. Despite receiving less than a majority vote, Perry has been determined to proceed with the TTC-35 project. Plans to build TTC-35 are fully disclosed on www.keeptexasmoving.org, an official Texas Department of Transportation (TxDOT) website.

On March 11, 2005, The TxDOT signed a "comprehensive development agreement" to build the "TTC-35 High Priority Corridor" parallel to Interstate 35.[3] The contracting party involved a limited partnership formed between Cintra Concesiones de Infraestructuras de Transporte, S.A.,[4] a publicly listed company headquartered in Spain, and a San Antonio–based construction company, Zachry Construction Corporation.[5] The Madrid-based construction company Groupo Ferrovial, one of Spain's largest builders, is in control of Cintra.[6] Grupo Ferrovial manages airports in Australia, Chile, and the U.K., as well as toll roads in Spain, Portugal, Canada, Chile, Ireland, and the United States.[7]

Cintra's contract with TxDOT to build the TTC was the biggest move in the United States so far in a growing trend to sell public infrastructure to foreign investors. In October 2004, Cintra along with Macquarie,[8] an Australian private investment consortium, bid $1.83 million to the city of Chicago to take over operations of the Chicago Skyway toll road on a ninety-nine-year lease.[9] In April 2006, the same group completed an agreement to lease for seventy-five years the Indiana Toll Road for an initial payment of $3.8 billion to the state of Indiana.[10] Cintra's successful bid to build and operate the TTC was the largest such contract negotiated to date.

Once the TTC is completed, U.S. citizens who want to drive on the superhighway from one Texas site to another will have to pay an investment consortium in Spain for the privilege. While the ownership rights of projects like the TTC will be retained by the state of Texas, Cintra will own the leasing rights to the superhighway for decades.

Under the terms of the TC comprehensive development agreement with TxDOT, Cintra-Zachry agreed to provide private investment of $6 billion "to fully design, construct and operate a four-lane, 316-mile toll road between Dallas and San Antonio for up to fifty years as the initial segment of TTC-35.[11] For this, Cintra-Zachry paid the state of Texas $1.2 billion for the long-term right to build and operate the initial segment as a toll facility. The initial payment was made when the contract between Cintra and TxDOT was signed, with no further approval needed by the voters or tax-payers of Texas. TxDOT received the authorization to undertake this massive project through a series of modifications to Texas law that were passed in previous years. Whether Texas voters realized it or not, in approving the proposed modifications to Texas law, they gave TxDOT the authority to proceed with a foreign entity to build the TTC. Texas voters would have no recourse to claim they did not understand the full implications of the authorizing laws when they were passed.

The TxDOT contract envisioned that Cintra-Zachry would de-velop a plan to build the entire TTC from Laredo, Texas, to the bor-der of Oklahoma, parallel to Interstate 35, a route that passes San Antonio, Austin, and Dallas. The development plan called for Cin-tra-Zachry to specify the near-term five-year plan (2005–2010), mid-term (2010–2025), and long-term (after 2025), in what was en-visioned to be a fifty-year project involving the construction of a network of some four thousand miles of TTC roads throughout Texas. The comprehensive development agreement calls for Cintra to fund all TTC superhighways with private funding. As joint ven-ture partner with Cintra, Zachry will presumably build the TTC throughout the fifty-year development period.

In April 2006, TxDOT released a four-thousand-page Envi-ronmental Impact Statement (EIS) for what was described as the "Trans-Texas Corridor-35 Oklahoma to Mexico/Gulf Coast Ele-ment."[12] The April 2006 EIS made clear that Cintra-Zachry planned to build a twelve-hundred-feet-wide complex involving ten lanes of highway—five lanes in each direction, north and south, with three lanes in each direction reserved for passenger vehicles and two separate lanes reserved for trucks. The EIS de-sign included six rail lines running parallel to the highway, with separate rail lines in each direction for high-speed rail, commuter rail, and freight rail. Finally, the design called for a two-hundred-feet-wide utility corridor that included pipelines for oil and natu-ral gas, pipelines for both water, cables for telecommunications and data, as well as electricity towers running the length of the

TTC.[13] An artist's rendering of the system is included from the Environmental Impact Statement.[14]

Figure 2. The concept for the Trans-Texas Corridor, shown here in an artist's rendering, calls for separate lanes for cars and trucks; rail with separate lines for passenger, high-speed freight, and commuter traffic; and a utility zone.

Source: U.S. Department of Transportation, Federal Highway Administration, article authored by Antonio Palacios, "Public Roads: Trans-Texas Corridor," July/August 2005. (http://www.tfhrc. gov/pubrds/05jul/07.htm)

TTC Designed for International Trade

Why does Texas need such a transportation system? The EIS statement of purpose made it clear that the TTC was designed to facilitate international trade:

> The purpose of TTC-35 is: To improve the international, interstate, and intrastate movement of goods and people; address the anticipated transportation needs of Texas from the Texas/Oklahoma state line to the Texas/Mexico border and/or Texas Gulf Coast along the I-35 corridor for the next twenty to fifty years; and, sustain and enhance the eco-

nomic vitality of the State of Texas. (EIS Executive Summary, page ES-3)

The proposed system is not without its costs. The concept for
the TTC system dates back to a TxDOT Trans-Texas Corridor
Plan adopted in June 2002. TxDOT ultimately plans to build some
four thousand miles of highway-railway-utility superhighways
throughout Texas over the next fifty years, using some 584,000
acres of what is now Texas farm and ranchland, at an estimated
cost of $184 billion.[15] The four-thousand-mile TTC system will
crisscross Texas from north to south and east to west. The system
reaches up into the panhandle of Texas and stretches across the
border with Oklahoma, and runs from El Paso on the west and
Laredo in the south. The network circles every major Texas city,
including San Antonio, Austin, Houston, and Dallas-Ft. Worth.

The TxDOT produced a conceptual map of the full TTC system to illustrate how the fifty-year build-out would network
Texas.[16] In addition to following the path of I-35, the TTC route

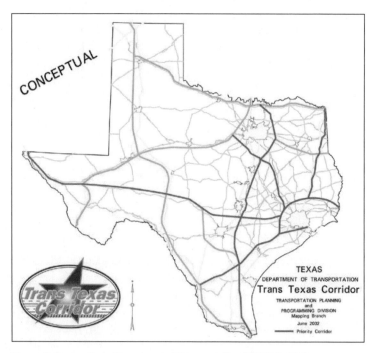

Figure 3. *Source: Texas Department of Transportation (TxDOT), 2002*

would proceed north from Laredo along the path of Interstate 69, heading east toward Indianapolis, where the route is intended to pass into Canada north of Chicago, through Michigan.

The TTC is designed to be an alternative to the existing interstate system, a separate toll road network that abandons the existing interstate structure without attempting to supplement it. It is apparently the beginning of a continental network designed to move intermodal goods that derive from global trade.

There are significant problems, however, with this plan. For one, the TTC corridors, nearly a quarter-mile in width, will be difficult to cross. These superhighways will virtually divide the land through which they pass. If the real intent of the TTC was to relieve congestion on existing interstate highways, then it seems

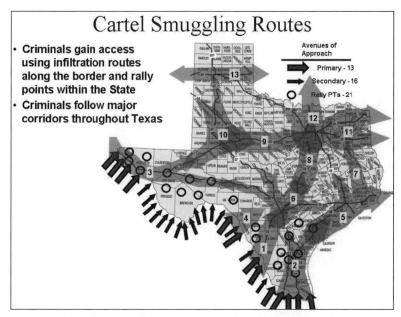

Figure 4. Note how similar this map is to the previous map showing the full 4,000 mile build-out of the TTC system. The planned Trans-Texas Corridor routes almost exactly parallel the drug cartel's smuggling routes in Texas.

Source: "A Line in the Sand: Confronting the Threat at the Southwest Border," a report prepared by the majority staff of the House Committee on Homeland Security, Subcommittee on Investigations, October 10, 2006. http://www.house.gov/mccaul/pdf/ Investigaions-Border-Report.pdf

the new transportation systems should interface with existing highways, especially in Texas's major cities. Instead, TxDOT designed TTC routes to go around important cities, leaving intracity transport largely to the existing network of limited access interstate highways. Connections to I-35 or other local highways in Dallas or Ft. Worth, where I-35 rush hour congestion can be a serious problem, are the responsibility of the cities themselves, not TxDOT, and certainly not Cintra or Zachry.

The construction of the TTC will have a staggering impact on the lives of many Texans. Consider the impact of one million eminent domain notices. Communities will be cut in half, necessitating driving tens of miles to get to the nearest overpass to see a neighbor or to get to the other side of a ranch. Families that have owned farms or ranches for generations will be thrown off their land so the superhighway can come through. When the 4,000 miles of TTC construction are complete, Texas will be crisscrossed by a network of superhighways that divide the state into pockets bridgeable only on overpasses or underpasses. Gone forever will be the Texas of Wild West lore. Gone forever will be the ranches and farms that have produced food for generations of Americans.

Texas will make use of the recent Supreme Court case *Kelo v. City of New London* (545 U.S. 469 [2005].[17]) In this case, the Supreme Court decided that eminent domain could be used to seize private property from U.S. citizens even though the purpose of the land seizure was to benefit a private corporation. The Supreme Court case said nothing that would imply the private corporation involved would have to be a U.S. corporation, which allows the Spanish-owned group backing the TTC to operate.

What is even more distressing is that eminent domain procedures in Texas severely mitigate resistance by homeowners. In a question-answer format on the TTC website, a "myth vs. reality" answer explains how the TxDOT plans to use what is known in Texas as "quick-take" eminent domain authority.[18] There TxDOT explains that a Texas state law (passed as HB3588) allows a quick-take seizure of private property "if TxDOT and the property owner cannot reach an agreement" on just compensation for the land involved. Under current Texas law, TxDOT can seize a property on the ninety-first day after the landowner is served with an official notice of quick take. As TTC construction begins on an aggressive schedule, more and more quick-take seizures of private property can be anticipated. Under quick take, no property owner who wants to block TTC progress will be able to do so for long. On the ninety-first day of a compensation disagreement, TxDOT under quick take will have the legal authority to step in and seize the land, regardless how vociferously the landowner protests.

It is hard to imagine that one million Texans will stand by and watch their land be taken from them. Perhaps this is a reason the TxDOT plans to build the highways over a period of forty years. Little by little, resistance will be worn away. The first land seized will be explained as a necessary cost of progress. Government officials, transportation planners, and politicians will find ways to prevent their own homes, ranches, farms, and business from being confiscated while leaving other Texans powerless to protect themselves.

The TTC is clearly not concerned with the preservation of Texas farm and ranch land. Those envisioning a regional or hemispheric economy imagine that the United States will import all the fruit, produce, and meat it consumes from lower-cost ranches and farms in Spanish-speaking countries south of the border. Texas ranches and farms are unfortunately dispensable if the United States intends to import the bulk of its good from another nation. The DOT, through the Federal Highway Administration (FHWA), has been involved at every step in the development of the TTC plans.[19] Published agreements between the FHWA and the TxDOT paved the way for TxDOT to proceed with its plans. Through the FHWA, the Bush administration recognized and approved of the TxDOT plans, recognizing that the development of the TTC as a "high-priority trans-Texas corridor" was consistent with the FHWA vision of how NAFTA superhighways should be developed in the United States.

Food moving from Spanish countries south of the border will largely enter the U.S. market through Texas. The decision to reconfigure Texas highways is consistent with the idea that

Texas will be a primary transportation gateway for free trade within the hemisphere.

A Mexican Customs Office in Kansas City

The goods that these TTC superhighways are carrying up from Mexico have to go somewhere. As SENTRI and FAST lanes are employed, many trucks will bypass customs at the border. In order to address that problem, a Mexican customs port is being built in the heartland of the United States: Kansas City.

The Council of Kansas City voted on May 18, 2006, to name the Mexican customs facility the "Kansas City Customs Port," despite the fact that it is actually a Mexican possession, staffed by Mexican government customs officials.[20] The $3 million facility will be paid for by Kansas City taxpayers, not by the Mexican government.

KC SmartPort is a nonprofit economic development organization dedicated to promoting Kansas City as "America's Inland Port Solution." A brochure on the organization's website[21] states that the ultimate goal is to bring containers from the Far East and China into Mexican ports, such as Lázaro Cárdenas, by-passing the Longshoremen's union in the ports of Los Angeles and Long Beach. Mexican trucks and Mexican railroads can then transport the containers into the United States over the NAFTA super-highways, bypassing the United Transportation Union and the Teamsters, as well as independent truckers who are owner-operators. The brochure, entitled "Two Worlds … One Route," includes a graphic that leaves no doubt about KC SmartPort's goal. A panel on the left of the graphic identifies four cities in the Far East—Tokyo, Bussan, Hong Kong, and Singapore—which are connected with a red line to the right panel, where the red lines enter North America at Lázaro Cárdenas. From there the red lines extend up through Texas, where they terminate in Kansas City.

Kansas City business leaders are determined to position themselves to profit from the global trade that is expected to flow through Mexico. The reasoning is simple. In the first ten years under NAFTA the volume of trade coming from Mexico did not prompt KC SmartPort to argue for the Mexican customs facility. Anticipating an increase in the volume of containers from the Far

East and China coming to our shores, the KC SmartPort expects many of those containers to enter mid-continent at Mexican ports on the Pacific. The TTC superhighway provides the needed truck and rail corridor and the logical mid-continent destination is Kansas City.

Unrestrained free trade means U.S. manufacturing will inevitably give way to the lowest cost of labor. Today, China has truly abundant slave labor and near-slave labor to meet the demand. Even in Mexico, an increasing number of manufacturing jobs are going to China, where the cost of labor is lower than that in Mexico and Central America.

In order to make this plan work, the cost of transporting those goods needs to be as near zero as possible. The mid-continent route to Kansas City is an inexpensive route because cheap goods from the Far East and China need not be transported by truck or train across the Rocky Mountains and the great expanse of the U.S. West. The use of Mexican dockworkers and transportation labor will save on U.S. labor union expenses. The logic is simple. First, the Far East and China reduce the cost of labor to as close to zero as is humanly possible. Then, floating the goods on huge container ships to Mexican ports on the Pacific transporting the containers up through Texas to Kansas City reduces the transportation costs of the goods to as little as possible. The distance the containers from the Far East and China have to be transported across land is reduced, thereby reducing costs. Then, to the extent that Mexican dockworkers and transportation workers replace U.S. workers, the more expensive cost of labor union employees and U.S. workers in general can be avoided.

The true social cost of cheap goods becomes more apparent when one considers the squeeze on middle class earnings represented by the plan. It is clear that multinational corporations seeking to maximize profits will continue to move U.S. manufacturing to foreign countries. Allowing multinational corporations free reign will not insure uninterrupted economic expansion, even if it allows corporations to reduce their costs and maximize profits.

Middle-class workers would suffer tremendously in the event of the inevitable business downturn. Should the housing bubble burst as did the dot-com high tech stock market of the late 1990s, many middle-class workers across the United States would be trapped with high-value mortgages they could no longer afford. Many of these hard-pressed mortgage holders might not be able to sell without substantial losses.

If this happens, the United States will be de-industrialized and the loss of manufacturing jobs will damage the middle class. Unions in the United States will be further damaged as Mexican dockworkers replace longshoremen and Mexican truck drivers replace Teamsters. Even non-union truck drivers will have to lower their earnings in order to compete. While Mexican train workers might not be able to replace United Transportation Union workers in the United States, the downward earnings pressure of Mexican train workers will embolden U.S. railroad companies who want to reduce the size of train crews. If UTU workers cannot be completely eliminated, their numbers can be reduced.

This plan is already in action. According to the SmartPort website, in March 2005, Kansas City signed a cooperative pact with representatives from the Mexican State of Michoacan to increase the cargo volume between Lázaro Cárdenas and Kansas City.

> Shipments will be pre-screened in Southeast Asia and the shipper will send advance notification to Mexican and American Customs with the corresponding "pre-clearance" information on the cargo. Upon arrival in Mexico, containers will pass through multiple X-ray and gamma ray screenings, allowing any containers with anomalies to quickly be removed for further inspection.

> Container shipments will be tracked using intelligent transportation systems (ITS) that could include global positioning systems (GPS) or radio frequency identification systems (RFID) and monitored by the ITS on their way to inland trade-processing centers in Kansas City and elsewhere in the United States.

> Kansas City offers the opportunity for sealed cargo containers to travel to Mexican port cities with virtually no border delays. It will streamline shipments from Asia and cut the time and labor costs associated with shipping through the congested ports on the West Coast. [22]

The international trade that Kansas City anticipates, then, is not made up of goods flowing between the United States and Mexico, but from China into America. If this continues long term, middle-class wages will drop due to job outsourcing and the lucrative American market will dry up. The multinational corporations involved are largely unconcerned about the long-term effects of their work. In the short run, boards and top officers can reasonably expect to boost quarterly profits by lowering costs. Mass-market distributors will benefit from selling "always low-priced" goods in the United States, which is still the world's largest retail market.

The federal government has been supportive of the Kansas City SmartPort. U.S. congressman Sam Graves (R-MO) has been successful in receiving federal funding for the project. Congressman Graves secured $500,000 in the 2003 fiscal year federal appropriations budget and another $750,000 in the 2005 fiscal year omnibus spending bill.[23] In September 2005, KC SmartPort received an additional $4 million from the Federal Highway Bill SAFETEA-LU to create Intelligent Transportation Systems that would tie into highway corridors linked to the SmartPort.

These funding initiatives reflect strong federal government support for the KC SmartPort effort to establish the city as the first inland port in the United States.[24]

Kansas City Southern: The NAFTA Railroad

The plan to make Kansas City the hub for international trade involves more than the development of a better highway system. Rail will also figure prominently in bringing Chinese goods into America through Mexico. Through a series of acquisitions including Mexican railroads, Kansas City Southern[25] has been declared the nation's first NAFTA railroad. Kansas City Southern (KCS) is a holding company consisting of three railroads: The Kansas City Southern Railway Company (KCSR), Kansas City Southern de Mexico, S.A. de C.V. (KCSM), and Panama Canal Railway Company (PCRC).

KCS has been called the "NAFTA railroad" ever since the acquisition of Mexican railroads. Mexican railroads play a key role in the KCS's NAFTA-focused marketing plan. The plan is to develop a U.S.-Mexican railroad network that connects to Mexican ports. This network can then supplement Mexican trucks in the effort to deliver to North America the goods manufactured in China and the Far East.

> The 2,661-mile KCSM operates the primary rail route in northern and central Mexico, linking Mexico City and Monterrey with Laredo, Texas, where more than 50 percent of the U.S.-Mexico trade crosses the border. The line also connects the major population centers of Mexico City and Monterrey with the heartland of the U.S. and serves the ports of Veracruz, Tampico, and Lázaro Cárdenas, a primary alternative to West Coast ports for shippers in the route between Asia and North America. [26]

A map on the KC SmartPort website calls the KCS system "NAFTA Rail." The map shows not only the KCS network, which reaches down into Mexico consolidate rail, but also displays the logos of the three railroads which it operates: the Kansas City Southern Lines, the Texas Mexican Railway Company, and TFM.

Kansas City SmartPort acknowledges the important place of the NAFTA Railroad in the Kansas City "inland port" plan. The

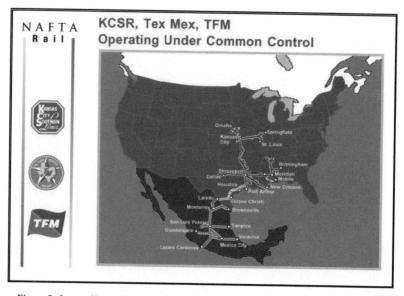

Figure 5. Source: Kansas City SmartPort website, "Two Worlds…One Route," a brochure available at http://www.kcsmartport.com/pdf/ SmtPrtOneRoute.pdf.

KC SmartPort website outlines the marketing plan:

> Kansas City offers the opportunity for sealed cargo containers to travel to Mexican port cities such as Lázaro Cárdenas with virtually no border delays. It will streamline shipments from Asia and cut the time and labor costs associated with shipping through the congested ports on the West Coast.

> In April 2005, Kansas City Southern completed purchase of a controlling interest in *Transprotacion Ferroviaria Mexicana* (TFM), enabling TFM, the Kansas City Southern Railroad, and the Texas Mexican Railway Company to operate under common leadership, creating a seamless transportation system spanning the heart of North America known as "The NAFTA Railway."[27]

A key goal of the SPP working groups has been to create "trusted traders," both rail and trucking connections that would permit the "free market" movement of goods between Mexico and the United States—a coming together of "free market" NAFTA thinking and the global "free market" thinking of the World Trade Organization.

This sort of open movement between countries for the sake of economic gain is exactly the sort of system that currently exists within Europe. A coherent transportation system is essential for the integration of large geographical areas, which is the reason why the Federal Highway Administration built an extensive freeway system throughout the United States in the second half of the twentieth century. Greater mobility between states allowed for greater economic prosperity. Such a strategy is now being adopted on an international level. While this may result in short-term economic gain for international corporations, it poses serious threats to American security and the enduring prosperity of America's middle class.

NASCO: A Trade Association for Super Corridors

The move to integrate trade within North America is not a random, isolated process. One organization that is working to further integrate North America's economies is the "North America Super Corridor Coalition, Inc.," or NASCO. NASCO is a

> Nonprofit organization dedicated to developing the world's first international, integrated and secure, multimodal transportation system along the International Mid-Continent Trade and Transportation Corridor to improve both the trade competitiveness and quality of life in North America.[28]

Note that this quote from the NASCO website says nothing about the United States. NASCO is intent on establishing North American super corridors, establishing travel and trade routes linking the three NAFTA countries.

As recently as May 2006, NASCO's website presented a map that emphasized the I-35 corridor's place as the central focus of NASCO's trade association activities. Curiously, this map was changed when concerns were raised about NASCO's activities. On the map, a yellow "Y" runs up from Lázaro Cárdenas in Mexico, north to Des Moines through Texas. The yellow "Y" next enters Oklahoma and passes through Oklahoma City on the way to Kansas City. In Canada, the yellow "Y" branches out to Vancouver on the west coast and Montreal in the east. While the NASCO map did present the United States, Canada, and Mexico as three distinct countries, the continental nature of the NASCO super-highway was clear. The map made it clear that NASCO intends to connect Mexico, Canada, and the United States into one super-corridor transportation system.

The NASCO website documents the receipt of $2.5 million in Congressional earmarks from the DOT for the development of a technology to track containers moving along the NASCO super corridor. The website goes to great length to distinguish the group as a trade association, not a government agency. NASCO also emphasizes that it will not build any highway. The building of the super corridors will presumably be left to the various NASCO members supported by the trade group.

The NASCO website places the organization's mission in the context of NAFTA trade. Consider the following language from the website:

> From the largest border crossing in North America (the Ambassador Bridge in Detroit, Michigan, and Windsor, Canada) to the second largest border crossing of Laredo,

Texas, and Neuvo Laredo, Mexico, extending to the deep water Ports of Manzanillo and Lázaro Cárdenas, Mexico and to Manitoba, Canada, the impressive, tri-national NASCO membership truly reflects the international scope of the Corridor and the region it impacts.[29]

NASCO has merged with what formerly was the North American International Trade Corridor Partnership (NAITCP), previously a Mexican nonprofit group. The North American Inland Port Network (NAIPN), a subcommittee of NASCO, has "been tasked with developing an active inland port network along our corridor to specifically alleviate congestion at maritime ports and our nation's borders." In addition to the KC SmartPort and the TxDOT, NASCO membership includes the Port of San Antonio and the Free Trade Alliance San Antonio, another private trade group that advances the idea that an inland city can also be an inland port.

NASCO's home page in May 2006 made it clear that the group was no longer looking at highways simply as U.S. freeways, and that its free trade vision was not limited to NAFTA. NASCO's goal is to support North American superhighways that link the United States, Mexico, and Canada into world trade via Mexican ports.

Plan for Superhighway Ripped as Urban Legend

Because organizations like the TxDOT, Kansas City SmartPort, and NASCO do not specifically label the highway concepts they are advocating as "NAFTA superhighways," officials of these organizations deny their intended creation. Such protests deny the obvious. The intermodal truck and rail transportation corridors and highways these organizations advocate would not be necessary unless North America had been opened up into a free trade organization.

On Wednesday, January 24, 2007, a congressman and a policy official of the DOT discussed whether NAFTA superhighways were a threat to U.S. sovereignty or an imaginary concern. Jeffrey N. Shane,[30] the under secretary of transportation for policy at the U.S. Department of Transportation, addressed these issues at a meeting of the Subcommittee on Highways and Transit of the

U.S. House of Representatives Committee on Transportation and Infrastructure.

During the questioning by committee members, Congressman Ted Poe (R-TX) asked Mr. Shane about the existence of plans for a NAFTA superhighway.

Shane responded that he was "not familiar with any plan at all, related to NAFTA or cross-border traffic." After further questioning by Poe, Shane stated that reports of NAFTA superhighways or corridors were "an urban legend."

At this, the chairman, Congressman Peter DeFazio (D-OR) questioned aloud whether Shane was just "gaming semantics" when responding to Poe's question.

"Mr. Shane was either blissfully ignorant or he may have been less than candid with the committee," Poe told *World Net Daily* in a telephone interview.[31]

When asked about the DOT's work with NASCO and the TxDOT, Poe told *WND*,

> The NAFTA superhighway plans exist to move goods from Mexico through the United States to Canada. It appears to be another one of the open-border philosophies that chips away at American sovereignty, all in the name of 'so-called trade.'
>
> There are security obstacles to this whole project that have to be addressed. I don't understand why the federal government isn't getting public input on this. We get comments like Mr. Shane's instead of our own government asking the people of the United States what they think about all of this. This big business coming through Mexico may not be good business for the United States.[32]

Poe continued to insist, "the public ought to make this decision...So, I don't understand, unless there's some other motive why the public isn't being told about these plans and why the public is not invited to make input."

On January 22, 2007, Congressman Virgil Goode (R-VA) introduced House Concurrent Resolution 40 to express the sense of Congress that the United States should not build a NAFTA superhighway system and should not enter into an agreement with Mexico and Canada to form a North American Union.

When asked to comment on Shane's response to Poe, Goode dismissed Shane's claim that NAFTA superhighways were just an urban legend

"Let's take Mr. Shane at his word. Let Mr. Shane come over here from the Department of Transportation and endorse House Concurrent Resolution 40," he said.

> If...he's not doing anything to promote a NAFTA super-highway and he's not doing anything to promote the Security and Prosperity Partnership of North America, then he won't mind joining his voice with ours to be in opposition to any such "urban legend," as he so calls it.

Congressman Goode objected to Mr. Shane's attempts to play what he agreed was a game of semantics:

"When President Bush had the meeting in Waco, Texas, the three leaders called the new arrangement the 'Security and Prosperity Partnership of North America,' SPP for short," Goode said. "But, as is suggested by Congressman DeFazio at the hearing, the intent of people like Mr. Shane is to use different words and different names as a way to deflect attention from what they are really doing."

Asked about White House Press Secretary Snow's denial that there was any White House plan to create a North American Union, Goode's reply was also direct:

"I guess Mr. Snow is saying that a Security and Prosperity Partnership and a North American Union are not one and the same," he said. "That's just the use of his words, but is he denying that President Bush, President Fox, and Prime Minister Martin had the meeting and came up with the Security and Prosperity Partnership in 2005? I doubt it."

Also present in the audience at the subcommittee meeting was Rod Nofzinger, director of government affairs for the Owner-Operator Independent Drivers Association.[33] Mr. Nofzinger told *WND* that Mr. Shane's denial struck him as less than genuine. In an email to WND, Mr. Nofzinger commented:

> Considering what we know about the Bush administration's efforts to open the border to Mexican trucks and that DOT officials have met with groups such as NASCO, I was

truly surprised to hear Mr. Shane say flat out that he had no knowledge of plans or meetings related to NAFTA or cross-border surface trade corridors.

Substantiating Mr. Nofzinger's argument is a speech given by Secretary of Transportation Norman Y. Mineta on April 30, 2004, at a NASCO forum in Ft. Worth, Texas.[34] There Mr. Mineta told the NASCO meeting, "NAFTA has opened the doors to expanding and flourishing trade across our border." He continued, "And to our friends from Mexico who are here today, I say, 'Welcome, and get ready.' Opening the border is of mutual benefit."

Specifically referring to Interstate Highways 35, 29, and 94, the core highways supported by NASCO as a prime "North American Super Corridor," Mineta mentioned NASCO:

> The people in this room have vision. Thinking ahead, thinking long term, you began to make aggressive plans to develop the NASCO trade corridor—this vital artery in our national transportation through which so much of our NAFTA traffic flows.

In a statement provided to *WND* by email, DeFazio cut past Shane's attempt to dismiss the subject by ridicule. DeFazio wrote that he was inclined to disregard Secretary Shane's statement of ignorance. "Whatever the case," DeFazio wrote, "it is a fact that highway capacity is growing to and from the border to facilitate trade, and there is no doubt that the volume of imports from Mexico has soared since NAFTA, straining security at the border." DeFazio was also aware of the plans to import an increasing number of containers from China. He continued, "Plans of Asian trading powers to divert cargo from U.S. ports to Mexico will only put added pressure on border inspectors. The U.S. needs to invest in better border security, including enhanced screening of cargo crossing our land borders."

Here Come the Mexican Trucks

While Congress wrangles over whether NAFTA superhighways are an urban legend, and while the public remains uninformed about the problems surrounding the growing integration of North America's economies, the federal government is pushing ahead with plans to open U.S. transportation systems to companies from other countries. The Department of Transportation has been determined to move ahead with a "pilot test" to allow one hundred Mexican trucking companies to run their long-haul rigs throughout the United States. The DOT and the Department of Homeland Security intend for Mexican trucking companies participating in the pilot test to be identified as SPP trusted traders. Accordingly, the Mexican trucks will be equipped with the necessary electronic identification systems needed to use FAST lanes.

On February 23, 2007, the DOT announced the launch of a year-long pilot program designed to allow one hundred Mexican trucking companies unlimited access to U.S. roads for the purpose of hauling international cargo.

As a reciprocal part of the pilot program, one hundred U.S. trucking companies will be allowed to operate in Mexico, but at a later date.

The February 23 DOT announcement set off a firestorm of criticism from within the trucking industry and from Congress.

In a press release issued by the Teamsters calling for congressional hearings, General President Jimmy Hoffa compared this announcement to the "Dubai Ports debacle," charging that President Bush is "playing a game of Russian Roulette on America's highways."

A spokesperson from the office of U.S. Senator Patty Murray (D-WA), chairman of the Senate Appropriations Subcommittee on Transportation, Housing, and Urban Development and Related Agencies, told *WND* that she plans to hold hearings on the DOT pilot program on March 8, 2007.[35]

A press release from Murray's office said, "I am holding this hearing to find out if the administration has really met the safety requirements that the law and the American people demand before long-haul Mexican trucks can travel across all our highways."

Todd Spencer, spokesperson for the Owner-Operator Independent Drivers Association, told *WND*:

> To reach a conclusion that the safety regime in Mexico is
> compatible in any way, shape, or form with what we have
> here in the U.S. is ignoring reality. Mexico has never had

hours in service regulations or drug testing of drivers. We still can't verify the accuracy of somebody's commercial driver's license in Mexico for safety or compliance.

Spencer stressed that this decision is not just a border decision. "Once Mexican trucks are in the United States on this pilot program, they can operate everywhere in the U.S.," Spencer told *WND*.

> If some state highway policeman in Vermont or Iowa stops a Mexican commercial truck in their state, they have absolutely no idea of deciding if that vehicle is in compliance with federal safety requirements. Who's going to provide the training or the equipment for state police to verify the legality of a commercial truck from Mexico, in terms of its cargo, its haul, its logbook, or even the driver? Local police aren't going to have a clue.

Hoffa cited Mexico's inability to satisfy the DOT inspector general's requirements for safety that have been mandated to the Federal Motor Carrier Safety Administration (FMCSA).

WND had previously reported that applications of some 678 Mexican motor carriers seeking long-haul authority to operate about four thousand vehicles had been held up pending the completed DOT inspector general's review of proposed FMCSA rules.[36]

The DOT spokesperson affirmed to *WND* that, after an audit of the enforcement mechanisms and regulations created by the FMCSA, the FMCSA has now drafted regulations that have been accepted by the DOT inspector general.

The Teamsters Union posed to *WND* a series of unanswered questions, including:

- Will the drivers be checked against the terror watch list or will our borders be open to anyone with a Mexican driver's license?

- Will the drivers be required to carry a Mexican passport as U.S. citizens are required to present their passports when entering the country from Mexico?

- Will all U.S. standards be applied to Mexican drivers, including the requirement that U.S. drivers undergo regular physicals and meet minimum age requirements?

- Will Mexican truck drivers participating in the pilot program be required to undergo drug and alcohol testing in U.S. labs? Who will oversee the collection of random samples for drug and alcohol testing of the Mexican drivers while they are in the U.S.?

- Will U.S. wage and hour laws be enforced for Mexican drivers during the pilot program? How will the DOT enforce hours of service rules and prevent false logbooks and fatigued drivers from entering the U.S.?

- How can the DOT assure the U.S. public that all trucks will be inspected by U.S. officials in Mexico and at the U.S. border when fewer than 10 percent of all Mexican trucks entering the commercial zone are inspected today?

According to a DOT spokesperson, the pilot program…

> …is predicated on the notion that Mexican trucks operating in the U.S. under the pilot program will operate pursuant to every single requirement that pertains to U.S. trucks operating in the United States, including both safety and security requirements on both the state and federal level.

The DOT has increased its inspection staff by some 270 inspectors to implement the pilot program and plans to continue the on-site inspection activities in Mexico. The DOT spokesperson confirmed that there is no limit to the number of trucks the one hundred Mexican trucking companies can operate in the United States. They may travel on any road within the United States once they are admitted in the pilot program at the border.

The Mexican trucks, however, were initially limited to carrying international cargo. The DOT pilot test specified that Mexican trucks be prohibited from picking up cargo in the United States for delivery within the United States. On their return home, the Mexican trucks would be allowed to pick up American-made cargo destined for delivery back to Mexico.

DOT insisted that Mexican trucks operating in the pilot test would meet all requirements for U.S. truck drivers. The DOT spokesperson specified that under agreements with Mexico already in effect, Mexican and U.S. commercial driver's licenses will be considered equivalent during the pilot program. Mexican trucks operating in the United States would be required to have U.S. insurance coverage for all liabilities, including traffic accidents.

"The intent is for the Mexican trucking operations in the U.S. to be indistinguishable from U.S. trucking operations," the DOT spokesperson affirmed, "except that the driver and the truck began their route in Mexico." Still, the controversy continued to rage, despite DOT reassurances.

U.S. Infrastructure Reconfigured for World Trade

Whether or not government and trade association officials wish to acknowledge the true intent of their actions, they are transforming U.S. highways and railroads into continental trade routes that can accommodate increasing NAFTA and WTO trade, anticipating a continued shift of U.S. manufacturing overseas.

The goal of those working on projects like the TTC is to restructure the transportation infrastructure of North America fundamentally—not so that Americans can move more quickly and efficiently between U.S. cities, but so that the vessels of global trade can arrive in North America and move throughout North America more cheaply and efficiently. With billions of dollars at stake in the effort to increase the volume of international trade brought into North America, there is plenty of international capital available to accomplish this restructuring. The international capitalists and the politicians who support them do not seem to care if the United States loses manufacturing jobs in large numbers, or if thousands of U.S. middle-class workers see their livelihoods undermined by slave labor or near-slave labor from China and the Far East.

To understand the magnitude of the international capital effort being mobilized to support the reconfiguration of the U.S. transportation system, the next section of the book will examine what the Bush administration has promoted as "public-private-partnerships," or PPP. The idea is to bring billions of dollars in foreign investment capital into the United States to finance transportation infrastructure programs (including the construction of the super corridors already discussed) as central to opening the United States to foreign manufacturers and foreign goods. The PPP concept is that, in exchange for their investment, foreign investment interests would own the management rights of their infrastructure projects under a contract that would permit the foreign investment source to collect tolls or other fees from the users of PPP infrastructure projects.

CHAPTER SEVEN

PUBLIC-PRIVATE PARTNERSHIPS

"There is no new, proposed 'NAFTA Superhighway.'"
NASCO (North America's SuperCorridor Coalition, Inc.)[1]

"On July 23, 1997, the NAFTA Superhighway Coalition was formed."
The NAFTA Superhighway Coalition, the Ambassador Bridge[2]

NORTH AMERICA'S PROGRESSION toward political integration is clearly moving forward on two related fronts. On the one hand, there is a clear move to improve the transportation links between Mexico and the United States in order to facilitate the influx of goods from the Far East and China into the American market. On the other hand, this further opens the American economy to international businesses, such as Mexican trucking companies. While international businesses have always been present in the United States market, this is the first time the construction of new American transportation infrastructure has been outsourced to foreign investment companies.

International companies have a strong economic interest in the integration of North America. Not only will companies from the Far East and China be able to transport goods more cost effectively into the U.S. market, but international infrastructure financing consortiums will have the opportunity to redesign the American infrastructure around the idea of international, rather than intra-national, trade.

The Bush administration has strongly encouraged the development of PPPs, or public-private partnerships. The model for these PPPs is the TTC agreement with Cintra, the investment consortium in Spain that will finance the construction of the Trans-Texas Corridor. Private investment capital will pay to develop multiple trade corridors throughout the United States under "comprehensive development agreements" in which the investment consortium will operate the corridor and collect tolls. Not surprisingly, many of these participating investment consortiums are foreign.

Foreign investors, through PPPs, stand to take advantage of an increasing number of investment opportunities in America's infrastructure. While government transportation officials at the national and state levels are planning multiple NAFTA superhighways throughout the United States, investment bankers are busy ensuring that international investors are available to fund the deals and that state officials know how to structure PPPs to take advantage of the international capital.

When examining the ways that foreign investments fit into the picture, it is important to understand that the TTC discussed in previous chapters is not the only superhighway intended to facilitate the cheap movement of international trade into the United States.

I-69—The Second NAFTA Superhighway

The I-69 corridor has already advanced into the funding and construction stages. As listed on the U.S. Department of Transportation's Federal Highway Administration's (FHWA) website, the corridor will connect Mexico and Canada through Texas, Louisiana, Arkansas, Mississippi, Tennessee, Kentucky, Indiana, Illinois, and Michigan.[3] The TxDOT's TTC website openly links the two projects: "Interstate 69 is a planned 1,600-mile national highway connecting Mexico, the United States, and Canada."[4]

> Congress passed several pieces of legislation defining the I-69 corridor. Legislation included ISTEA (1991), 1993 DOT Appropriations Act, 1995 National Highway System Designation Act and TEA-21 (1998).[5]

The website further indicates that TxDOT anticipates the completion of the I-69/TTC environmental impact statement in Fall 2007 and expects to receive federal approval in Winter 2007.[6]

States Describe I-69 as a NAFTA Superhighway

The Louisiana Department of Transportation and Development (LaDOTD) acknowledges that it conducted an I-69 environmental and location study in conjunction with the FHWA to study a proposed route through Bossier, Cado, and DeSoto Parishes. As described on the LaDOTD website, "The proposed highway is part of the I-69 Corridor, which will link Indianapolis, Indiana, to the lower Rio Grande Valley in Texas."[7] The description of the I-69 Corridor on the LaDOTD website echoes the description on the TxDOT website: "Interstate 69 is a 1,600-mile long national highway that will ultimately connect Canada to Mexico." LaDOTD openly states that the I-69 Corridor's purpose is to "improve international and interstate trade."[8] Federal highway funds have enabled the group to begin construction.[9]

Similar I-69 Corridor discussions may be found on the state department of transportation websites in Arkansas,[10] Mississippi,[11] Tennessee,[12] Kentucky,[13] Indiana,[14] and Michigan.[15] The only state DOT website that does not have a specific discussion of the I-69 Corridor is Illinois. The FHWA specifies that the involvement of Illinois in the I-69 corridor is limited and that the current plan is that the corridor in Illinois will utilize existing roads, particularly I-94 from Chicago to Detroit.[16] The I-69 Corridor will cross the U.S. border with Canada in Port Huron, Michigan, continuing in Canada as Highway 402 in Ontario.

The Federal Highway Administration's Strategic View of I-69

The FHWA has called the I-69 corridor as a "megaproject," defined as "a major transportation project that costs at least $1 billion and attracts a high level of public attention or political interest because of their impact on the community, environment, and State budgets."[17] As was noted in the previous chapter, the FHWA considers the four thousand miles of TTC superhighways planned for construction in the next fifty years to be an essential component of hemisphere trade expected to come through Texas in coming decades. These Texas superhighways, including I-69, constitute a NAFTA/CAFTA gateway into the United States. Should the Free Trade Act of the Americas (FTAA) ever be passed, the gateway through Texas would open up the United States for hemispheric trade reaching down to the tip of Argentina.

FHWA reports reveal how the I-69 Corridor fits into the planned TTC network. Antonio Palacios, an engineer in FHWA's Texas Division, provides the following explanation in a FHWAY publication:

> Although part of a national project, I-69/TTC is being developed in Texas under the Trans-Texas Corridor master plan. I-69 is a 2,570-kilometer (1,600 mile) national highway that, once completed, will connect Mexico, the United States, and Canada.

The FHWA has created a website to instruct state highway managers how to create PPPs within their own jurisdictions.[18] The close similarity between this FHWA language and the language used by states such as Texas and Louisiana in describing the I-69 corridor is striking. A section of the TxDOT TTC website has been created to feature I-69 planning.[19]

Anyone doubting the support of the Bush administration for PPP highway construction should recall President Bush's nomination on September 5, 2006, of Mary Peters as secretary of transportation.[20] Ms. Peters served as the head of the FHWA in the Bush administration as the TTC and I-69 Corridor projects were being developed.

Multiple Corridors and
Multiple Corridor Trade Associations

The home page of the nonprofit organization North American Forum on Integration (NAFI) displays a map that shows four North American corridors—Pacific, West, East, and Atlantic.[21] Robert Pastor is a member of the NAFI board of directors.

The NAFI website notes that following the implementation of NAFTA, "coalitions of interest have been formed to promote specific transportation channels, to develop the infrastructures of these channels and to propose jurisdictional amendments to facilitate the crossing of the borders."[22] The website explains that these coalitions include businesses, government agencies, civil organizations, metropolitan areas, rural communities, and individuals who wish "to strengthen the commercial hubs of their regions."

Put simply, this means that government and business groups have come together to support the development of four north-south corridors that will span North America east to west. The planned corridors are intended to be similar to the Trans-Texas Corridor, in that they are multimodal, moving containers in both trucks and trains, and moving people in cars and trains.

The NAFTA superhighway/corridor concept has been well advanced since 1994, involving extensive government, business, and trade organization activity that is thoroughly documented on dozens of official websites. One must examine the NAFI corridors one by one, to see how much extensive government-business planning has already been done to make these NAFTA corridors a reality.

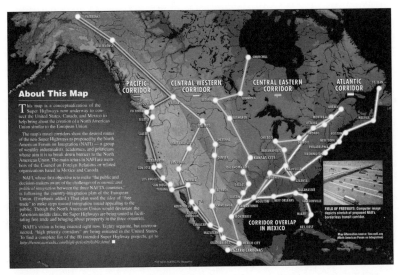

Figure 6. *Source: Map by Jim Capo, Reproduced with Permission from* New American Magazine.

The Pacific Corridor

The Pacific Corridor is intended to span both the Pacific coast and the west side of the Rocky Mountain routes.

The key organizing group for the Pacific Corridor is the U.S.-Canadian International Mobility Trade Corridor Project (IMTC), a coalition of business and government interests formed in 1997. The IMTC has received funding from both the U.S. and Canadian government.[23]

CANAMEX

CANAMEX is a proposed NAFTA superhighway that would extend from Edmonton, in Alberta, Canada, to Mexico City. The route would connect Salt Lake City and Las Vegas on the western slope of the Rocky Mountains. On the eastern slope, a superhighway called "Camino Real" would connect Billings, Montana; Cheyenne, Wyoming; Denver, Colorado; and El Paso, Texas. Both routes would connect in Canada, extending to Fairbanks, Alaska, and in Mexico where they would terminate at Mexico City.

In 1995, CANAMEX Corridor (www.canamex.org) was founded as a trade organization. The FHWA identifies CANAMEX and the Camino Real routes as High Priority Corridors under federal highway law.[24]

The Atlantic Corridor

The Atlantic Corridor runs down the eastern seaboard roughly along Interstate 95. The I-95 Corridor Coalition is one of the more advanced trade corridor business and government groups in existence.[25]

Investment Bankers and Foreign Investors Stand Ready

Private investors have a vested interest in the completion of the superhighway projects. Not only will the new infrastructure increase trade, but there is a considerable amount of money to be made from toll payments. The projects will require private financiers in order to go forward. A study by the National Chamber Foundation of the U.S. Chamber of Commerce[26] concluded that the Highway Trust Fund will have a zero cash balance in 2008 after meeting the highway capital improvements mandated by the 2005 Safe, Accountable, Flexible, and Efficient Transportation Act—A Legacy for Users (SAFETEA-LU) legislation. The only obvious solution to this budget shortfall is to raise gasoline taxes.

Key players, including the investment bankers and the worldwide capital investors, have a plan to address these fiscal shortcomings with their own resources. On April 30, 1992, President George H. W. Bush signed Executive Order No. 12803 on infrastructure privatization, a move that cleared the way for private capital to invest in U.S. infrastructure projects. As noted by C. Kenneth Orski, the editor and publisher of the transportation industry publication Innovation Briefs,[27] the model has been well established in Europe. Italy's Autostrade SpA was sold to private investors in the 1990s and in France the three largest toll roads in which the government had a controlling interest were put up for sale in 2005. In Spain and Portugal, all major roads are today in private hands.

Capital groups such as Cintra Concesiones de Infraestructures de Transport in Spain and the Macquarie Infrastructure Group and Transurban in Australia are positioned to make substantial investments in the building of NAFTA superhighways within America.

With trillions in investment dollars needed to build the next generation of highways in the United States, investment bankers and those who run capital investment funds stand to make hundreds of millions in fees. This alone is enough to drive forward the NAFTA superhighway movement and to make sure politicians willing to support the movement have ample funds with which to run their campaigns and live their lives comfortably. Each superhighway project proposed will involve huge quantities of foreign capital, much of which will be paid as initial fees.

The TTC may be viewed as a test case. The investment world is watching carefully, anticipating that the TxDOT will succeed. The growing momentum behind PPPs virtually guarantees that highway departments in all fifty states will soon consider leasing existing or planned highways to foreign investment interests.

Carlyle Group Forms Infrastructure Investment Project

In March 2006, the Carlyle Group, a global private equity firm headquartered in Washington, D.C., announced the organization of an eight-person investment team that will raise a multi-billion dollar fund to purchase public infrastructure projects, including U.S. highways that can be operated as toll roads.[28]

The team is headed by two experienced leaders: Robert W. Dove, who spent ten years with Bechtel Enterprise, the financing and development arm of the Bechtel Group, a global engineering construction company, and by Barry Gold, the former Managing Director and co-head of the Structured Finance Group of Citicorp/Salomon Smith Barney. As described by the Carlyle Group's website:

> Carlyle's Infrastructure team will invest primarily in the U.S. infrastructure in transactions ranging from $100 million to more than $1 billion. The team will engage in public-private partnerships (PPP) with governments at all levels as well as purchase projects outright or through long-term concessions.

As reported in the *Guardian*, President George H. W. Bush has been compensated substantially by the Carlyle Group for giving speeches and reportedly advising on various Carlyle Group investments.[29] Dubai International Capital also coinvests in Carlyle Group private equity deals.[30] In 2006, Dubai International Capital surfaced in the U.S. press as Dubai Ports World sought to acquire P&O Ports, the port operations subsidiary of the London-based Peninsular & Oriental Steam Navigation Co. In the resulting controversy over port security and Dubai's history of involvement with terrorism, Dubai Ports World agreed to divest the U.S. port operations involved in the acquisition.

Frank Carlucci, secretary of defense under President Reagan, originally created the Carlyle Group. When he organized the Carlyle Group in 1987, the plan was to bring together a group of former government and military officials who had extensive experience with defense and national security. The Carlyle Group was to be a private capital group that would quietly invest in defense industry projects, seeking to leverage the insider status of

Carlyle Group principals to benefit financially from government contracts in their areas of expertise. In 1993, James Baker III, former secretary of state under President George H. W. Bush, joined the Carlyle Group. The Carlyle Group has not been limited to conservative Republicans. In September 2003, George Soros invested $100 million in Carlyle Partners II, one of the Carlyle Group's most successful funds.[31]

The group also has a Mexican investment operation with ties to President Clinton. In January 2004, the Carlyle Group put together a new team to begin investing in Mexico. The 3-person team managing the group's Mexican office included Mark McLarty, the chief of staff to and special envoy to the Americas for President Bill Clinton.[32]

"PPP" — Investment Bankers Put America Up for Sale

As was noted earlier, on April 30, 1992, President George H. W. Bush signed Executive Order No. 12803 on infrastructure privatization, clearing federal barriers for cities and states to lease public works infrastructure to private investors. Although the action involved no law passed by Congress, the executive order allowed cities and states to generate substantial one-time payments for leasing existing public facilities or for entering into "comprehensive development agreements" with private investors to build new public infrastructure. Without this action by President George H. W. Bush, the TTC project would never have been possible. Now, investment bankers worldwide are rushing to benefit from the huge fees they know will be realized as PPP projects in the United States privatize a wide range of public infrastructure, including highways, schools, water departments, and prisons.

In September 2006, the Euromoney Seminars, a division of the London-based Institutional Investor PLC, held a PPP conference in New York at the Waldorf Astoria hotel. The organizers of the North American PPP 2006 conference[33] charged attendees $2,000 to hear talks by investment bankers from some of the world's largest and most prestigious investment banks, including Lehman Brothers, Goldman Sachs, the Royal Bank of Scotland, HSBC, JPMorgan Asset Management, and AIG Highstar Capital.

Cintra, Macquire, and the Carlyle Group (in the person of Barry Gold) attended as well.

The Waldorf Astoria conference brought multi-billions in capital finance capability together with state and federal highway officials, tax attorneys, accountants, and municipal officials to discuss how more of the U.S. infrastructure could be sold to private investors, expanding the TTC model developed in Texas. Government representatives included attendees from the U.S. DOT and the government of Mexico. Additionally, some ten different state departments of transportation sent representatives to the conference, including DOT government representatives from the states of Virginia, Wisconsin, Louisiana, Florida, Oregon, Alaska, Indiana, and Texas.

Topics at the conference included "providing state government with access to quick capital," and "To toll or not to toll: When, where, and how?" The PPP conference made it clear that ample private capital worldwide was available for applying the TTC model to highways across the United States. All aspects of private finance and management of state highways in the United States were considered, including fees, tax considerations, legal issues, and environmental considerations.

Noting that $90 billion is required each year just to maintain U.S. infrastructure up to current standards, the conference brochure made clear that in the United States much more than highways was available for PPP private capital infusions:

> In order to adequately improve the network, a cash investment is required that would upgrade transportation networks, highways, airports, ports, municipal buildings, housing, and schools. Federal and state governments alone are not in a position to fund this injection. Going to the municipal bond finance markets is becoming more difficult as public debt grows even larger. Moreover, an inability to raise funds through higher taxes means public revenue will continue to remain flat.[34]

The PPP intends to make virtually all public infrastructures available for private investment and management. U.S. citizens accustomed to viewing their roads, schools, water departments, hospitals, ports, airports, municipal buildings, and prisons as public institutions owned by all residents in the state are in for a surprise. Given the direction PPP is headed, America is up for sale and there is no assurance taxes will go down as a result. The U.S. taxpayer has paid for current public infrastructures. Now the federal government is encouraging states and local governments throughout the country to sell those facilities to private investment consortiums, under the direction of private investment bankers who will earn billions of dollars in fees in the process.

Euromoney Seminars held a second PPP conference in Miami, Florida, from March 19–21, 2007.[35] Entitled, "PPP: The North American Public Private Partnerships Intensive Seminars," the conference is subtitled, "A three-day intensive learning seminar featuring twenty hours of lectures, presentations, and guidance from field-leading experts in North American PPP and PFI." PFI stands for private finance initiative, a companion concept to the public-private partnerships.

The cost of the 2007 Euromoney Seminars PPP program is $3,499 per participant. The conference brochure reassures attendees that the expense is worth it, noting "Attendance guarantees you instruction in the need-to-know aspects of PPP deals."

Responses to the PPP System

The influx of private investment funds into public projects has created mixed reactions. On the one hand, the federal government has embraced the new sources of funding. The FHWA website enthusiastically promotes the use of PPPs to build transportation infrastructure.[36] The FHWA states clearly that under PPP the "private sector assumes a greater role in the planning, financing, construction, operation, and maintenance of a transportation facility compared to traditional procurement models."[37]

The site shows legislators and administrators what changes in state law are required to make transportation PPPs possible. Five of the seven sample PPP projects listed are in Texas, including both the TTC project and I-69, listed for the Texas segment as TTC 69.[38] A FHWA manual issued in November 2005 on using PPPs for highway projects is provided as a PDF download on the website "to provide a one-stop resource" for states that want to develop highway projects in conjunction with the FHWA.[39] The website also provides as "templates" the agreements that were made to lease the Chicago Skyway and the Dallas to San Antonio segment of the TTC project.[40]

Conservatives have recently cooled toward the new arrangements. At first, many conservatives supported PPPs, on the premise that private enterprise groups could build and operate public infrastructure more efficiently than government bureaucracies. If private investment capital could be mobilized to develop, maintain, and operate public infrastructure projects, then perhaps taxes could be cut. As NAFTA has developed, however, conservatives are now questioning these presumptions. For one thing, the sell-off of U.S. public infrastructure raises national security issues. The U.S. public was unwilling, largely because of security concerns, to see a port operations company with Dubai take over operations at major U.S. ports. Are the American people really ready for U.S. highways to be reconfigured into global trade corridors? How does anyone know that the foreign interests investing into U.S. public infrastructure will not have hostile disagreements with the United States at some time in the future? How certain is it that terrorists will not penetrate the management structures set up by foreign investors to manage their U.S. infrastructure projects?

President George W. Bush has made abundantly clear that his administration has no objection to foreign entities purchasing major U.S. corporations, including U.S. airlines.[41] The Department of Defense has suggested that foreigners might be recruited to the U.S. military, in return for receiving preference on becoming U.S. citizens.[42] How far will this national defense outsourcing go?[43] These questions should be subject to national public debate as the PPP momentum builds.

The transportation restructuring of America, if ultimately completed, will be a joint enterprise between government, represented by the SPP, and private enterprise, represented by the various international and American corporations involved in the intended creation of the Trans-Texas Corridor. This restructuring favors the very global capitalists who stand to make the most money. Behind the goal of integrating North America through a comprehensive transportation system is the goal of increasing the profit margin for large businesses. This economic drive is taking America's infrastructure out of American hands and placing it in the hands of global companies, who will only be sympathetic to America's interests as long as it is profitable for them.

As we will see in Part Three, this is only one of the many consequences stemming from the gradual adoption of the integrationist policies espoused by Pastor and others. These theories have slowly entered the realm of government policy through the SPP working groups, and the realm of legal jurisprudence with the creation of the NAFTA Chapter 11 tribunal. As theory becomes action, and as action becomes law, what will be the impact on America's economy and sociopolitical culture?

PART III

THE EFFECTS OF GLOBALIST POLICY ON AMERICA

CHAPTER EIGHT

RED CHINA OPENS PORT IN MEXICO

"With the collapse of the Soviet Union, and the internal disarray of the Russian Federation, the People's Republic of China sees itself as the sole Communist superpower in the world."

Edward Timberlake & William Triplett, *Red Dragon Rising*, 1999.[1]

INTEGRATIONISTS would have us believe that moving the United States toward a supra-national marketplace will benefit America. Not only would such policies make goods and services cheaper for average Americans, they claim, but building and staffing super corridors and other major capital projects necessary for the integration would add jobs, give the United States a radically improved infrastructure, and decrease wait times at the border.

But the sword of global capitalism cuts both ways. China is the true beneficiary of increasing global "free trade" with the United States. China stands to gain the most from the widening of American markets that would result from the formation of a North American community. Cheap goods from the Far East and China already undercut jobs in the United States, Canada, and Mexico—integrating North America would only accelerate this process. Giving China unprecedented access to North American ports will undercut the economies of all three North American nations and make North American economies less able to compete in the global marketplace.

In fact, the loss of manufacturing in North America has already begun to jeopardize the long-term health of the United States' economy. Unfortunately, "free trade" agreements we have made with China have not been "fair trade" agreements. In our enthusiasm to trade with China, our "free trade" arrangements, including those negotiated under the World Trade Organization (WTO), continue to be one-sided, decidedly in favor of China.

Today, in order to access the lucrative United States market, China must deal with unionized longshoremen at Los Angeles, New York, Seattle, and other port cities throughout the United States, which they perceive as far too costly. With the advent of super corridors, the Chinese will circumvent expensive U.S. labor unions by shipping their goods to Mexico, which will then travel by truck to the rest of North America.

Cities such as Kansas City and San Antonio are declaring themselves to be "inland ports," ready to receive the containers from China coming into North America through the rapidly developing Mexican ports on the Pacific. A new, deeper and wider Panama Canal will permit megaships with goods from the Far East and China to sail directly to Gulf ports and East Coast ports such as Miami. Sailing Chinese goods a longer distance is cheaper than unloading Chinese containers in West Coast ports and transporting them by truck and train into the heart of the United States. Development plans in Gulf ports and East Coast ports such as Miami are preparing to position for a share of the megaship container traffic the multinational corporations are planning to bring into the United States over the next twenty-five years.

China enjoys important structural advantages in international "free trade" with the United States. America's exported goods are taxed twice when they are exported to China under a value added tax system that unfairly removes VAT taxes when Chinese goods are exported to the United States.

But structural advantages alone are not China's only means of gaining leverage. Their willingness to exploit their own workers in ways unthinkable in the United States gives them a massive labor pool. International businesses looking to maximize profits keep millions of Chinese workers in slavery, or near-slavery, in order to use them as workers. By allowing ourselves to become dependent upon cheap Chinese goods and labor, the United

States has largely lost our moral authority to reprimand China and correct these human rights abuses.

In the final analysis, it is China and those who are able to invest in Chinese companies that stand poised to profit from the integration of North America as a free trade marketplace. Perhaps that is why the Chinese are working so hard to ensure such integration happens.

China Invests in NAFTA Ports in Mexico

In order to solidify its economic superiority over North America, Red China is working to restructure the North American transportation infrastructure. To that end, they are investing heavily in developing deep water ports in Mexico in order to bring an unprecedented volume of containers into the United States along the emerging NAFTA super corridor.

Hutchison Ports Holdings (HPH), a wholly owned subsidiary of China's giant Hutchison Whampoa Limited (HWL),[2] is investing millions to expand the deep water ports on Mexico's Pacific coast at Lázaro Cárdenas[3] and Manzanillo.[4] Now Hutchison Ports is pledging millions more to develop Punta Colonet, a desolate Mexican bay in Baja California. Mexico plans over the next seven years to dredge and convert Punta Colonet into a ten- to twenty-berth-deep water port capable of processing some six million standard Twenty-Foot Equivalent Units (TEUs).[5]

It is not just any Chinese company, however, that owns Hutchinson Ports Holdings. According to Judicial Watch, "Hutchison, Whampoa, Ltd., is the holding company of billionaire Li Ka-Shing, a well-known businessman whose companies make up 15 percent of the market capitalization of the Hong Kong Stock Market." A Judicial Watch complaint[6] filed in 2002, when HWL was purchasing the then-bankrupt Global Crossing,[7] notes that Li Ka-Shing's holdings includes ports, telecom, and energy assets around the world.

Ka-Shing is more than a typical corporate tycoon; he has some very interesting friends. A declassified intelligence report that Judicial Watch obtained in a Freedom of Information Act (FOIA) request reported that, "Li is directly connected to Beijing and is willing to use his business influence to further the aims of the Chinese Government." Judicial Watch objected that "Li Ka-Shing's agency relationship to the Communist Chinese should disqualify him from owning Global Crossing's network, which controls a significant percent of all the fiber optics currently leaving the United States."

Global Crossing was a Clinton administration darling noted for turning Democratic National Committee chairman Terry McCauliffe's $100,000 investment into an $18 million personal fortune. But Global Crossing's bold move to control the U.S. fiber-optics network overreached, ending in a corporate melt-down that was an unfortunate prelude to the Enron debacle. Hutchison Ports dropped the bid to purchase Global Crossing when the Committee on Foreign Investments in the United States (CFIUS) refused to approve the transaction on national security grounds.[8]

HWL also has business dealings with the China Ocean Shipping Company (COSCO), China's largest shipping line, which is owned by the Chinese People's Liberation Army.[9] In 1998, Congress blocked on national security grounds an attempt by the Clinton administration to allow COSCO to lease the abandoned Long Beach Naval Station.[10]

Despite the ongoing security concerns, HWL has established a North American beachhead. Remarkably, in the aftermath of the Dubai Ports World blowup in Congress, the Bush administration hired HWL in the Bahamas to operate sophisticated equipment designed to detect nuclear material inside containers headed for the United States.[11] By investing millions to deepen Mexico's ports, HWL has found perhaps the most effective back door of all for gaining access to the continental U.S. market.

San Antonio's Inland Port Pursues China

Hutchinson Port Holdings is not the only party interested in expanding the ports in Mexico. The Port Authority of San Antonio[12] has been working actively with the Chinese to open and develop the Mexican coast to more Chinese shipments.

In April 2006, officials of the Port Authority of San Antonio traveled to China with representatives of the Free Trade Alliance

San Antonio,[13] the Port of Lázaro Cárdenas, and Hutchison Port Holdings to develop the Mexican ports. The goal of the meetings in China was described by the March 2006 e-newsletter of the Free Trade Alliance San Antonio:

> In January of 2006, a collaboration of several logistics entities in the U.S. and Mexico began operation of a new multimodal logistics corridor for Chinese goods entering the U.S. Market. The new corridor brings containerized goods from China on either Maersk[14] or CP Ships[15] service to the Mexican Port of Lázaro Cárdenas. There, the containers are off loaded by a new world class terminal operated by Hutchison Ports based in Hong Kong. The containers are loaded onto the Kansas City Southern Railroad de Mexico where they move in-bound into the U.S. The containers clear U.S. customs in San Antonio, Texas, and are processed for distribution.[16]

The Free Trade Alliance San Antonio is self-described as a "public-private" organization created in 1994 to lead the development of San Antonio as a competitive "inland port" and international trade center.

A Mexican Customs Office in San Antonio?

San Antonio's inland port is crucial for a developing NAFTA super corridor along Interstate I-35. According to reporter Rick Alm, San Antonio envisions the opening of a Mexican customs office in their inland port, a move that has been pioneered by Kansas City SmartPort:

> Under this area's arrangement [establishing a Mexican customs facility in the Kansas City SmartPort], freight would be inspected by Mexican authorities in Kansas City and sealed in containers for movement directly to Mexican destinations with fewer costly border delays. The arrangement would become even more lucrative when Asian markets that shipped through Mexican ports were figured into the mix. "We applaud the efforts of Kansas City and the Mexican government in developing a Mexican customs facility there," said Jorge Canavati, marketing director for Kelly USA [former name for San Antonio's inland port established on the former site of Kelly Air Force Base]. He said a

Mexican customs function for Kelly USA "is something that is still far away…We may be looking at that" in the future.[17]

The Free Trade Alliance San Antonio 2005 summary of goals and accomplishments documents the direct involvement of the Bush administration in the development of San Antonio's inland port plans. The following were among the bullet points:

- Organized four marketing trips to Mexico and China to promote Inland Port San Antonio and met with prospects. Met with over fifty prospects/leads during these trips.

- Continued to pursue cross border trucking by advocating a pilot project with at least two major Mexican exporters as potential subjects. Worked with U.S. Department of Transportation, Dept. of Homeland Security, and U.S. Trade Representative on this concept.

- Working with Mexican ports to develop new cargo routes through the Ports of Manzanillo and Lázaro Cárdenas.

As already noted, San Antonio is on the planned route of Trans-Texas Corridor 35.

In October 2006, representatives of the Free Trade Alliance San Antonio, together with officials of the Port Authority of San Antonio and officials from the Mexican Port of Lázaro Cárdenas, visited China again on a corridor marketing trip. According to a press release put out by the Free Trade Alliance San Antonio, the primary purpose of the trip was "to promote the new multimodal logistics corridor developed by Port San Antonio that runs between the Mexican Port of Lázaro Cárdenas and San Antonio."[18] The press release further specified the savings anticipated by using this new route, instead of the more traditional route through Los Angeles or Long Beach:

> Opened in early 2006, the new corridor offers Chinese exports a competitive alternative for entering the U.S. market. Since its inception, the new corridor has consistently saved shippers 3–5 days on delivery times and an average of $100 on shipping costs for Chinese containerized goods transiting into the Texas market. New changes in steamship service may further reduce the transit time by another thirty hours.

While in China, the group anticipated making their presentation to another three to four hundred Chinese logistics and exporting companies.

The development of a China-Mexico trade route reflects a fundamental shift since NAFTA's passage. In the mid-1990s, there were some three thousand *maquiladoras* located in northern Mexico, employing over one million Mexicans in low-paying, assembly sweatshops. Today, even Mexican labor is not cheap enough for international corporations. According to the Federal Reserve Bank of Dallas, the *maquiladora* activity is down over 25 percent from its peak, as international corporations have found even cheaper labor in China.[19] William Hawkins estimates that six hundred *maquiladora* assembly plants have now relocated to China, leaving 250,000 unemployed Mexican workers behind.[20]

As the Port of San Antonio suggests, linking inland ports with NAFTA super corridors and NAFTA railroads is an important part of the development plan for the emerging global economy. Multinational corporations are now determined to exploit cheap Mexican labor, not so much for manufacturing and assembly, but as a means of saving port and transportation costs in the North American market.

The Plan to Deepen and Widen the Panama Canal

The move to import Chinese goods even goes as far south as Panama. Panama plans to build a deeper, wider Panama Canal in order to allow Chinese ships direct access to the Gulf of Mexico and key ports such as Miami, Florida. At present, the Suez Canal is the primary passage for ships from the Far East to reach the East Coast of the United States. Deepening and widening the Panama Canal would provide the Far East a second option.

The shipping industry defines Panamax container ships as those that are able to fit through the 1,000-feet-long and 110-feet-wide lock chambers of the 92-year-old Panama Canal.[21] The Panama Canal allows ships that are a maximum of 965 feet long and 106 feet wide.[22] Typically, the largest Panamax containerships today carry forty-five hundred twenty-foot containers, which is the standard length. The first generation of post-Panamax container ships carry up to 9800 containers. Today, a new class of super-post-Panamax vessels is under construction. These will carry 12,500 such containers.

Panama's President Martin Torrijos has decided to put to referendum a $6 billion project to build new locks in the Panama Canal sufficiently deep and wide to accommodate post-Panamax ships.[23] President Bush, while visiting Panama during November 2005, supported the plan to expand and modernize the Panama Canal, a plan then estimated to cost $10 billion.[24] Critics such as the Council on Hemispheric Affairs have argued that the cost of expanding the Panama Canal could be as high as $25 billion.[25] Hutchison Ports Holding, through its subsidiary Panama Ports Company, operates the ports of Cristobal and Balboa located at each end of the Panama Canal.[26]

Citing the increasing congestion in West Coast ports, shipping industry experts have argued that either the Panama Canal must expand to accommodate the huge volume of Chinese imports or the canal will simply become obsolete. Otherwise, post-Panamax ships containing Chinese goods will be forced to utilize the Suez Canal to access the U.S. market.

In 2003, West Coast ports handled approximately 80 percent of the more than $100 billion in goods imported from China. Atlantic ports accounted for about 19 percent and Gulf Coast ports picked up the extra 1 percent. As noted by Michael Bomba of the Center for Transportation Research at the University of Texas at Austin, "the volume of Chinese import trade handled by East Coast ports has more than doubled between 2000 and 2003, with the largest jump occurring in 2002, when shippers began to search for alternative routes."[27] Shipping industry experts widely regard the Longshoreman Union's West Coast strike a primary reason importers of goods from China have sought to open Mexican ports and a variety of East Coast ports as alternative ports of entry.[28]

Huge Post-Panamax Megaships

The post-Panamax fleet in service at the end of 2000 consisted of some three hundred container ships.[29] Experts expect that container ships with nine to ten thousand container capacity will soon dominate main arterial shipping, such as between China and the United States. Ships with twelve thousand and over capacity will be phased into operation between 2009 and 2010.[30] Super container ships with the capacity to carry 12,500 containers have to be built with twin engines to maintain the twenty-five-knot speed required for a maximum load, which will involve at least twenty-one containers stacked across the weather deck.[31]

Post-Panamax container ships carrying seven thousand containers require cranes 250 feet tall, equivalent to a twenty-story-tall building. In March 2005, the Port of Oakland, California, installed a second post-Panamax crane that was 241 feet tall, which the city described as being "as tall as a twenty-four-story building at its apex."[32] The $7 million crane was designed with a boom that can extend to unload ships stacked twenty-three containers wide. The week after the crane was installed, the Port of Oakland was expecting one of the world's largest container ships, the eighty-two hundred container "Hugo." The Hugo is able to carry enough cargo "to completely fill a one million-square-foot regional shopping center with TVs, toys, clothes, shoes, and other products stacked eight feet high."[33]

Preparing to handle super post-Panamax containerships with 12,500 TEU capacity requires reengineering just about every deep-sea port in North America. None of this would be necessary except that it seems the Bush administration plans to continue the work started by President George H. W. Bush and Bill Clinton. If the plan were to strengthen manufacturing within the United States, there would be no need for post-Panamax ships and ports with post-Panamax cranes for unloading.

Global shipping companies are working to increase the size of their ships in order to achieve economies of scale, thereby reducing transportation costs. Even goods produced by cheap Red Chinese labor would not be competitive in the United States if transportation costs from Asia could not also be reduced dramatically. Just as China has sought to capture the world market on cheap labor, so they are pushing to reduce transportation costs to and within the United States to the cheapest levels possible. For the unbridled capitalists, the "best" cost of labor and transportation is zero, or as close to zero as possible.

Port of Houston Positions for Post-Panamax Trade

Jim Edmonds, chairman of the Port of Houston, has said that the Port of Houston is the Gulf port most likely to benefit from the expansion of the Panama Canal.

"The Port of Houston has 73 percent of the container market in the Gulf of Mexico and about 94 percent of the container market in Texas," Edmonds explained. "So, it would be logical to assume that whatever growth in Gulf container traffic that comes from the expansion of the Canal would most likely come into Texas."

A Cambridge Systematics study[34] completed in October 2006 confirms that the impact of the Panama Canal expansion "will be felt most heavily on and around the Port of Houston, the state's largest container port and a key trading partner for goods shipped via the Panama Canal." Cambridge Systematics also documented the move away from West Coast ports, noting that:

> The Panama Canal's share of total container shipments between Asia and the United States has increased from 11 percent in 1999 to over 38 percent in 2004 and container volumes through the Canal are expected to grow by nearly 6 percent annually over the next several years.

On February 8, 2007, the Port of Houston opened the Bayport Container Terminal, which was built in anticipation of an ever-increasing volume of container traffic coming through the port.

Cambridge Systematics concluded that the Bayport Container Terminal "will approximately triple the available capacity for containerized traffic at the Port and allow it to more effectively handle Panamax and post-Panamax ships." The $1.4 billion Bayport Container Terminal, when fully developed, will have seven container berths with the capacity to handle 2.3 million containers on a complex which includes a 376-acre container yard and a 123-acre intermodal facility.

Edmonds confirmed that the Trans-Texas Corridor plans to develop I-69 are part of the Port of Houston's plan.

"I am hopeful that the south Texas segment of I-69 will be among the first to be upgraded," Edmonds said. I see I-69 over time as a real improvement to the ability to move cargo from Canada to Mexico and the Port of Houston needs to be a player in that."

Big Easy Gets Ready for Megaships from China

"The Panama Canal is very important to the Port of New Orleans," said Chris Bonura, communications manager of the Port of New Orleans.

> Just because of geography, if you want to get from the Far East to the Port of New Orleans, you have to go through the Panama Canal. So, this expansion project will be beneficial to the Port of New Orleans, and truly to all the ports in the Gulf of Mexico.

Bonura explained that the Mississippi River is the main channel for the Port of New Orleans: "The Mississippi River is maintained to a depth of forty-five feet," Bonura said, "and we believe we can serve as a conduit through the Mississippi River to the whole middle section of the United States."

"Instead of coming to the East Coast or the West Coast and carrying containers into the center of the U.S. by train or truck," Bonura continued, "we believe we have a direct route through the Mississippi River to go right up into the nation's heartland. On the Mississippi River, you can get to thirty states without touching dry land."

"The whole concept of the transport of containers on barges has not taken off as much in the United States as it has in Europe," Bonura conceded. "Still, there are various types of cargo that are not time-sensitive and there is a considerable cost savings to barge transport. The Mississippi River adds a dimension to the Port of New Orleans that make us truly a full intermodal, allowing for containers to be transferred to barges, trucks, or rail for transport into the interior of the country.

"The shipper at our port has a full range of modal choices once their cargo gets to the Port of New Orleans—truck, train, and barge," Bonura stressed. "Once the container to the port, that's only half the story. How are you going to get the container to the final destination? At the Port of New Orleans, we accommodate all the modes."

The shift in Asian trade to East Coast ports via all-water routes through the Suez and Panama canals, however, resulted in the Far East being the fastest-growing region for the port in 2005, reflecting an increase of 34.96 percent over fiscal 2004. Trade with Asian countries represented 22.71 percent of the total tonnage handled at the Port of Miami during 2005, second only to South America, which accounted for 23.42 percent of total trade.[35]

Sensors to Track Containers on I-35 NASCO SuperCorridor

This influx of goods from China demands a faster system of processing them. In order to accommodate the increased number of containers coming into the United States, developers are working on a system that would expedite both the processing and shipping processes. At first glance, the program seems innocuous enough, but further research revealed a surprising backer of this new development.

In order to track containers once they are within the North America, Lockheed Martin[36] has begun working with NASCO (North America's SuperCorridor Coalition, Inc.) to build a system of sensors to track cargo remotely along a super corridor stretching across North America from Texas to Canada.

On November 30, 2006, John Mohler, a senior vice president at Lockheed told the "North America Works II" transportation conference in Kansas City that his company would establish ten to fourteen sensor locations early in 2007 to track specific cargo shipments along the NASCO corridor that involves Interstate Highways 35, I-29, and I-94. The sensor locations would include the Mexican port of Lázaro Cárdenas; Laredo, Texas; Kansas City, Missouri.; and Winnipeg, Canada. Containers coming into Lázaro Cárdenas from China and the Far East would be equipped with these sensors for tracking in trucks and trains.

Lockheed plans to use tracking technology the company developed as the primary contractor in a program with the U.S. military called Global Transportation Network, which has been in operation since the first Gulf War in 1991.[37] For the program, Lockheed developed the sensor technology to track military cargo from the United States to the war zone in the Middle East. The Global Transportation Network tracking technology is intermodal in that it tracks containers wherever they are located—onboard ships, in trucks or trains, or in warehouses.

Mohler told the conference that the full network would cost $40 million and involve three hundred and fifty to four hundred sensor locations along the NASCO corridor, as well as a "command and control center" to monitor information on the tracked shipments, including cargo location, temperature, and weight changes. Mohler explained that Lockheed is designing the program to "integrate electronically the NASCO Corridor, north to south, from Winnipeg down into Mexico, to create an electronic backbone through the center of North America."

The purpose of the joint venture with NASCO, according to Mohler, is to achieve

> full visibility of freight moving along the NASCO corridor through the center of the United States, ultimately integrating both coasts with data on all freight moving north and south, ultimately as well from east to west, to get full integration of all data on the entire supply chain moving throughout North America.

NASCO plans to use the project with Lockheed to generate enough revenue so NASCO can become self-sustaining. Generating a private revenue flow is strategically important to NASCO in that the trade organization wants to find an alternative for keeping the organization financially alive other than continued dependence upon federal earmark funding.

On December 6, 2006, Leslie Holoweiko, a spokesperson for Lockheed Martin, confirmed that, "We are working with NASCO to propose a cargo tracking system that we think will make our super-corridor highway systems more secure without impeding the flow of commerce." Holoweiko also acknowledged that Lockheed has not yet signed a contract with NASCO. "Currently, we are pursuing a proposal," she said. "Nothing is firm as of yet and we should have more details in the next few months."

On December 5, 2006, Tiffany Melvin, the executive director of NASCO, confirmed that NASCO was pursuing a sensor contract with Lockheed, suggesting that the proposal "is a great opportunity for improving the efficiency and security of cargo as it moves along highways and rail." She also confirmed that Jim Bergfalk was being hired by NASCO to be the president of the International Mid-Continent Trade and Transportation Corridor Association, a new 501(c)3 nonprofit organization NASCO is forming to administer the Lockheed contract.

Mohler told the Kansas City conference that Lockheed plans to contribute $5 million of the $7 million needed to complete the pilot-project phase of the NASCO sensor project. The rest of the funds, according to Mohler, would come from the Department of Transportation. These funds would create the first ten to fourteen sites and establish the Lockheed Martin control center capability to capture and integrate the data. Lockheed and NASCO declined to explain how they planned to fund the $40 million required to build the full sensor system. Lockheed and NASCO also declined to say who would own the cargo tracking sensor system once it is completed.

China's Hutchison Port Holdings Aligned with NASCO

While the plan to build a sensor system to expedite the flow of goods from China into the United States is problematic in its own right, there is another wrinkle that is even more disturbing. Research revealed that Hutchison Port Holdings owns 49 percent of the Lockheed Martin subsidiary that was involved in implementing the corridor technology project with NASCO. Not only does Hutchinson Port Holdings operate the Mexican ports at both Manzanillo and Lázaro Cárdenas; it is also a subsidiary of Hutchison Whampoa Limited, which has close ties to the Communist Party in China.

On April 21, 2005, Savi Technology, a Lockheed Martin owned subsidiary, announced the formation of a new $50 million joint venture company, called Savi Networks LLC.[38] Savi Technology owned 51 percent of the joint venture company and Hutchison Port Holdings owned 49 percent. The announced purpose was to deploy a Radio Frequency ID (RFID) network to track and manage ocean cargo shipments.

Lockheed Martin spokesperson Leslie Holoweiko confirmed that Savi Networks LLC is the company named in the contract currently being negotiated with NASCO to provide cargo sensors along I-35. If successfully negotiated, the contract would appear to give Hutchison Port Holdings operational involvement all along the emerging I-35 NAFTA super corridor.

Apparently, the plan is to integrate data from Savi Networks Radio Frequency Identification (RFID) equipment with sensor data along the NAFTA super corridor, in order to track and manage cargo at any stage in its transportation. According to the press release announcing the formation of the joint venture company formed with HPH, Savi Networks LLC was created to install "active RFID equipment and software in participating ports around the world to provide users with information on the identity, location, and status of their ocean cargo containers as they pass through such ports."[39]

Conceivably, the Savi-installed RFDI software would permit NASCO to track containers from the time the containers leave ports in China and the Far East, to when the containers enter North America at Mexican ports such as Lázaro Cárdenas. From Mexico to Windsor and Winnipeg, NASCO could then track containers along the super corridor. This is the methodology Lockheed and NASCO plan to use to accomplish their goal of making the I-35 corridor an "electronic backbone" of the continent, capable of integrating all "supply-side" data regarding all global trade containers approaching or within North America.

Not surprisingly, the NASCO plan to use cargo tracking technology is consistent with the plans Security and Prosperity Partnership (SPP) of North America has put forth to rely primarily on technology, instead of in-person inspections, to track and monitor containers entering the United States. The NASCO container tracking system would integrate with the FAST lanes and SENTRI electronics that SPP is using "to streamline the secure movement of low-risk traffic across our shared borders" with Mexico and Canada."[40]

THE LATE GREAT USA

NASCO and SPP present this electronic tracking capability as a management efficiency tool. Yet never in our history have we managed the movement of millions of containers that originated in foreign nations. Can we assume that criminal elements, including the drug cartels that dominate Mexico, or terrorists will not access the containers? Are we truly secure in knowing that a company with close ties to the Communist Chinese could have access to a database that would disclose the precise location of Chinese containers in the United States? The multinational corporations driving this agenda are concerned about maximizing profits, even if maximizing profits involves turning over huge segments of the U.S. economy to the management of Chinese companies. Who in the equation is concerned that Communist China might not always be our ally?

Is China a Trustworthy Ally?

Obviously, those promoting China's interests are spending a huge amount of capital to reconfigure North American ports and transportation infrastructure. William Hawkins concludes:

> It is well past time to rethink the sophistry of "free trade" with China. Instead of spending billions of private and public funds aiding Chinese traders, a major effort should be launched to rebuild and expand the production base of North America. A key part of that effort would be to renegotiate NAFTA to create a true trade bloc that would drive Chinese goods off the continent, rather than into its heartland.[41]

Even though China was never a part of negotiating NAFTA, it is emerging as the clear winner, to the detriment of manufacturing and assembly in both Mexico and the United States alike. Unexpectedly, the Bush administration is plunging into a Security and Prosperity Partnership of North America, "integrating" and "harmonizing" administrative law and regulations with Canada and Mexico and promoting policies such as the deepening of the Panama Canal that will only increase our dependence upon China and advance their agenda.

Under SPP, electronics seem to be the solution for establishing the security of containers moving into the continent, just as electronics were the solution for "trusted traders" and "trusted travelers" moving within North America. Under SPP, only a small fraction of global trade containers entering North America or passing through North America will ever be inspected manually. Instead, the sophisticated electronics SPP is relying upon to identify "trusted travelers" and "trusted traders" is being extended to identify "trusted containers."

In the process, Hutchison Port Holdings with its ties to China has positioned itself to control not only the ports of entry, but also the sophisticated data collected throughout North America to track the progress of China's containers throughout the continent. How can we be so blindly reliant on China as a trustworthy business partner when we cannot be certain China will forever be our ally in international politics?

CHAPTER NINE

THE USA IN TWILIGHT

*"For America itself, the cost of so-called free trade has
been exorbitant and destructive."*

Lou Dobbs, *War on the Middle Class*, 2006[1]

SECURITY CONCERNS SHOULD be enough to cause conster-
nation about the push to harmonize North American transportation systems. Such moves not only further the work of integrating North America economically, but make North America dependent on China. Handing our security over to technology that is
developed, owned, *and managed* by Chinese companies that have
ties to their government is, to put it mildly, problematic.

The integration of the transportation system is a part of the
overall vision of the Security and Prosperity Partnership of North
America. There is no small irony, then, that not only have these
policies decreased our security, they have endangered our prosperity. Fundamentally, the United States' economy is not strong
enough to sustain growth and outsource jobs to China and else-
where. Pursuing policies that make America dependent on Chinese imports only exacerbates the problem.

The causes for this precarious situation are clear: First, "free
trade" agreements favor multinational corporations at the expense of American manufacturing and labor. Under NAFTA,
even Mexico is being inundated with cheap Chinese goods, to the
detriment of low-cost Mexican manufacturing and assembly
plants. Put simply, the "free trade" agreements negotiated in recent decades are not "fair trade" agreements. Instead, multina-

tional corporations have used "free trade" agreements to stack the deck against the United States.

Second, the open border policy of the Bush administration has allowed millions of uneducated, low-skilled Mexicans to flood into our country. As a result, union employees must compete with workers willing to accept much lower levels of pay.[2] At the same time, the American taxpayer subsidizes this Mexican underclass by providing ample social benefits. The range of benefits include free medical care at hospital emergency rooms, free public education, and a variety of welfare benefits that are especially generous for those children of illegal aliens who are born in the United States.

Third, the federal budget deficit is likely to increase as the U.S. population grows older. This deficit will only compound if the Bush administration "totalizes" U.S. Social Security benefits to include Mexicans who work in the United States, both legally and illegally. These trends promise a growing income gap in the United States between the very rich and the very poor, to the clear detriment of the middle class.[3]

As more jobs go overseas, the United States stands to lose the most economically successful middle class in the history of the world. The U.S. economy is transforming into a service economy where only the well-educated have any reasonable chance of economic advancement. This, however, raises questions about America's future. Can the United States remain strong if our budget and trade deficits continue to grow? Is North American integration the only solution to continued U.S. prosperity?

Through maintaining devastating budget deficits, pursuing open border policies and entitlement programs, and not correcting the structural advantages enjoyed by China and other countries, America has done serious economic harm to itself. What's more, it has given China a strong economic advantage, which may be used by them as political leverage.

The Real Federal Budget Deficit in 2006: $4.6 Trillion

The 2006 federal budget deficit was $4.6 trillion. But not according to the federal government. According to the *2006 Financial Report of the United States Government*, which was released by the U.S. Department of Treasury on Friday, December 15, 2006,[4] the deficit was *only* $248.2 billion, prompting the Bush administration to hail the fact that the deficit is shrinking.[5]

The enormous size of the actual deficit, though, puts the government in a bind. "The 2006 federal budget deficit of $4.6 trillion is $1.1 trillion more than the 2005 federal budget deficit," says John Williams, who publishes the Internet website Shadow Government Statistics.[6] "The Bush administration is in an untenable situation with a budget deficit this dramatic. Taxing 100 percent of all wages, salaries, and corporate profits would not eliminate a deficit of this magnitude, and cutting Social Security and Medicare spending is politically impossible."

But why the disparity between the two numbers? Williams commented that the Treasury Department's *2006 Financial Report of the United States Government* shows that when the budget deficit is examined based on generally accepted accounting practices (GAAP), "the actual deficit number was nearly 19 times the size of the gimmicked 'official' deficit for 2006 of $248 billion. Total obligations were 4.2 times annual U.S. gross domestic product (GDP)." This data is presented in Table 1.

TABLE 1: U.S. Government Federal Budget Deficits

U.S. Treasury, *Financial Report of the United States*, 2002–2006

Fiscal Year	Formal Cash-Based Deficit	GAAP w/o SS or Medicare Deficit	GAAP with SS and Medicare Deficit	GAAP Federal Negative Net Worth	Gross Federal Debt	Total Federal Liabilities GAAP
	(Billion)	(Billion)	(Trillion)	(Trillion)	(Trillion)	(Trillion)
2006	$247.7	$449.5	$4.6	$53.1	$ 8.5	$54.6
2005	318.5	760.0	3.5	49.4	7.9	50.9
2004	412.3	615,6	3.4	45.9	7.4	47.3
2003	374.8	667.6	3.7	34.8	6.8	36.2
2002	157.8	364.5	1.5	32.1	6.2	32.7

Table 1. Source: John Williams, Shadow Government Statistics, on *ShadowStats.com*

The difference between the "official" budget deficit of $248 billion and the $4.6 trillion deficit reported in the *2006 Financial Report of the United States Government* is that the "official" deficit is calculated on a cash basis, where the government uses all tax receipts, including Social Security tax receipts, to pay liabilities as they occur. But generally accepted accounting practices include year-for-year changes in the net present value of unfunded liabilities in social insurance programs such as Social Security and Medicare, which results in a significantly larger deficit number.

In other words, under cash accounting, the government makes no provision for future Social Security and Medicare benefits. "Truthfully," Williams pointed out, "there is no Social Security 'lock-box.'" He continued:

> There are no funds held in reserve today for Social Security and Medicare obligations that are earned each year. It is only a matter of time until the public realizes that the government is truly bankrupt and no taxes are being held in any set-aside reserve where they can only be used in the future to pay the Social Security and Medicare benefits taxpayers are earning today.

Calculations from the *2006 Financial Report of the United States Government* also show that the negative net worth of the federal government has increased to $53.1 trillion, while the total federal obligations now total $54.6 trillion.

"The Treasury is right in that Social Security and Medicare must be shown as liabilities on the federal balance sheet in the year they accrue," Williams argued.

> To do otherwise is irresponsible, nothing more than an attempt to hide the painful truth from the American public. The public has a right to know just how bad off the federal government budget deficit situation really is, especially since the situation is rapidly spinning out of control.

"The federal government is bankrupt," Williams explained. "In a post-Enron world, if the federal government were a corporation such as General Motors, the president and senior treasury officers would be in a federal penitentiary."

In a letter included in the *2006 Financial Report of the United States Government*, David M. Walker, the Comptroller General of the United States, clarified the $53 trillion negative net worth; "This translates to a current burden of about $170,000 per American or approximately $440,000 per American household."

Remarkably, the U.S. Government Accountability Office refused to certify or render an opinion on the consolidated financial statements contained in the *2006 Financial Report of the United States Government*. They noted serious financial management problems at the Department of Defense, the federal government's inability to adequately account for and reconcile intra-governmental activity and balances, and the federal government's ineffective process for preparing the consolidated financial statements.

In his letter, David Walker commented that until these financial reporting problems were resolved within the federal government, the problems outlined in the audit report "will continue to have adverse implications for the federal government and American taxpayers."

"That's an understatement," Williams replied. He continued:

> What the Comptroller of the United States is telling us is that as bad as a $4.6 trillion federal budget deficit and a $53.1 trillion GAAP negative net worth are, the situation with the Bush administration federal budget deficit might even be worse yet, hard as that may be to imagine.

The Decision to "Totalize" Social Security

However, the budget deficit is only the beginning of the federal government's financial problems. After refusing to release the document for three and a half years, in January 2007 the Social Security Administration finally complied with a Freedom of Information Act (FOIA) request filed by the TREA Senior Citizens League and released the first public copy of the U.S.-Mexico Social Security Totalization Agreement. According to the TREA Senior Citizens League, a nonpartisan seniors' advocacy group, the totalization agreement "would allow millions of illegal Mexican workers to draw billions of dollars from the U.S. Social Security Trust Fund."[7] While the Social Security Administration signed the agreement with in June 2004, at the time of its disclosure President Bush had not yet signed it. Once President Bush signs the agreement, the House of Representatives or the Senate would have sixty days to vacate the agreement by voting to reject it.

The United States currently has totalization agreements with twenty-one countries. The agreements allow workers to combine earnings from foreign countries with earnings in the United States to qualify for Social Security benefits. The agreement with Mexico would allow a Mexican worker to qualify for Social Security benefits after only six quarters (eighteen months) of employment in the United States. A U.S. worker typically needs forty calendar quarters (120 months) to receive U.S. Social Security benefits.[8]

The agreement reveals the Bush administration's determination to incorporate illegal workers from Mexico into the U.S. economy. Furthermore, keeping the U.S.-Mexico Totalization Agreement from the public suggests the Bush administration has something to hide.

In September 2003, the U.S. General Accounting Office estimated that a Social Security totalization agreement with Mexico would cost $78 million in the first year and would grow to $650 billion (in constant 2002 dollars) in 2050. The GAO admitted that even this estimate was low given that the totalization agreement provides an additional incentive for millions more Mexicans to enter and work in the United States.[9]

With the addition of this totalization agreement, the federal deficit would be even larger than the $4.7 trillion the U.S. Department of Treasury calculated for 2006.

Bush Administration Mortgages USA to China

As distressing as the financial outlook is for the federal government, it gets worse. Under the Bush administration, the U.S. trade deficit with Communist China has expanded dramatically.

Since 2000, our trade deficit with China has grown from $83.8 billion to $201.6 billion in 2005. During that same period, imports from China grew nearly 250 percent, from $100.1 million to $243.5 million. Meanwhile, in 2005, America exported only $41.8 billion, despite a nearly 400 percent increase since 2000.

A Congressional Research Service (CRS) report presenting these data in May 2006 concluded that the "U.S. trade deficit with China is now larger than that of any other U.S. trading partner, and in 2005 it was nearly equal to the combined U.S. trade deficits with Japan, China, and Mexico ($209 billion)."[10] Moreover, the gap is widening. As the CRS report noted, the "U.S. trade deficit with China in 2005 was about 24 percent higher than it was in 2004."

At the same time, China hit $1 trillion in foreign exchange reserves, holding some $700 billion in U.S. assets, about half of which were in U.S. Treasury securities.[11] Before 1979, China never had more than $1 billion in foreign exchange reserves, and even sometimes reported a negative in dollar holdings. Since then, China has become an investor, a creditor nation, while the United States has become its debtor.

This too, though, is merely indicative of a larger trend. U.S. treasuries are increasingly held by foreign interests. In 1965, foreigners owned just 4.7 percent of outstanding government debt, but in 2005 some 42.8 percent of Treasury securities were in foreign hands.[12] Of outstanding marketable Treasury securities totaling over $4 trillion, approximately 49 percent were in the hands of foreign holders in 2006. China still holds approximately 70 percent of their foreign exchange reserves in dollar-denominated assets, including $327.7 billion invested in U.S. Treasury bonds as of August 1, 2006. This makes China the second largest lender to the United States, after Japan's $635.3 billion of foreign exchange holdings in U.S. Treasury bonds.[13]

While 70 percent may seem high, China has moved away from the dollar. In 2003, 83 percent of their foreign exchange reserves were in dollars. They are seeking to protect themselves against the impact of a dollar that depreciated 12 percent against the euro between November 2002 and August 2005.[14] Should China decide to reduce this percentage to some 65 percent or lower, the U.S. Treasury could have a difficult time subsidizing its budget deficits.

How Much Treasury Debt Will China Buy?

The U.S. Treasury has tried to link our budget deficits to our trade deficits in order to benefit the United States. How? The U.S. Treasury sells securities to countries that invest in the dollar as a way of financing our federal budget deficits.

The problem with this strategy, however, is that nothing says that our trading partners must hold their reserves in dollars. If China, or other large holders of U.S. dollar reserves, decides to move away from the dollar, the Treasury could find that financing the deficit becomes much more difficult and expensive. Not only that, the Treasury's reliance on Chinese investments could give China leverage over U.S. foreign policy.

For instance, if Taiwan continues its bid for UN membership as expected,[15] what will be the United States' response? Will we support them in the face of a clearly disapproving China that owns $1 trillion in foreign exchange reserves, some 70 percent of which is held in U.S. dollar assets? How about when China owns $2 trillion, or $3 trillion?

How ironic it would be if Red China were to dominate the United States without firing a shot. The cheap Chinese imports that we value so much may end up costing far more than we pay at the store.

World Moves Away from the Dollar

The move away from the dollar has already begun. China announced around Thanksgiving 2006 that their central bank had decided to hold fewer dollar assets in their foreign exchange account. As a result, the dollar dropped dramatically on world markets.[16] In the third quarter of 2006, the U.S. current account balance deteriorated even further, increasing to a $225.6 billion deficit versus a $217.1 billion deficit in the second quarter.[17]

In his newsletter of December 31, 2006, Bob Chapman explained that, "Central bankers in 2007 will begin to move away from the dollar in their foreign reserve holdings."

Chapman documented that the international move away from the dollar has already begun. China, the second largest holder of U.S. debt, reduced purchases of U.S. bonds 1.7 percent in the first ten months of the year. "Central bankers in Venezuela, Indonesia, and the UAE have said they will invest less of their reserves in dollar assets," Chapman explained. Iran's switch to euros is the greatest threat yet to the dollar. The usage of the euro is now universal in Iran and it will spread to other Islamic oil-producing countries as well. The share of dollars as a percentage of OPEC foreign reserves has fallen from 67 percent to 65 percent in the first half of 2007. Yet the Federal Reserve finds itself in a dilemma. As Chapman put it:

> The Fed has to make continued attempts to tighten rates in an effort to make yields more attractive and stem the tide of central banks fleeing the dollar...But tightening interest rates will only expedite the fall of the U.S. housing market which could well quicken a U.S. recession, which I believe began in February 2006.

As the stock market entered 2007, investors wondered how long the economic expansion would continue without a major correction. Should the Federal Reserve decide to control inflation by tightening interest rates, the U.S. economy could easily enter a recession. If the Federal Reserve decided to reduce interest rates to provide the economy a "soft landing," those holding large accumulations of U.S. dollar-based assets in their foreign exchange reserves might be encouraged to move a portion of their portfolios to other currencies to hedge their downside risk.

Made in China

The fiscal difficulties of the Federal government are compounded by the loss of high paying American jobs. Since 2000, the manufacturing sector has lost three million jobs. The availability of cheap labor is a significant factor in shifting manufacturing to China.[18]

The Congressional Research Service correctly warned that backlash from Congress in inevitable:

> The continued rise in the U.S.-China trade imbalance, complaints from several U.S. manufacturing firms over the competitive challenges posed by cheap Chinese imports, and concerns that U.S. manufacturing jobs are being lost due to unfair Chinese trade practices have led several

> Members (of Congress) to call on the Bush Administration to take a more aggressive stance against certain Chinese trade policies deemed to be unfair.[19]

Senator Charles Schumer (D-NY), a strong critic of the Bush administration, has consistently charged that China is unfairly manipulating the yuan for trade advantages[20] and that the Bush administration is responsible for losing a growing number of manufacturing jobs to China.[21] On March 15, 2006, Senator Schumer released a study documenting the loss of 104,000 manufacturing jobs across upstate New York since 2001.[22] Schumer attributed the job loss to China's unfair international trade practices.

Over the past few years, major U.S. automakers, including Ford and General Motors, have announced plant closings and job layoffs in the United States. The loss of steel and other factory jobs have severely impacted many states in the industrial Midwest, including those in Michigan and Ohio. Many blue-collar towns have vacant plants that are no longer on the tax rolls, which in turn impacts city services, schools, and hospitals in the area.[23]

Meanwhile, U.S. automakers are looking to manufacture cars in China, where health benefits and pensions won't add to labor costs. China's auto exports doubled in 2006, as Daimler-Chrysler signed a letter of intent with China's Chery Automobile Co. that calls for the Chinese automaker to make subcompact cars to be sold by Chrysler in the United States and Europe.[24] The Bush administration's determination in demanding that foreign automakers establish plants in the United States to make cars intended for sale in the U.S. marketplace is gone.

China's Currency Advantage

Senator Schumer's criticism that China manipulates the yuan is not without merit. China has consistently refused to allow its currency, the yuan, to float freely on world trade markets. China's goal is to keep the yuan artificially low, thereby making China's exports more attractive to U.S. capitalists, while making imports from other countries more expensive in China.

On July 21, 2005, the PRC government finally gave in to U.S. pressure and announced that the yuan would be allowed to float according to market forces. Yet China proceeded cautiously. Rather than allowing the yuan to float freely on international currency exchanges, China decided to peg the value of the yuan to a carefully selected basket of currencies.[25] The yuan would go up or down in value in accordance with the performance of the selected currencies. This fluctuation in value, however, is much more limited than if China subjected the yuan to the free market.

This concession was less than the United States had hoped for. China's central bank could still support the yuan, as the indexing formula would not necessarily require an automatic resetting of the yuan's value. By controlling which countries' currencies set the value of the yuan, China is still able to artificially keep its value low. In contrast, a free floating currency would have its value reset constantly by international monetary exchanges in which market forces would determine the yuan's value *vis-à-vis* currencies of other nations.

In an unusual move, the Bush administration sent virtually the entire economic "A-team" to visit China for a "strategic economic dialogue" in Beijing on December 14 and 15, 2006. Treasury Secretary Henry Paulson and Federal Reserve Chairman Ben Bernanke led the delegation, which consisted of five other cabinet-level officials, including Secretary of Commerce Carlos Gutierrez. Also in the delegation were Labor Secretary Elaine Chao, Health and Human Services Secretary Mike Leavitt, Energy Secretary Sam Bodman, and U.S. Trade Representative Susan Schwab.

The results of the discussions were disappointing. In an important speech before the Chinese Academy of Social Sciences in Beijing, Federal Reserve Bernanke decided to revise the printed version of his remarks, backing away from calling China's currency policy a "subsidy" for its exports. International traders would have perceived such a comment as inflammatory. Observers on the scene strongly suspected that the change had been recommended by Treasury Secretary Paulson, who in his previous career had made himself a multi-millionaire at Goldman Sachs by promoting trade with China.[26] Bernanke's printed text, which had

had been released to the press in China before the speech, was blunt, charging directly that China's undervalued currency functions as "an effective subsidy" benefiting Chinese firms that focus on exporting.[27]

At the end of the meetings, the Chinese acknowledged that they had listened politely, suggesting they would consider the proposals made, without making any definite commitment to allowing the foreign exchange value of the yuan to be set by market forces. In other words, the Chinese said, "No." Their central bank would continue to keep the value of the yuan artificially low. In the weeks following, the value of the yuan was allowed to creep a bit upwards. Still, since introducing the reforms in July 2005, the value of the yuan had only risen 6 percent by the beginning of 2007.[28] This was a small increase in the value of the yuan, especially considering that the Chinese GDP grew in 2007 at a rate of approximately 10.5 percent, while the U.S. GDP grew approximately 3.5 percent.[29]

Despite the Bush administration jawboning with China, the value of the yuan remained artificially low. Our growing foreign trade deficit with China plus our continuing budget deficits put the Bush administration in an uncomfortable position. Increasingly the goods being sold by our top mass merchandisers are made in China, while we are going into debt to China to finance our federal budget deficits.

The Bush administration has followed the theory that allowing China free and open access to penetrate (and perhaps dominate) the North American marketplace will engage the Chinese such that their political allegiance to the United States is more firmly secured. But several key military developments in the past decade suggest the Chinese are engaged in a military buildup,[30] which would increase their leverage over the United States.

China's Military Buildup

China has devoted much of its newly found economic strength to building one of the most modern armies in the world. In 2006, the U.S. intelligence community acknowledged that China has developed and deployed a series of missiles that would give them second-strike capability in any nuclear confrontation with the United States. Specifically, China has now equipped and launched their first Type 94 nuclear powered submarines, each of which carry sixteen JL-2 (DF-31) ballistic missiles, with a range of eight thousand kilometers. This capability allows Chinese submarines to target large portions of the continental United States from areas near the Chinese coast. As late as May 2004, the Pentagon had argued that the Type 94 submarine would not be operational until 2010.[31]

Second-strike capability means that the Chinese mainland could absorb a U.S. nuclear attack, but China could still retaliate against the United States. In other words, the Chinese could launch a nuclear ballistic missile from the ocean, even if all ballistic missiles on the Chinese mainland were destroyed. Possessing second-strike capability provides China more dangerous options in any military or political showdown with the United States.

In December 2006, at a meeting of delegates to a Communist Party conference on the navy, Chinese president and commander-in-chief Hu Jintao urged building a powerful, modern Chinese navy that would be prepared for military struggle "at any time."[32] In comments that were published in the PRC's *People's Daily* and *People's Liberation Army Daily* newspapers, Hu Jintau said: "We should strive to build a powerful navy that adapts to the needs of our military's historic mission in this new century and this new stage." A strong ocean-going Chinese navy would secure China's international trade and energy routes and present a strong challenge to the United States over Taiwan. China has consistently maintained that it would attack Taiwan if the island dared to formally proclaim its independence.

A United States strapped by historically large and growing trade and budget deficits will be increasingly hard-pressed to compete militarily with China, especially as the United States remains militarily engaged in the Middle East. Allowing China to exert an increasing role in North American trade, with a trade balance constantly flowing in China's favor, is risky policy. What assurance do we have that China will remain a friend and ally of the United States?

The VAT Menace

Advocates of "free trade" have hailed treaties such as NAFTA and the WTO. Yet, because most of our "free trade" partners use a value added tax (VAT), America has been placed at a severe disadvantage. The United States, virtually alone among the world's major international trading countries, does not use a VAT. "Free trade" is certainly not "fair trade" when VAT structural advantages stack the deck against the United States before any cards are dealt.

The impact of the value added tax (VAT) on international trade is complicated. Yet it may be the most important variable in explaining our expanding trade deficits. The average U.S. citizen can no longer afford not to understand the VAT, especially in an era where free trade agreements dominate our international trade agenda.

The modern VAT was created by French economist Maurice Lauré in the 1950s. The basic concept is that a "value added" tax is imposed at each stage in the chain of production of a good or service.

In a sense, this hides the tax from the consumer. The producer builds the price of the tax into his selling price, which passes the tax along to the consumer at the point of sale. The amount of the VAT, then, is included as a percentage of the final value of the good or service. The VAT is not reimbursed to the consumer, so at the final point of purchase, the government gets to keep the VAT once and for all.

A VAT and a sales tax are both "indirect" taxes, in that the consumer, rather than the producer, pays them. Income taxes, in contrast, are "direct" taxes in that the tax cannot be shifted to someone else other than the person producing the income. The main difference between a VAT and a sales tax is that the VAT is applied at each stage of production, whereas sales taxes are usually imposed once, at the final point of sale.

In international trade, countries do not treat indirect taxes and direct taxes the same, and that differential puts the United States at a decided disadvantage. The United States does not use a VAT system. Some 137 countries, including the EU countries, China, Canada, and Mexico, have VAT systems. A simplified example may clarify how VAT systems disadvantage American goods.

On the one hand, an American made car that sells for $23,000 in the United States includes profit for the company and covers the various tax obligations and expenses for the company. When the manufacturer exports that car to Germany, the German government adds 16 percent VAT to the $23,000 price, meaning that the car will be sold in Germany for $26,680.

On the other hand, consider a German car that is sold in Germany for $23,000 after the 16 percent VAT is imposed. When the German manufacturer exports that car to the United States, Germany *rebates the 16 percent VAT to the manufacturer*, allowing the export value of the car to be $19,827.59. Moreover, when the German car is imported to the United States, the U.S. government does not assess any comparable tax, so the car is allowed to enter the U.S. market at a price under $20,000.

The system disadvantages U.S. producers two ways. When exported, the U.S. car starts off with a disadvantage of $3,680 in Germany because of the VAT. At the same time, the German car, which sells at home for the same price as the American car sells in America, sells in America for $3,172.41 less than the U.S. car. In this example, the total disadvantage American car companies face is $6,852.41.

In effect, the rebate of the VAT to German exporters serves as a German subsidy for exports, while the imposition of a VAT on American imports serves as a German tariff. Still, free trade agreements do not define the VAT as either a subsidy or a tariff, even though the system demonstrably disadvantages U.S. manufacturers both in exporting to VAT countries and in competing with other countries' exports in the U.S. market.

Here are the crucial points:

- Companies operating in VAT countries enjoy rebates of VAT taxes on the goods they export. Companies that manufacture goods in the United States get no refunds of the state and federal taxes they pay on the goods they export.

- Imports into VAT countries are subjected to VAT at the border, while imports into the United States are not taxed at the border.

- As a result, U.S. exports are taxed twice, while exports from VAT countries are traded free of certain types of taxes.

In an interview with *Human Events*, Congressman Duncan Hunter (R-CA) expressed the VAT disadvantage as follows:

> We practiced what I call "losing trade"—deliberately losing trade—over the last 50 years. We need to reverse that. Today, other countries around the world employ what they call a value-added tax, in which foreign governments refund to their corporations that are exporting goods to the United States the full amount of their value-added taxes that that particular company pays in making a product. They subsidize them. Japan's VAT, I think, is 5 percent or 6 percent. I believe China's is 17 percent.
>
> When American products hit their shores, they charge a value-added tax in the same amount. So they enact a double hit against American exporters. One is that they subsidize their own imports going out, and the second is that they tax us going in. The United States doesn't do this.[33]

As we are the only major international trade country without a VAT, the VAT system uniquely hampers American exports. The U.S. simply has no border-adjustable mechanism that can rectify the disadvantage.

On May 17, 2005, while testifying to the Subcommittee on Trade of the House Committee on Ways and Means, attorney Terence Stewart of the Washington firm Stewart and Stewart estimated the impact of differential taxation as follows:

> On the issue of differential treatment of tax systems, the U.S. is seriously disadvantaged by the application of WTO rules on taxes. With 137 countries applying a VAT tax and a worldwide VAT tax advantage of 15 percent, the U.S. faces up to $450 billion total disadvantage to U.S. exports ($180 billion) and export subsidies to import competition ($270 billion).[34]

The VAT differential puts U.S. exporters in a huge hole, out of which it is almost impossible to dig. At the same time, the VAT differential gives those who import into the United States a significant edge, virtually assuring their dominance in our domestic market.

"Every major trading country in the world economy, except for the U.S., has a VAT system," notes Auggie Tantillo, executive director at the American Manufacturing Trade Action Coalition (AMTAC).[35] As Tantillo explained:

> The important thing to understand is that the VAT disadvantage is a structural impediment or distortion, just like the currency manipulation China currently exploits by refusing to allow the value of their currency to freely float on world currency exchanges. The VAT differential is not simply a tangential, frivolous, or superficial thing that a few countries do here or there, just a minor irritant. The VAT differential is a core, driving aspect as to why U.S. companies find themselves continuously at a disadvantage. If you extrapolate to the next step, the VAT differential is a core reason for why we see this escalating growth in the U.S. trade deficit on an annual basis.

Ironically, Tantillo argues that the VAT differential is a key reason many U.S. companies move their manufacturing off shore, as it is more lucrative for them to export into the U.S. market rather than to operate as U.S. domestic producers. Right now, U.S. automakers are contemplating closing U.S. plants in favor of opening plants in China and importing cars to the U.S. market.

Tantillo elaborated:

> When you add everything up and start to look at the cumulative effect, the board of a U.S. company sitting around a table has to say, "We can cut our labor costs by 'x' percent, we can get rid of our health care, we don't have to produce a pension plan, and then we have this VAT situation where our taxes are rebated to us when we ship to the U.S., the market we want to impact anyway, so why do we stay here in the United States? Why not move our manufacturing to Asia?" The economic analysis just becomes compelling for many U.S. companies.

In other words, the VAT differential functions as an additional structural incentive for U.S. companies to move manufacturing to foreign countries where they can participate in the VAT advantages as importers into the U.S. market. A U.S. company, in other words, could seek to act as a foreign company in order to get the benefit of VAT refunds.

CHAPTER TEN

CHEAP LABOR AND CHEAP MONEY

"The fading of communist ideology in China, in contrast, has posed no threat to the unity of a country with a core Han culture going back thousands of years and, to the contrary, has spurred a new Chinese nationalism."

Samuel Huntington, *Who Are We?* 2004[1]

THE LOSS OF ECONOMIC POWER to China is troubling, but we have lost something far more precious than political and economic leverage. Now that the American economy is largely dependant upon China, America has lost the moral power to demand that China end its human rights abuses. Indeed, U.S. "free trade" agreements have put the United States in a morally questionable position, as they have given multinational corporations permission to push labor costs to levels at or below the minimum standards of human dignity.

A young peasant in China may face dire choices between nearly starving in poverty or going into an urban area to work for pennies an hour. The cruel master of necessity forces these young people into a dormitory work setting, strips them of human rights, and subjects them to a grueling schedule where discipline and loss of pay are an almost inevitable. As the worker "ages" beyond twenty years old, multinational corporations throw them once again into the streets, as there is a line of younger, nearly starved peasants ready to step into the job.

In addition, some of the labor in China comes from concentration camps for political and religious prisoners. As the government forces them to live in circumstances that amount to life-long incarceration on minimum diets and minimum human amenities, these political and religious prisoners in China face a dire fate from which they will not emerge alive. The Chinese may even kill those less fortunate among the concentration camp "workers," should they identify markets in which their internal organs can be sold for profit.

China, in the final analysis, is still a rigid totalitarian state controlled by communists. That China has combined profit with communism does not mean that human rights are suddenly being honored for its citizens. Religious and political persecutions occur in China on a daily basis, even if the government keeps them from the eye of the media. What's more, the reality of China's situation does not confirm the hype about China developing a middle class. Citing statistics from the banking group BNP Paribas, the Chinese Embassy touts that by 2010, some 100 million families will qualify as "middle class," with assets of 620,000 yuan (U.S. $74,700) and an annual income of 150,000 yuan (U.S. $18,000). Bank Paribas defined this "middle class" group as "well-educated professionals and white-collar employees (brain workers)," who "participate in the decision making and management of companies."[2] This analysis leaves little promise that China's "middle class" prosperity will extend to the near-slave labor that does the manual work.

The United States has rightly decided that slavery of African Americans is and was morally wrong. Is it now free from moral blame simply because multinational corporations are exploiting slaves and near-slaves in a distant country? Are Chinese human beings less deserving of human respect and human rights than other races? Multinational corporations intentionally keep these uncomfortable questions beneath the surface, as they want to convince U.S. shoppers that the cheap price of retail goods is worth any human price.

Wage Exploitation: The Unspoken Goal of U.S. "Free Trade"

The differential in wages to manufacture goods between the United States and China is extraordinary. The website of the CANAMEX Corridor Coalition, a trade association that wants to form a transportation super corridor in the central eastern United States, highlights this disparity:

- $0.25 Average hourly manufacturing wage in India and China

- $2.10 Average hourly manufacturing wage in Mexico

- $17.20 Average hourly manufacturing wage in United States[3]

Interestingly, CANAMEX presents these numbers first. Somehow, CANAMEX concluded that these wage differences would make their argument for super corridors indisputable. The opportunity to exploit these cheap wages in China demands better means to transport Chinese goods into America. Or so the argument goes.

With these wage discrepancies and a free trade policy that does not prohibit corporations from exploiting labor in foreign nations, moving manufacturing to China should be a "no-brainer" for any multinational capitalist whose only concern is the bottom line.

Red Chinese Slave Labor

Though most Americans do not want to acknowledge it, the difficult truth is that China uses slave labor as a means of keeping its wages as low as possible, so that it can produce goods for the U.S. market. Much of that slave labor involves political, ethnic, and religious "criminals."

It was Mao, in the 1950s, who first established the Chinese slave labor camps known as the *Laogai*. Writing for the *Human Rights Brief* at American University's Washington College of Law, Ramin Pejan explains that the *Laogai* system consists of three distinct types of reform: convict labor (*Laogai*), reeducation through labor (*Laojiao*), and forced job placement (*Jiuye*).[4] The political nature of these Chinese prison labor camps is clear: "The PRC [People's Republic of China] uses Laojiao to detain individuals it feels are a threat to national security or it considers unproductive."[5]

Even when prisoners complete their sentences, the government still forces some 70 percent to live in assigned locations, where they continue to work in the prison camps.

Laogai is an abbreviation for *Laodong Gaizao,* which translates from Mandarin as "reform through labor." This cruel slogan echoes the twisted phrase *"Arbeit Mach Frei"* ("Work Will Make You Free") that the Nazis placed in iron over the entrance to the concentration camp at Auschwitz.

Despite efforts by the U.S. government to keep Chinese goods produced by slave labor from entering the U.S. market, the Laogai Research Foundation maintains that China represses open investigation of forced labor camps. As a result, importing goods created through slave labor continues:

> Due to strong resistance from Western nations against forced labor products, in 1991 China's State Council re-emphasized the ban on the export of "forced labor products" and stipulated that no prison is allowed to cooperate or establish joint ventures with foreign investors. However, the State Council's move was merely a superficial one, and prisoners today still produce forced labor products in great numbers. The Chinese government grants special privileges to enterprises using labor camps and prisons, to encourage and attract foreign investment and export. Prisoners are forced to manufacture products without any payment, and are often forced to work more than 10 hours a day and sometimes even overnight. Those who cannot fulfill their tasks are beaten and tortured. The forced labor products these prisoners produce are exported throughout China and the world.[6]

The Laogai Research Center "believes that as long as the Chinese Communist Party's dictatorship exists, the Laogai will continue to serve as its essential mechanism for suppression and prosecution." The Laogai Research Foundation's *2005–2006 Laogai Handbook* documents over 1,000 Chinese slave-labor prison camps still operating today, with a prison population that they estimate at several million.[7] Even a brief review of the individual prison camps listed makes clear that the camps produce a wide variety of products for export, including food products, small manufacturing or assembly products, shoes, and other articles of clothing.

The Laogai Research Foundation stresses that the Laogai system, like the Soviet Gulag, violates human freedom: "The Laogai is incompatible with freedom and democracy."[8] As unpopular as this information may be, the reality is that the Chinese economy exploits slave labor to produce the goods that mass marketers sell to their customers across the United States. Nor should we ease our consciences by assuming that China will necessarily develop its own strong middle class, despite China's exploitation of workers. The Laogai Research Foundation dismisses the position many scholars advance that economic development is a catalyst for democratization and liberalization, arguing that, "The more China advances, the more its people are restricted politically and socially."[9] The Laogai prison system is both an important tool of repression for the Chinese Communist Party, as well as an important source of revenue.[10]

The Laojiao (reeducation through labor) continue to round up political and religious prisoners, including the Falun Gong and Christian movements. The Laogai Research Foundation continues to believe that the Chinese are using lethal injections in hospitals and "execution vans" to harvest the organs of political prisoners. This is the dark underside of the Communist Chinese exploitation of its own population for economic gain. U.S. business leaders like to project our own ideas and values on their Chinese counterparts, assuming that as the Chinese understand capitalism, they also accept our moral values. Instead, the Chinese see only our hypocrisy. American capitalists, government leaders at the highest level, and consumers are willing to ignore China's egregious human rights abuses as long as the entrepreneurs make profits, the government officials get campaign contributions, and the consumers are able to buy cheap goods.

A U.S.-China Security Review Commission Policy Paper on Prison Labor and Forced Labor in China concluded that the U.S. Customs Service "cannot conduct independent investigations in China" to determine if goods imported into the United States were made in Chinese forced labor camps.[11] Despite numerous treaties, memoranda of understanding, and laws, the commission concluded that China simply refuses to supply the information needed to make factual determinations.

The 2005 Annual Report of the Congressional-Executive Commission on China concluded that: "Forced labor is an integral part of the Chinese administrative detention system, and child labor remains a significant problem in China, despite being prohibited by law."[12]

Chinese "Under-Market" of Near-Slave Labor

Just above the slave labor camps is a vast Chinese under-market where millions of Chinese work for meager wages under abusive work conditions. Today China makes approximately 75 percent of the world's toys.[13] As noted by the Asian Human Rights Commission (AHRC),[14] U.S. companies such as Disney, Mattel (maker of the Barbie doll), Hasbro, McDonald's (Happy Meal toys), and Warner Brothers utilize factories in China to produce toys for virtually every major U.S. retailer, including Toys-R-Us, Wal-Mart, and Target.[15] Still, the AHRC documents that working conditions in the Chinese toy manufacturing industry are abysmal, just one notch above twenty-first century slave trade standards. The AHRC's description of the situation included the following list:

- Average age of a worker in a typical Chinese toy factory: between twelve and fifteen years old

- Typical wage of workers in Asian toy factories: from as little as six cents an hour up to forty cents an hour

- Typical number of hours worked in a day during busy periods: up to nineteen

- Typical number of days worked per week: six

- Young workers work all day in 104-degree temperature, handling toxic glues, paints, and solvents

- Workers weakened by illness and pregnant workers, who are supposed to have legal protection, are forced to quit

- The typical profile of workers in these factories is single young women migrants from rural areas who have come to the cities in search of jobs

With over one billion Chinese vying for existence, the Chinese under-market thrives in a competitive environment that results from an over-supply of labor. One mistake can exclude an un-educated and unskilled worker from future employment, especially when thousands wait in line for the job.

What's more, it is clear that the Communist Chinese are continuing to persecute Falun Gong cult practitioners. Canadian human rights lawyer David Matas and former Canadian MP David Kilgour released a report in July 2006 alleging that the Communist Chinese harvest organs by murdering imprisoned Falun Gong practitioners.[16] The report's conclusions were clear:

> We believe that there has been and continues today to be large scale organ seizures from unwilling Falun Gong practitioners.
>
> We have concluded that the government of China and its agencies in numerous parts of the country, in particular hospitals but also detention centres and "people's courts," since 1999 have put to death a large but unknown number of Falun Gong prisoners of conscience. Their vital organs, including hearts, kidneys, livers, and corneas, were virtually simultaneously seized involuntarily for sale at high prices, sometimes to foreigners, who normally face long waits for voluntary donations of such organs in their home countries.[17]

The black market in organ purchases remains largely underground, hidden from public view. But do we really think a bright moral line exists between using Chinese slave labor—a form of slow death for the abused under-market workers—and outright murder of political prisoners to meet the market's demand for human organs?

Michael Wolf's[18] photographs of under-market labor in China are not so different from the photographs of Lewis W. Hine[19] and Jacob Riis,[20] who documented the human exploitation in this country prior to the rise of the U.S. labor movement. But if China ever introduced human rights considerations into their labor markets, capitalists would simply move on to the next market where slaves could be found—Indonesia, the Middle East, or Africa.

New Balance Athletic Shoes Made in China—A Case Study in Workers' Rights Abuse

An international workers' advocacy report by the National Labor Committee (NLC) and China Labor Watch (CLW) charges that New Balance is still making athletic shoes for the U.S. market in a Chinese sweatshop where the human rights of workers are regularly abused.[21]

Despite these allegations, The La Salle Bank Chicago Marathon on October 22, 2006, accepted New Balance for the ninth year as the official apparel and footwear sponsor for the marathon.[22]

Published in February 2006, the NLC and CLW workers' advocacy report analyzes the Li Kai Factory Number 5, using worker testimony and extensive photographs. The Li Kai Factory Number 5 produces shoes for New Balance in China. The workers' advocacy report documents the low wages the company pays workers:

> The major component in the Li Kai Factory Number 5, which produces for New Balance, is the very low wages, which are well below subsistence levels. The base wage at Factory Number 5 is just 40 cents an hour and $3.22 a day. After mandatory deductions are taken out for dorm and food expenses, the workers' wages actually drop to 32 cents an hour, $2.55 a day, and only $12.92 a week.

In response to these charges, New Balance management pointed out their company's code of conduct with respect to Chinese workers:

> The New Balance Athletic Shoe, Inc., operates with the highest ethics and stands for integrity of people and product. We have a strong compliance program and aggressively promote our standards and monitor supplier factories continuously with a full compliance team in China. Our standards are rigorously applied through a process which includes training, establishes standards of performance, sharing of ideas and methods for compliance, monitoring by New Balance, and monitoring by an independent third party.

Interestingly, the NCL/CLW report comments that New Balance's corporate compliance policy tends to suffer when translated into Chinese:

> In fact, when it comes to the core internationally recognized right to organize independent unions, New Balance allowed subtle but significant changes to be made in the Mandarin translation of its code of conduct. Whereas the English version reads: "There shall be no discrimination against workers based on political affiliation or union membership," the Mandarin translation removes "union membership" and inserts "membership in a social organization." It is the same with the right to freedom of association. The English version reads: "employees shall respect the right of workers to join and organize associations of their own choosing, and to bargain collectively." The Mandarin version reads: "...join and organize legal associations or social organizations including the right to bargain collectively." Of course, independent unions are not legal in China.

The report notes that these subtle changes are not innocent: "The Li Kai workers have no rights, least of all the right to form an independent or real union and to bargain collectively."

On August 30, 2006, Charles Kernaghan, executive director of the National Labor Committee explained that compliance statements such as that issued by New Balance are intended primarily for public relations in the United States. "The companies like New Balance do not take seriously their own compliance statements," Kernaghan said.

The workers' advocacy report details human rights abuses at the Li Kai factory. Like many other shoe, garment, and toy factories in China, Li Kai prefers to hire young women. Approximately 80 percent of Factory Number 5 workers are women, and the vast majority of those are between eighteen and twenty-three years old. Researchers found two workers who were just fourteen years old, a clear violation of China's own labor law.

The NCL/CLW report produces a sample worker's pay stub, which documents the mandatory deductions for room and board. Workers at the New Balance factory work ten hours a day, Monday through Friday, with an additional eight-hour overtime shift required on Saturdays. As the report notes:

> Many women—especially those who had to work standing up all day—complained about the exhaustion of regularly working a ten-hour shift with just a half hour off for lunch. When these workers end their shift, their legs and backs are "unbearably sore."

New Balance workers at the Chinese factory who are getting married or attending funerals "are either forced to skip work or to request special time off—of course, without pay." The workers do not receive annual vacations, even though the Li Kai Company manual specifies that workers are entitled to paid annual vacations. The company does not give employees pensions, and it was "unclear" to NCL/CLW researchers whether New Balance workers received any health insurance or work injury insurance.

The penal code makes the harsh conditions explicit. New Balance fines workers if:

> they walk off the sidewalk, drop a candy wrapper, leave a shirt on their bunk bed, use electricity for personal reasons, talk back to supervisors, try to organize or fail to sweep and mop their room three times a day. The military-like lists of factory rules and regulations are long, intrusive, and demeaning, and the fines are harsh.

Deductions of wages for disciplinary purposes further reduce the pay of workers at Li Kai.

The report's conclusion on the dehumanization of New Balance workers in the Li Kai environment was severe:

> At the center of the new corporate world order—as evidenced by the collaboration of New Balance and the Li Kai Shoe Company in China—is the complete dehumanization of the workforce. In this new corporate world order, young workers living and working in huge gated industrial zones have no rights and no voice, with every second of their lives micro-managed in a demeaning and humiliating manner through an endless list of military-like rules and regulations, backed up by serious fines and punishment. New Balance says these are "model factories," but in reality they far more resemble minimum security prisons.

Not only is the work environment oppressive; life in the dorms is equally punitive. Again, quoting from the NCL/CLW report:

Of course, by forcing the workers to clean the company's dormitories—or risk serious fines—Li Kai management saves money in cleaning bills. But management is also using a shell game, with the workers' own money, to pit the workers against each other to make certain they go about their cleaning with real enthusiasm. Management has developed a point system of merits and demerits to judge each room's cleanliness. So a "dirty floor," "stuff on or under the bed not put away," "using electricity for personal purposes," and "dirty doors or windows" will each be met with one or two point demerits for each roommate.

In this punitive environment, fines and demerits can easily cost the worker what amounts to one or more days' pay.

The NCL/CLW report also documents a January 16, 2006, meeting where a New Balance corporate team from the United States was met by upwards of four thousand cheering Li Kai Factory 5 workers in a carefully rehearsed show designed for the sake of public relations. As the report makes clear, in the days leading up to the arrival of the New Balance management team, "the workers were required to practice twice daily, including getting up early, rehearsing how to assemble in huge color-coordinated blocks and rows according to their uniform colors."

At the public meeting with New Balance managers, a group of workers made up their own chant: "New Balance, New Balance is the number one hirer of prostitutes! Li Kai has the lowest wages! Di Chang, Di Chang manufactures crap!" "Di Chang" is a pejorative reference to the factory, roughly translated as "last factory." A photograph shows the U.S. executives sitting in chairs at the front of the group meeting, applauding as the workers chanted.

Charles Kernaghan explained that the markup on New Balance athletic shoes manufactured in China is enormous:

We find the shipping documents on the sneakers entering the U.S. and the total cost of production—direct labor, indirect labor, materials, shipping costs, and profit to the factory—including every conceivable cost the sneaker comes into the U.S. at something like $14.61 a pair. The sneakers then sell at retail for $135.00. So this is an 824 percent markup. That's why the sneaker companies go to China. The workers are paid at below subsistence levels and are

> made to live in dormitories in inhuman conditions, charged
> for their food, utilities, and housing in the dorm.

A statement on the New Balance website notes that worldwide sales in 2005 totaled $1.54 billion, while domestic U.S. sales totaled $1.09 billion.[23]

The message on the website of the 2006 La Salle Bank Chicago Marathon seems inconsistent with New Balance's record of workers' human rights and labor rights abuses.

> The word is out in many languages about a magnificent
> marathon that is run each October in one of the world's
> great cities, situated in America's heartland. The message to
> runners from Afghanistan to Zimbabwe, Alabama to Wyo-
> ming and all points in between is "come to Chicago, enjoy
> all that the city has to offer, have a memorable race and tell
> your friends about it."

Unfortunately, none of the workers making New Balance sneakers could reasonably expect to attend the festivities at the marathon.

America Outsources Manufacturing

Not only have "free trade" agreements placed America in a questionable moral situation: they have also been a disaster for U.S. manufacturing. As a result of NAFTA, CAFTA, and the World Trade Organization (WTO), millions of manufacturing jobs in the United States have gone overseas.

According to the Economic Policy Institute (EPI), as a percentage of our economy, international trade has doubled. This growth, though, has come only at the expense of massive U.S. trade deficits and a rapid out-flow of manufacturing jobs. EPI documents that, "For working Americans, the effects of the enormous growth in foreign trade have been mostly negative, resulting in the loss of good-paying manufacturing jobs, significant downward pressure on wages, and increased inequality." Between 2000 and 2005, more than three million manufacturing jobs have disappeared from the U.S. economy. Today, about half of all U.S.-owned manufacturing production is now overseas.[24]

Even though productivity in the U.S. economy has grown dramatically over the past twenty-five years, the wages and benefits of non-supervisory workers—who constitute about 80 percent of the U.S. workforce—have been stagnant. EPI notes that "in the past twenty-five years, the economy has expanded steadily and a better-educated workforce has become far more productive but without sharing the nation's economic growth."[25] Open borders increase the impact on the bottom tiers of U.S. employment, as millions of uneducated Mexicans pour into the labor market at the lower skill levels.[26]

The American Manufacturing Trade Action Coalition (AMTAC) documents that the United States now has fewer manufacturing jobs than we had in 1950.[27] Job creation has been in the government sector or in the lower skilled, lower paying job classifications. Even those areas where America is currently thriving may be in danger. Recent reports indicate that China's "soaring spending on technology research and development now exceeds that of Japan," and will pass the EU in four years and the United States in seven years. This is bad news for technology industries, where until recently the United States has maintained a lead.[28]

U.S. Middle Class Squeezed in Income Gap

The loss of jobs overseas has widened the income gap in America. The income gap is a measure of the earnings and net worth of the top tiers of society versus the middle class and the poor. According to Federal Reserve Bank data, in 2004 the top one-fifth of American households held 80 percent of the nation's net worth and 50 percent of the nation's income.[29] The Economic Policy Institute rankings of states according to the income gap between the top 5 percent of families and the bottom 20 percent reveal that Arizona has the worst income gap; the average income of the top 5 percent of families is $223,081 and the average income of the bottom 20 percent is $15,719.[30] The state with the least wide income gap is Wyoming, but even the top 5 percent earns an average of $145,587 and the bottom 20 percent earns $18,171.

Put simply, the U.S. economy is losing middle-class jobs. Union manufacturing and construction employees who once could earn upwards of $20 an hour must now compete with illegal immigrants for non-union jobs that may pay $8 an hour. Middle-class workers who lose manufacturing jobs may not be permanently unemployed, but the replacement jobs are typically lower skilled and lower paying opportunities. As the U.S. economy moves toward a global economy, the very middle class to whom the multinational corporations are expecting to sell under-market goods will continue to erode. Evidently, the anticipation of the multinational corporations is that the retail market is large enough that erosion in middle-class jobs and a growing income gap will not undermine their ability to sell internationally manufactured goods at a profit.

But while the middle class has been shrinking, the Federal Reserve has kept interest rates low, stimulating the post-9/11 economic recovery and buoying the stock market. Profits and bonuses in the multinational corporations and Wall Street investment banks have been at all time highs since around 2004 or 2005.

Still, the party at the top cannot go on forever, not if the current trend to outsource manufacturing overseas continues and the bottom rungs of employment classifications continue to deteriorate. No one should have any doubt that the higher income opportunities in the future will be primarily for the well educated and the higher skilled. CEOs and Wall Street investment bankers will be compensated in the millions, while blue collar workers in states like Ohio and Michigan will wonder how they are to survive.

Even Federal Reserve Chairman Ben Bernanke has begun sounding the alarm bell. In a speech to the Greater Omaha Chamber of Commerce on February 6, 2007,[31] Bernanke warned that rising income inequality in the United States "has been evident for at least three decades, if not longer." In the speech, Bernanke directly discussed effects related to globalization. He noted, for instance, that the influx of low-skilled immigrants into the United States has reduced the relative wages of less skilled U.S. workers. Yet, expectedly, Bernanke concluded on the side of favoring globalization. He grudgingly acknowledged that "the advent of new technologies and increased international trade can lead to painful dislocations as some workers lose their jobs or see the demand for their particular skills decline." Yet he held the line that "hindering the adoption of new technologies or inhibiting trade flows would do far more harm than good, as technology and trade are critical sources of overall economic growth and of increases in the standard of living."

Still, that the Federal Reserve chairman would comment on the income gap at all was significant. In the first term of the Bush administration, liberal Democratic Party politicians who typically wanted to attack the Bush tax cuts were the only ones to raise concern about the income disparity in America. That Chairman Bernanke has delivered a speech on the topic strongly suggests that the concern has percolated over to the more conservative Republican Party base.

A robust stock market since 2005 indicates that multinational corporate profits have been high. At the same time, housing starts in the U.S. economy have declined and home foreclosures are increasing. The rates of middle-class household debt and debt payments are at record levels. If the economy were to go into recession, we would most likely experience the unusual phenomenon of seeing high rates of inflation accompanied by increasing unemployment, especially among middle-income workers.

China's enormous population and its blatant disregard for its citizens' most basic rights give it an enormous advantage over the American economy. The more companies move to China for the cheap labor, the more they compromise their moral status. At the same time, they endanger the livelihood of the very middle class to which they typically sell their products.

China's advantage is a result of the globalization policies pursued in America over the course of the last several years, and it is an advantage that is not going to go away soon. This advantage has already given China a significant upper hand in the economies of North America, and further opening North America to trade from China will only increase that advantage at the expense of the poorest North American workers.

Supporters of a North American community argue that, once the United States enters the supra-national marketplace, Americans stand to reap great economic benefits. However, the cost is too high in terms of national security and in terms of the loss of American jobs to foreign workers—especially from China. Giving

China so much control over our trade—especially imports—and other nations so much control over our transportation systems, as proposed under the SPP, means also giving foreign entities control over American security and the economic and political futures of American citizens. In effect, Americans would hand over our sovereignty and our very way of life to those whose only incentive to protect our rights will be their own economic interests.

CONCLUSION

CHINA'S ECONOMIC ADVANTAGE would only widen with the emergence of a North American Union. In a North American Union, the economic future of the United States would be closely tied to that of Mexico and Canada. The creation of an NAU would lead to greater political and judicial integration with our North American neighbors, as well—just as it did in Europe beginning fifty years ago. If Americans do not wish to follow the EU model, we must demand accountability from our politicians and business leaders. We must demand our right to see the prospect of entering a North American Union brought before the American people and their elected representatives for an open referendum and a national vote.

Robert Pastor has led the charge to establish the intellectual groundwork, arguing not only for the creation of a North American community, but for the adoption of the amero as a North American regional currency. Like Jean Monnet who coaxed Europe from an economic coal and steel agreement into a political regional government, Robert Pastor has championed the cause of following a similar incremental path on this continent. The theories Pastor nurtures and espouses are beginning to transform from mere talk among ivory tower elites to action within the governments and corporate structures of Mexico, Canada, and the United States.

Since the Waco Declaration established the SPP, a framework of bureaucratic working groups has systematically "integrated" and "harmonized" the administrative laws and regulations of Mexico, Canada, and the United States. This work has proceeded largely below the radar of public opinion, but the results are noticeable. The SPP is slowly evolving into the North American Union.

"Trusted trader" and "trusted traveler" programs are already firmly in place and Mexican trucks cross our borders in FAST lanes to run their long-haul rigs throughout the United States. Our transportation structures are being reconfigured to accept an unprecedented volume of international trade, largely witnessed in millions more containers from China pouring into north-south super corridors linked to ports in Mexico, along the Gulf of Mexico, and on the East Coast. While a North American Union is not inevitable, it is plausible given the actions of current and previous administrations.

The profound changes in the United States should be apparent to any American who has seen their job travel overseas or who has already lost their job to illegal immigrants at home. In the spring of 2006, hundreds of thousands of illegal immigrants filled our city streets, marching under the Mexican flag and demanding all the rights U.S. citizens enjoy. Meanwhile, the income gap between the very rich and the very poor is growing. How many generations will it take for the American economic profile to resemble that of Mexico?

Skeptics, of course, have charged that the Trans-Texas corridor is just another highway project, and that the amero is nothing more than the idle speculation of a few economists. So what if free trade eliminates an increasing number of manufacturing jobs, the critics argue. The middle class will benefit from the cheaper consumer goods that will result from improved transportation routes.

But several lingering questions have upset the calm of even the most determined skeptics.

- Why are our borders still open, despite serious threats?

- Why are law enforcement agents on the border prosecuted while U.S. attorneys protect the civil rights of fleeing drug smugglers, all at the insistence of the Mexican government?

- Why does China enjoy one-sided advantages, built into the very fabric of every "free trade" agreement?

When examining these controversies, the light bulb finally turns on for many skeptics who realize that the three presidential administrations since the passing of NAFTA have pursued strategies consistent with precipitating a merger of the United States, Mexico, and Canada. While this realization can be disconcerting, recent developments at the grassroots and at the policy and political leadership levels are encouraging. Among these is a strong grassroots reaction to recent outrages involving the policing of our border with Mexico.

Mexico Demands Prosecutions of U.S. Border Patrol Agents

Two separate cases have focused many Americans' attention on the Bush administration's lack of protection of our Southern border. In both cases, U.S. Attorney Johnny Sutton in El Paso decided to protect "the civil rights" of illegal immigrants, even when they were involved in smuggling large quantities of marijuana into the United States.

Sutton has close ties with President Bush. From 1995 to 2000, Sutton served as the criminal justice policy director, advising Governor George W. Bush on criminal law. Sutton has also served as chairman of the Attorney General's Advisory Committee, which plays an important policy role in making sure the Department of Justice carries out the president's objectives in federal criminal law enforcement.

On February 17, 2005, just south of El Paso, Border Patrol agents Ignacio Ramos and Jose Compean fired their weapons on a fleeing illegal alien, Osvaldo Aldrete-Davila. Aldrete-Davila had abandoned a Ford Econoline van filled with 743 pounds of marijuana. He was hit in the left buttocks by a shot that traversed his groin and lodged in his right thigh. The medical evidence was consistent with him being shot from the side, not from behind as some of his apologists had claimed. The Border Patrol officers both maintained that Aldrete-Davila was armed and that he had pointed a shiny object at them that they had taken to be a weapon. Aldrete-Davila escaped into Mexico and was picked up south of the Rio Grande. Since he was not apprehended on the scene and frisked, no one will ever know if Aldrete-Davila was armed that day.

Because they discharged their weapons, officers Ramos and Compean were convicted in a criminal trial and sentenced to eleven and twelve years in federal prison respectively. Aldreta-Davila retained a U.S. attorney and sued the Border Patrol for $5 million for violating his civil rights.

In another case, on April 14, 2005, in Rocksprings, Texas, one Ms. Garcia was an occupant of a speeding blue Chevrolet Suburban full of illegal Mexican aliens. The driver of the car attempted to run over Sheriff's Deputy Hernandez after he stopped the vehicle for running a stop sign. When Hernandez fired his weapon at the rear tires of the Suburban, a bullet fragment hit Ms. Garcia in the mouth, cutting her lip and breaking two teeth. Deputy Hernandez was convicted of violating her civil rights.

Both cases produced outrage in the United States. Why were the Border Patrol agents in federal prison while the illegal aliens were set free and, in one case, stood to gain as much as $5 million from a lawsuit contesting civil rights supposedly reserved for U.S. citizens? Why was a twenty-five-year-old deputy's sheriff sent to federal prison for shooting at the tires of a speeding van full of illegal aliens after the van refused to stop *and* the driver attempted to run him down?

In both cases, the explanation was the same. The Mexican consulate had intervened, formally demanding that the U.S. Justice Department prosecute the law enforcement officers to protect the "rights" of Mexican citizens illegally in the United States.[1] In both cases, President Bush and the Department of Justice under Attorney General Alberto Gonzales complied with Mexico's demands. Investigations in both the Gilmer Hernandez case and in the Ramos-Compean case began only after the Mexican consulate intervened and demanded that President Bush take action.

Congress was outraged when the Mexican consulate's involvement came to light. Representative John Culberson (R-TX) said he had "long suspected that Mexican government officials ordered the prosecution of our law enforcement agents." Culberson's explanation was that "Mexico wants to intimidate our law enforcement into leaving the border unprotected, and now we have confirmation of it in writing."[2] Congressman Ted Poe (R-TX) concurred. "The Mexican government should do more to keep illegals from Mexico from crossing into the United States, especially drug dealers, rather than be concerned about our border agents." Poe was angry at seeing written confirmation of Mexico's interference. "The U.S. Justice Department should not be working for the Mexican government," he told the press.[3]

Mexico's intervention into American border law enforcement is another indication of our gradual ceding of our sovereignty. Our government has lost the resolve to secure our borders and to enforce our laws. The message from the White House to the Border Patrol and all other law enforcement officers couldn't be clearer: When it comes to illegal aliens, "hands off." After the Hernandez case and the Ramos-Compean imprisonment, all law enforcement officers encountering illegal aliens now must consider the political ramifications of their actions. If they discharge their weapons in the wrong situation, even if the officer has legitimate reasons to fear for their life or the lives of others, they could end up in federal prison

Of course, this "chilling effect" was exactly what Mexico hoped to achieve. After these very public prosecutions of U.S. law enforcement agents, the borders with Mexico and Canada were wide open.

Meanwhile, President Bush has continued his plea that Congress enact a "comprehensive immigration reform" bill that has become a codeword for legislation that includes both guest worker and "pathway to citizenship" provisions. Many conservatives continue to argue that both provisions amount to an amnesty. The prosecution of the law enforcement agents in the Ramos-Compean and the Hernandez cases forced many Americans to conclude that President Bush's determination to pursue open border policies has trumped backing enforcement of immigration laws.

Supporting law enforcement on the border should be one of America's top priorities. In addition, America needs to remind Mexico that it is primarily their responsibility to keep illegal immigrants out of the United States. That Mexican officials can make demands on the Department of Justice shows how diminished our will to enforce our own laws has become.

A Free Trade Advocate Reevaluates

Another recent development in the globalist debate is the shocking reversal of Princeton economist Alan S. Blinder on free trade.

For decades, Blinder had been one of the most influential advocates of free trade, while he served as a vice chairman to the Federal Reserve Board and as he advised Democratic presidential candidates. Yet on March 28, 2007, the *Wall Street Journal* published a front-page article broadcasting Blinder's sudden warning that the very outsourcing he had advocated could place as many as 40 million U.S. jobs at risk of being shipped out of the country in the next decade or two.[4] The warning was shocking, as 40 million jobs is *more than double* the total number of U.S. workers employed in manufacturing today.

Blinder further acknowledged that the economic pain inflicted when workers lose jobs to foreign countries may be far more disruptive than free trade globalists have so far admitted. As an aide to President Clinton, Blinder had helped sell NAFTA to Congress. Now, as the impact of outsourcing reaches beyond manufacturing to include high-tech production and technologically driven service support, Blinder has begun to worry that millions of Americans have only begun to experience the painful dislocations and readjustments that the very free markets he advocated often demand.

Furthermore, Blinder worried that the U.S. educational system would not be able to readjust fast enough, if at all, to train U.S. youths to compete in the type of global market our free trade agreements have created. In this global market, Blinder argued, even having a college education might not be a "silver bullet," not when computer-proficient labor in countries such as India is available to do the job for a fraction of the cost. Blinder cautioned politicians that as the impact of outsourcing expands beyond blue-collar manufacturing to include college-trained specialists, the vocal political opposition should be expected to intensify.

Opposition in Congress Grows

The good news is that opposition to the emerging North American Union is also growing in Congress. On January 22, 2007, Congressman Virgil Goode (R-VA) introduced House Concurrent Resolution 40 (HCR 40) to express the sense of Congress that the United States should not engage in the construction of a super corridor system or enter into a North American Union with Mexico and Canada.

HCR 40 charges that "the actions taken by the SPP to coordinate border security by eliminating obstacles to migration between Mexico and the United States actually makes the U.S.-Mexico border less secure because Mexico is the primary source country of illegal immigrants into the United States."

The resolution calls for Congress to express its sentiment that:

1. the United States should not engage in the construction of a North American Free Trade Agreement (NAFTA) Superhighway System;

2. the United States should not allow the Security and Prosperity Partnership (SPP) to implement further regulations that would create a North American Union with Mexico and Canada; and

3. the president of the United States should indicate strong opposition to these acts or any other proposals that threaten the sovereignty of the United States.

Congressman Goode introduced two additional bills into the 110th Congress, with the intent of blocking the North American integration the Bush administration is pursuing. The two additional resolutions are:

- **HCR 18**. Expressing disapproval by the House of Representatives of the Social Security totalization agreement signed by the commissioner of Social Security and the director general of the Mexican Social Security Institute on June 29, 2004. Joined by 27 co-sponsors. Introduced on January 4, 2007.

- **HCR 22**. Expressing the sense of Congress that the president should provide notice of withdrawal of the United States from NAFTA. Co-sponsored by Congressman Walter Jones (R-NC). Introduced on January 10, 2007.

HCR 40 drew five co-sponsors, all Republicans: Representatives John J. Duncan, Jr. (R-TN), Virginia Foxx (R-NC), Walter B. Jones, Jr. (R-NC), Ron Paul (R-TX), Cliff Stearns (R-FL), and Zach Wamp (R-TN).

Anti-NAFTA Superhighway Bills

Opposition is growing outside of Congress as well. On February 20, 2007, Oregon joined a growing list of states that have introduced motions opposing the North American Union and NAFTA super corridors. The state legislatures of Arizona, Missouri, South Carolina, Utah, Virginia, and Washington have introduced similar bills.

The resolutions introduced into state legislatures suggest that the anti-NAU, anti-NAFTA super-corridor movement is taking hold of the grassroots. Fifty years ago, no message permeated the United States unless the mainstream media covered it. Today grassroots movements can become major political forces as the word spreads through talk radio and on the Internet.

There is no reason to go blindly into the brave new world of the North American Union if the American people take the time and make the effort to inform themselves. An informed American people will demand that their politicians come out of the shadows and openly state their support for SPP and the North American integration occurring under its watch.

Those who want to make sure a North American Union never forms have a responsibility to support those in Congress who are introducing resolutions against it. Ultimately, if Congress lives up to its oversight responsibilities, congressional hearings examining the SPP are in order. With its power of subpoena, Congress should be able to get from SPP a full range of documents that have not been forthcoming despite vigorous FOIA requests launched by Judicial Watch and others. This documentary record is crucial to form a series of inquiries so questions can be asked of SPP participants and other government officials in public hearings.

Call to Action

Americans *can* still affect the political scene. Most congressional offices are relatively small, generally with room for only about a half dozen staffers. Even a dozen calls on a particular theme to a congressional office are typically noticed. One hundred calls in any given day can virtually tie up the congressional receptionist, threatening to throw the office into communications gridlock. Opposition to SPP is growing in Congress. Now is the time to add momentum to that movement!

Demanding congressional legislation that will repeal NAFTA is the surest way to bring a halt to North American integration. If congressional hearings can be held on the proposed legislation, the many important issues of integration will be brought into the public eye. NAFTA passed not as a treaty, but as simple legislation, and consequently can be overturned as such.

With NAFTA and CAFTA repealed, congressional authorization for SPP will clearly be erased. But in order to ensure that this is the case, any bill repealing NAFTA and CAFTA should also include a directive that the United States withdraws from the three country "working groups" now organized under SPP.

Next, all U.S. "free trade" agreements need to be modified to eliminate structural discrimination against U.S. exports, such as the differential application of value added taxes by over 137 nations. Key to these modifications should be language that prohibits the abusive use of human labor. In the aftermath of the Civil War, the United States declared that exploitation of African American slaves was morally wrong and that African Americans should receive full rights of citizenship. America must similarly declare that exploitation of Chinese slaves or near-slaves is also morally wrong, along with the exploitation of any other workers anywhere in the world. If we have to pay more for electronics, clothes, and food, so be it. The exploitation of labor for the maximization of profit has never been a morally acceptable proposition and it should not be today.

Withdrawing from the World Trade Organization would also make clear to globalists that the United States is going to protect its own economy first and make sure our political institutions remain sovereign. The United States can participate in world trade without being a member of the WTO. Rather than complying with WTO rules that impose an authority over U.S. laws and regulations, we should seek to work with free trade partners who are willing to accept our renegotiated "fair trade" agreements.

Ultimately, the best way to stop the incremental movement from NAFTA into a regional structure of administrative law and regulations is to shut down SPP. The United States has survived for over two centuries without reforming our executive bureaucracy into three country "working groups." Dialogue with Mexico and Canada can go forward, but in order to change U.S. regulations, the executive branch must submit new laws to Congress or ask the Senate to ratify the required treaties. The president and the executive branch must return to an environment in which congressional oversight and public disclosure are taken as serious obligations. A transparent executive branch openly communicating with Congress and the U.S. public will eliminate any concern that America is unwittingly handing over its sovereignty.

Under SPP, we face a "brave new world" where our borders will be open to unrestrained immigration while our infrastructure is auctioned off to international investment consortiums, packaged as "public-private partnerships," and sold as necessary to maintain our "security" and "prosperity." If our infrastructure is a good enough investment that investment bankers can package deals for foreign investors, why can't deals be packaged for U.S. citizens and our existing state and local governments? Multinational corporate profits are important, but not at the expense of a strong U.S. middle class or the destruction of a manufacturing base within the United States.

Reject the SPP, oppose the NAU, and say "no" to NAFTA super corridors. These are the steps we must take if we are to avoid a regional government along the lines of the European Union. Those of us who want to preserve, protect, and defend a sovereign United States of America see our future in building a strong U.S. economy. The merger of the United States, Mexico, and Canada can be reversed. Yet the time to do so is growing short. At stake is nothing less than the continuance of an economically strong and politically sovereign United States that we cherish for ourselves, for our children, and for generations to come.

ACKNOWLEDGMENTS

PHYLLIS SCHLAFLY and Eagle Forum led the way with her insightful writings about the Security and Prosperity Partnership of North America, seeing the risks to U.S. sovereignty long before I began to write about the subject. Howard Phillips and The Conservative Caucus were also pathfinders in bringing attention to the risk that NAFTA could evolve into the North American Union. Both have encouraged me in my efforts to write and speak out on this topic.

In coauthoring *Minutemen: The Battle to Secure America's Borders*, I began to appreciate how the Security and Prosperity Partnership was a reason our borders remain wide open. In many ways, this book is a sequel to that work, explaining why President George W. Bush has been willing to sit by idly while the United States is invaded by millions of illegal immigrants each year. Having voted for George W. Bush twice, I have been deeply disappointed that I felt compelled to write *Minutemen* and now this book, in an attempt to turn the tide.

Robert Bluey, while he was an editor at *Human Events*, had the insight and courage to encourage me to write many of the early articles that led to this book.

As always, I am grateful to Joseph Farah who as founder of *World Net Daily* hired me as a staff reporter. Joseph must also be recognized as one of the first to issue the warning that SPP would take us further down the road to a North America. Much of this book began as articles I investigated first for the readers of *World Net Daily*.

I would like to thank the talented and dedicated team at World Ahead Media for believing in this message and working with us over the last year to shape the statement of that message. This book benefited tremendously from the professional editing team organized by Norman Book. Matt Anderson and Rachel Motte did a

ACKNOWLEDGMENTS

wonderful job polishing the text of this book. World Ahead president Eric Jackson, marketing director Judy Abarbanel and her intern Cara Eshleman, and editorial project manager Ami Naramor also contributed greatly to the outcome of this book, as well as cover designer David Fideler.

Finally, I am indebted once again to the constant understanding, quiet patience, and unwavering encouragement of my wife Monica and my daughter Alexis for supporting me in the countless hours required to finish this book.

APPENDICES

NORTH AMERICAN FORUM

CONFIRMED PARTICIPANTS

Forum Cochairs

- Dr. Pedro Aspe
- Hon. Peter Lougheed
- Hon. George Shultz

Canadian Participants

- Col. Peter Atkinson, Special Advisor to Chief of Defence Staff
- Hon. Perrin Beatty, Canadian Manufacturers and Exporters
- Mr. Peter M. Boehm, Assistant Deputy Minister, North America, Foreign Affairs and International Trade Canada
- Mr. Thomas d'Aquino, Canadian Council of Chief Executives
- Hon. Stockwell Day, Minister of Public Safety, Government of Canada
- Dr. Wendy Dobson, the Institute for International Business
- Mr. N. Murray Edwards, Edco Financial Holdings, Ltd.
- Mr. Ward Elcock, Deputy Minister of National Defence
- Mr. Bill Elliott, Associate Deputy Minister, Public Safety
- Dr. John English, the Cdn Centre for International Governance Innovation
- Mr. Brian Felesky, Felesky Flynn, LLP
- Mr. Richard L. George, Suncor Energy Inc.
- Dr. Roger Gibbins, Canada West Foundation
- Rear Adm. Roger Girouard, Commander Joint Task Force Pacific, Cdn Forces

- Major Gen Daniel Gosselin, Director General, International Security Policy
- Mr. James K. Gray, Canada West Foundation
- Mr. Fred Green, Canadian Pacific Railway
- Mr. V. Peter Harder, Deputy Minister of Foreign Affairs
- Mr. Paul J. Hill, Harvard Developments Inc.
- General Rick Hillier, Chief of the Defence Staff
- Mr. Pierre Marc Johnston, Heenan Blaikie
- Mr. James Kinnear, Pengrowth Corporation
- Mr. Harold N. Kvisle, TransCanada Corporation
- Hon. John P. Manley, McCarthy Tetrault LLP
- Mr. Ron Mannix, Coril Holdings Ltd.
- Mr. Ron Mathison, Matco Investments
- Hon. Anne McLellan, Senior Counsel, Bennett Jones
- Hon. Greg Melchin, Minister of Energy, Government of Alberta
- Ms.Sharon Murphy, Chevron Canada
- Ms. Sheila O'Brien, President, Corporate Director, Belvedere Investments
- Hon. Gordon O'Connor, Minister of Defense, Government of Canada
- Mr. Berel Rodal, International Center on Nonviolent Conflict
- Mr. Gordon Smith, Chairman, the International Development Research Centre

American Participants

- Ms. Deborah Bolton, Political Advisor to Commander, U.S. Northcom
- Mr. Ron T. Covais, President, the Americas, Lockheed Martin Corporation
- Sec. Kenneth W. Dam, Max Pam Professor Emeritus of American and Foreign Law and Senior Lecturer, University of Chicago Law School
- Mr. Dan Fisk, Senior Director, Western Hemisphere, National Security Council
- Sec. Ryan Henry, Deputy Under Secretary of Defense for Policy
- Ms. Carla A. Hills, Chairman and CEO, Hills & Co.
- Ms. Caryn Hollis, DASD (Acting) Western Hemisphere Affairs
- Mr. Bill Irwin , Manager—International Government Affairs; Policy, Government and Public Affairs, Chevron Corporation
- Mr. Robert G. James, President, Enterprise Asset Management Inc.
- Admiral Tim Keating, Commander, U.S. Northern Command

APPENDICES

- Mr. Floyd Kvamme, Chair, President's Council of Advisors on Science and Technology; Director, Centre for Global Security Research
- Dr. Ronald F. Lehman II , Director, Center for Global Security Research, Lawrence Livermore National Laboratory
- Mr. William W. McIlhenny, Policy Planning Council for Western Hemisphere Affairs
- Dr. Peter McPherson, President, National Association of State Universities and Land-Grant Colleges
- Ms. Doris Meissner, Senior Fellow, Migration Policy Institute
- Dr. George Miller, Director, Lawrence Livermore National Laboratory
- Mr. George Nethercutt, Chairman, U.S. Section of the Permanent Joint Board on Defense, U.S.–Canada (Security)
- Mary Anastasia O'Grady, Journalist for the *Wall Street Journal* (Area Specialist)
- Dr. Robert A. Pastor, Director, Center for North American Studies, American University, Washington, D.C.
- Dr. William Perry, Co-Director, Preventive Defense Project
- Lt. Gen. Gene Renuart, USAF Senior Military Assistant to Secretary Rumsfeld
- Mr. Eric Ruff, Department of Defense Press Secretary
- Sec. Donald R. Rumsfeld, Secretary of Defense, U.S. Department of Defense
- Dr. James Schlesinger, Former Secretary of Energy and Defense
- Mr. William Schneider, President, International Planning Services
- Secretary Clay Sell, Deputy Secretary of Energy, U.S. Deptartment of Energy
- Dr. Thomas A. Shannon, Assistant Secretary of State for Western Hemisphere Affairs
- Dr. David G. Victor, Director, Program on Energy & Sustainable Development, Center for Environmental Science and Policy
- Maj. Gen. Mark A Volcheff, Director, Plans, Policy and Strategy, NORAD-NORTHCOM
- Ms. Jane Wales, President and CEO, World Affairs Council of Northern California
- Mr. R. James Woolsey, Vice President, Booz Allen Hamilton

Mexican Participants

- Emb Andrés Rozental, (Mexican Coordinator) Mexican Council on Foreign Relations

APPENDICES

- Silvia Hernández, Former Senator and Chair of the Senate Foreign Relations Subcommittee on North America
- Mario Molina, 1995 Nobel Laureate in Chemistry
- Fernando Chico Pardo, CEO, Promecap
- Juan Gallardo, CEO, Grupo GEUSA
- Gerónimo Gutiérrez, Deputy Foreign Minister for North America
- Luis de la Calle, Consultant, Former Deputy Minister of Economy
- Agustín Barrios Gómez, Solutions Abroad
- Vinicio Suro, PEMEX
- Eduardo Medina Mora, Secretary of Public Security
- Carlos Heredia, State Government of Michoacán
- Jaime Zabludowsky, Consultant, Former Trade Negotiator
- Manuel Arango, CEO, Grupo Concord
- Jorge Santibañez, President, El Colegio de la Frontera Norte
- Luis Rubio, CIDAC
- Mónica Serrano, El Colegio de México, Senior Fellow Oxford University
- Arturo Sarukhan, Coordinator of Inernational Affairs, Campaign of Felipe Calderon
- Juan Camilo Mouriño, General Coordinator of President Elect's Transition Team
- Ernesto Cordero, Coordinator for Public Policy Issues Ambassadors/Consul General
- Mr. Carlos de Icaza, Ambassador of Mexico to the United States
- Mr. Gaëtan Lavertu, Ambassador of Canada to Mexico
- Ms. Maria Teresa Garcia Segovia de Madero, Ambassador of Mexico to Canada
- Mr. Thomas Huffaker, U.S. Consul General in Calgary (on DOD's list)
- Mr. John Dickson, Deputy Chief of Mission, U.S. Embassy in Ottawa (representing Ambassador of U.S. to Canada)
- Mr. Colin Robertson, Minister and Head, Washington Advocacy Secretariat (representing Ambassador of Canada to U.S.)

NORTH AMERICAN FORUM

CONFIRMED AGENDA

Draft Detailed September 1, 2006
Agenda
Internal Document
North American Forum
Fairmont Banff Springs Hotel
Banff, Alberta, Canada
September 12–14, 2006

Under the Joint Chairmanship of:

- The Hon. George Shultz, Former U.S. Secretary of State
- The Hon. Pedro Aspe, Former Finance Minister of Mexico
- The Hon. Peter Lougheed, Former Premier of Alberta

Continental Prosperity in the New Security Environment

Session I: Opening comments by Messrs. Aspe, Lougheed and Shultz

Session II: A Vision for North America: Issues and Options

Session III: Toward a North American Energy Strategy

Session IV: Opportunities for Security Cooperation in North America (Parts I and II)

Session V: Demographic and Social Dimensions of North American Integration

Session VI: Border Infrastructure and Continental Prosperity

Session VII: Roundtable Conversation with the Co-Chairs

Draft September 1, 2006
Agenda
North American Forum
The Fairmont Banff Springs
Banff, Alberta, Canada
September 12–14, 2006

Under the Joint Chairmanship of:

- The Hon. George Shultz, Former U.S. Secretary of State
- The Hon. Pedro Aspe, Former Finance Minister of Mexico
- The Hon. Peter Lougheed, Former Premier of Alberta

Continental Prosperity in the New Security Environment

Tuesday, September 12th

3:00 pm	Advance Registration
4:30 pm	Location: Heritage Hall
5:00 pm	Registration Location: Oval Room
5:45 pm	Opening and Welcoming Reception Location: Conservatory in the Cascade Ballroom
6:45 pm	Dinner & Keynote Address Location: Cascade Ballroom
8:00 pm	Keynote Address "Energy and Environment: a vision for North America" Dr. Mario Molina, 1995 Nobel Laureate in Chemistry

Wednesday, September 13th

7:30 am	Continental Breakfast & Registration Location: Alhambra Room
8:15 am	Keynote Address Hon. Greg Melchin, Minister of Energy, Government of Alberta
8:45 am	Q&A
9:00 am	SESSION I: OPENING COMMENTS BY MESSRS. SHULTZ, ASPE, AND LOUGHEED Location: Alhambra Room
	SESSION II: A VISION FOR NORTH AMERICA: ISSUES & OPTIONS Location: Alhambra Room

9:30 am   PANEL

           Moderator: Dr. Thomas A. Shannon
                            Assistant Secretary of State for
                            Western Hemisphere Affairs

           Panelists: Robert Pastor,
                            Director, Center for North American Studies,
                            American University

                            Roger Gibbins,
                            President & CEO, Canada West Foundation

                            Andrés Rozental,
                            Mexican Council on Foreign Relations

10:05 am   ROUNDTABLE DISCUSSION

10:45 am   BREAK

           SESSION III: TOWARD A NORTH AMERICAN
                            ENERGY STRATEGY
                            Location: Alhambra Room

11:05 am   REMARKS: Secretary Clay Sell, Deputy Secretary of En-
                            ergy, U.S. Department of Energy

11:25 am   PANEL:

           Moderator: N. Murray Edwards
                            Vice Chairman
                            Canadian Natural Resources, Limited

           Panelists: Richard George,
                            President & CEO, Suncor Energy Inc.

                            David Victor,
                            Director, Program on Energy & Sustainable
                            Development, Center for Environmental
                            Science & Policy

                            Vinicio Suro,
                            Planning & Evaluation Subdirector, PEMEX

12 noon   ROUNDTABLE DISCUSSION

12:45 pm   BREAK

1:00 pm   LUNCH
           Location: Cascade Ballroom

1:30 pm   KEYNOTE ADDRESS

Secretary Donald H. Rumsfeld, Secretary of Defense,
US Department of Defense

SESSION IV: OPPORTUNITIES FOR SECURITY
COOPERATION IN NORTH AMERICA—
Military-to-military cooperation
Location: Alhambra Room

2:30 pm   PANEL:

    Moderator: William J. Perry
                former US Secretary of Defense

    Panelists: Admiral Tim Keating
               Commander NORAD/USNORTHCOM

               Major General Daniel Gosselin
               Director General, International Security Policy

               Gerónimo Gutiérrez
               Undersecretary for North America
               Ministry of Foreign Affairs

3:05 pm   ROUNDTABLE DISCUSSION

4:00 pm   BREAK

SESSION IV: OPPORTUNITIES FOR SECURITY
COOPERATION IN NORTH AMERICA
(CONTINUED)
Location: Alhambra Room

4:15 pm PANEL:

    Moderator: William Schneider
                President, International Planning Services

    Panelists: Ward Elcock
               Deputy Minister of National Defence

               Eduardo Medina-Mora
               Secretary of Public Safety

               Ryan Henry
               Principal Deputy Under Secretary of
               Defense for Policy

4:50 pm   ROUNDTABLE DISCUSSION

5:45 pm   WRAP-UP OF DAYTIME SESSIONS

6:30 pm   RECEPTION
           Location: Conservatory in the Cascade Ballroom

7:00 pm   Dinner & Keynote Address

8:10 pm   Keynote Address
The Hon. Stockwell Day, Minister of Public Safety,
Government of Canada

Thursday, September 14th

7:00 am   Breakfast

7:15 am   Keynote Address
Floyd Kvamme, Chairman, President's Council of
Advisors on Science & Technology

Q & A—7:40 to 8:00 a.m.

        SESSION V: DEMOGRAPHIC AND SOCIAL
                    DIMENSIONS OF NORTH AMERICAN
                    INTEGRATION
                    Location: Alhambra Room

8:00 am   PANEL: Moderator: Andrés Rozental, Mexican
Coucil on Foreign Relations

Panelists

- Dr. Wendy Dobson, the Institute for International Business

- Carlos Heredia, Chief International Affairs Advisor to the Governor of the State of Michoacán in Mexico

- Doris Meissner, Senior Fellow, Migration Policy Institute

8:35 am   ROUNDTABLE DISCUSSION

9:30 am   Break

        SESSION VI: BORDER INFRASTRUCTURE AND
                    CONTINENTAL PROSPERITY
                    Location: Alhambra Room

9:45 am   PANEL: Moderator: Hon. John P. Manley, McCarthy
Tetrault LLP

Panelists:

- Thomas d'Aquino, Canadian Council of Chief Executives

- Carla Hills, Chairman & CEO, Hills & Co.

- Luis de la Calle, Consultor

10:20 am ROUNDTABLE DISCUSSION

11:00 am SESSION VII: ROUNDTABLE CONVERSATION
WITH THE CO-CHAIRS
Location: Alhambra Room
Moderator: Jane Wales, President and
CEO, World Affairs Council of
Northern California

Presenters:

- George Shultz, Co-Chair, North American Forum

- Peter Lougheed, Co-Chair, North American Forum

- Pedro Aspe, Co-Chair, North American Forum

12:00 pm Adjourn

12:30 pm Informal lunch

NOTES

Introduction

1. Christopher Booker and Richard North, *The Great Deception: The Secret History of the European Union* (New York: Continuum Books, 2003), 5.

2. Quoted in "Jean Monnet: 1888–1979," in "The history of the European Union: The European citizenship," at http://www.historiasiglo20.org/europe/monnet.htm.

3. Europa, "Gateway to the European Union," the official Internet portal to the European Union, in a year-by-year timeline entitled "The History of the European Union," at: http://europa.eu/abc/history/1950/index_en.htm. Referred to hereafter as "Europa Timeline."

4. Documented in "A Timeline of the EU," BBC News, October 29, 2004, at: http://news.bbc.co.uk/1/hi/world/europe/3583801.stm. Referred to hereafter as "BBC News Timeline."

5. Europa Timeline at: http://europa.eu/abc/history/1951/index_en.htm.

6. Europa Timeline at: http://europa.eu/abc/history/1957/index_en.htm.

7. *Great Deception*, 86–87.

8. Europa Timeline at: http://europa.eu/abc/history/1992/index_en.htm.

9. BBC News Timeline, at: http://news.bbc.co.uk/2/hi/europe/3583801.stm.

10. Closing words of Jean Monnet's memoirs, quoted by Booker and North, op. cit. 1, 1.

11. *Great Deception*, 3.

12. Ibid., 1.

Chapter One

1. George Soros, *The Age of Fallibility: Consequences of the War on Terror* (New York: Public Affairs, 2006), "Prologue," xv.

2. For a description of Vicente Fox's "20/20 vision" plan, see: The North American Forum on Integration (NaFINA), "NAFTA Timetable: North American Agenda," at: http://www.fina-nafi.org/eng/integ/ chronologie.asp?langue= eng&menu=integ.

3. Press Release, "Remarks by President George W. Bush and President Vicente Fox of Mexico in Joint Press Conference," Rancho San Cristobal, at San Cristobal, Mexico, White House website, February 16, 2001, at: http://www.whitehouse.gov/news/releases/2001/02/20010216-3.html. The quotations in this paragraph come from this source.

4. Press Release, "Joint Statement by President Bush and President Fox Toward a Partnership for Prosperity: The Guanajuato Proposal," White House website, February 16, 2001, at: http://www.whitehouse.gov/news/releases/2001/02/20010220-2.html.

5. Robert L. Bartley, "Open NAFTA Borders? Why Not? Immigration is what made this country great," *Wall Street Journal*, July 2, 2001. http://www.opinionjournal.com/columnists/rbartley/?id=95000738.

6. State Visit by Mexican President Vicente Fox, White House website, September 5–6, 2001, at: http://www.whitehouse.gov/news/releases/2001/09/20010905.html.

7. Press Release, "Joint Statement between the United States of America and the United Mexican States," White House website, September 6, 2001, http://www.whitehouse.gov/news/releases/2001/09/20010906-8.html.

8. Fact Sheet, Office of the Press Secretary, "U.S.-Mexico Partnership for Prosperity," U.S. Department of State website, March 22, 2002, at: http://www.state.gov/p/wha/rls/fs/8919.htm. See also: "Evans Cites Benefits of NAFTA, U.S.-Mexico Trade Ties: Commerce secretary attends Partnership for Prosperity workshop," U.S. State Department website, June 28, 2004, for a discussion of subsequent meetings, at: https://usinfo.state.gov/wh/ Archive/2004/Sep/13-451509.html.

9. "The Future of North American Integration in the Wake of the Terrorist Attacks," Council on Foreign Relations, October 17, 2001, at: http://www.cfr.org/publiction/4280/future_of_north_american_integration_in_the_wake_of_ the_terrorist_attacks.html.

10. Ibid.

11. Ibid.

12. "Council Joins Leading Canadians and Mexicans to Launch Independent Task Force on the Future of North America," Council on Foreign Relations, October 15, 2004, at: http://www.cfr.org/publication.html?id=7454.

13. Chairmen's Statement, "Creating a North American Community," Council on Foreign Relations, Independent Task Force on the Future of North America," March 2005, at: http://www.cfr.org/publication/7912/creating_a_north_american_community.html. A copy of the report can be downloaded as a PDF file free of charge at this CFR webpage.

14. Ibid., 6.

15. Ibid., 9.

16. Ibid., 5.

17. Joint Statement by President Bush, President Fox, and Prime Minister Martin, "Security and Prosperity Partnership," White House Press Release, March 23, 2005, at: http://www.whitehouse.gov/news/releases/2005/03/20050323-2.html.

18. The White House, "President Meets with President Fox and Prime Minister Martin," March 2005, at: http://www.whitehouse.gov/news/releases/2005/03/images/20050323-5_wf1g2507jpg-515h.html.

19. Joint Statement by President Bush, President Fox, and Prime Minister Martin, "Security and Prosperity Partnership."

20. Ibid.

21. Council on Foreign Relations, "Building a North American Community," Independent Task Force Report No. 53, May 2005, available to be downloaded as a PDF file at: http://www.cfr.org/publication/8102/building_ a_north_american_community.html. Referred to hereafter as "CFR Task Force Report."

22. Ibid., 1.

23. Ibid., 2–3.

24. CFR Task Force Report, "Foreword," xvii.

25. Ibid., 3.

Chapter Two

1. Testimony of Dr. Robert A. Pastor, vice president of international affairs, professor, and director of the Center for North American Studies, American University, before a hearing of the Subcommittee on the Western Hemisphere, U.S. Senate Foreign Relations Committee, "A North American Community Approach to Security," June 9, 2005, archived on the Council on Foreign Relations website, at: http://www.cfr.org/publication/8173/north_american_community_approach_to_security.html.

2. William F. Jasper, "The Panama Canal Giveaway," The New American, Vol. 15, No. 13, June 21, 1999, at http://www.thenewamerican. com/tna/1999/06-21-99/vo15no13_panama.htm.

3. The Heritage Foundation Staff, "Institute for Policy Studies," May 1977, archived on the website of The Heritage Foundation at: http://www.heritage.org/Research/GovernmentReform/IA2.cfm.

4. Robert A. Pastor, *curriculum vitae* published on the American University website at: http://www.american.edu/ia/pdfs/pastorcv.pdf.

5. G. Russell Evans, Captain USCC (Ret.), "Reflections on Defending America's Honor at the Panama Canal," NewsMax.com, December 11, 2006, at: http://www.newsmax.com/articles/?a=1999/11/1/131341.

6. Patrick M. Wood, "Globalization: The Final Demise of National Security," Part 1 of 3, NewsWithViews.com, March 11, 2006, at: http://www.newswithviews.com/Wood/patrick14.htm.

7. Robert A. Pastor, "North America's Second Decade," Foreign Affairs, January/February 2004, at: http://www.foreignaffairs.org/ 20040101faessay 83112/robert-a-pastor/north-america-s-second-decade.html.

8. Robert A. Pastor, Testimony before the Standing Committee on Foreign Trade and International Trade, House of Commons, Government of Canada, Ottawa, Canada, February 7, 2002, at: http://www.american.edu/ia/cnas/pdfs/PastorTestimonyCanada.pdf.

9. Robert A. Pastor, *Toward a North American Community: Lessons from the Old World* (Washington, D.C.: Institute for International Economics, August 2001), 149.

10. *Great Deception*, 428.

11. *Toward an American Community*, 152.

12. Ibid., 162.

13. Ibid., 168.

14. *Great Deception*, 427–428.

15. Quoted in "Euroquotes" at Liebreich.com, http://www.liebreich.com/LDC/HTML/Europe/06-Democracy.html.

16. *Toward a North American Community*, 8-14.

17. *Toward a North American Community*, xii.

18. Ibid., 2.

19. Ibid., 60.

20. Ibid., 100.

21. Ibid., 102.

22. *Curriculum vitae.*

23. Testimony of Dr. Robert A. Pastor before a hearing of the Subcommittee on the Western Hemisphere, U.S. Senate Foreign Relations Committee.

24. Ibid., 104–108.

25. Ibid, 123.

26. Ibid., 121.

27. Ibid., 133–135.

28. Ibid., 140–142.

29. Ibid., 143.

30. Ibid., 137.

31. W. P. Kinsella, *Shoeless Joe* (Mariner Books, 1999).

32. The North American Development Bank (NADB) was founded under NAFTA and has failed to achieve Robert Pastor's dream of developing Mexico. For the NADB home page, see: http://www.nadb.org/about/about_ origins.html.

33. Robert A. Pastor, editor, "The Paramount Challenge for North America: Closing the Development Gap," Sponsored by the North American

Development Bank, March 14, 2005, page 1, at: http://www.american.edu/ia/cnas/pdfs/NADBank.pdf.

34. Ibid.

35. Diana Estévez, "El provocador," published in the Spanish magazine *Poder y Negocios*, October 24, 2006, archived on the American University website at: http://www.american.edu/ia/cnas/pdfs/pastor_pyn_10242006.pdf.

36. Ibid.

37. Jerome R. Corsi, "North American Leader Says Merger Just Crisis Away," *World Net Daily*, December 15, 2006, at: http://www.worldnetdaily.com/news/article.asp?ARTICLE_ID=53378.

38. Ibid.

39. American University, Center for North American Studies, "About Us," at: http://www.american.edu/ia/cnas/aboutus.html.

40. "Triumverate: The only North American model parliament," on the website of the North American Forum on Integration (NAFI), at: http://www.fina-nafi.org/eng/triumvirat07/default.asp?langue=eng&menu=triumvirat07.

41. "Helms Forces Out Nominee for US Ambassador to Panama," published by the Nicaragua Solidarity Network of Greater New York, "Weekly News Update on the Americas," Issue #262, February 5, 1995, at: http://www.tulane.edu/~libweb/RESTRICTED/WEEKLY/1995_0205.txt.

42. Ibid.

43. George Putnam, "Casteñada Would-be Mexican President," NewsMax.com, October 21, 2005, at: http://www.newsmax.com/archives/ articles/2005/10/20/154003.shtml.

44. Jorge G. Castañeda, Campanero: *The Life and Death of Che Guevara* (New York: Vintage, 1998). See a description of Castañeda's book on Che Guavara, written on the Allen & Unwin website: "Description: This is an account of Che Guavara, a man who became a cultural icon to a generation," at: http://www.allenandunwin.com/shopping/ProductDetails.aspx?ISBN=9780747535201.

45. Ibid, in their jointly coauthored final chapter entitled "Is Cooperation Possible?" page 371.

46. Ibid., 3.

47. Ginger Thompson and Tom Weiner, *New York Times*, "Mexico Struggles for the Attentions of a Preoccupied U.S.," October 13, 2002, archived on the website of the American Immigration Law Foundation, at: http://www.ailf.org/pubed/pe_mex_article2.asp.

48. *Curriculum vitae.*

49. "Statement by Robert A. Pastor supporting John Kerry for Presi-

dent," National Press Club, October 6, 2004, on the website of the Peace Corps at: http://www.peacecorpsonline.org/messages/messages/2629/ 2024094.html.

50. Ibid., 56.

51. Ibid.

52. "A North American Community Approach to Security." The council referred to in this quotation is the Council on Foreign Relations, in their report entitled "Building a North American Community," issued May 2005. http://www.cfr.org/publication/8173/north_american_community_approach _to_security.html.

53. Robert A. Pastor, Testimony before the Standing Committee on Foreign Trade and International Trade.

54. "Building a North American Community." The PDF version of the task force report can be read at no cost on the Internet. http://www.cfr.org/ content/publications/attachments/ NorthAmerica_TF_final.pdf.

55. Jerome R. Corsi, "Senator ditches bill tied to 'superstate,'" *World Net Daily*, July 25, 2006, at: http://www.worldnetdaily.com/news/article.asp? ARTICLE_ID=51222.

56. Center for North American Studies, Summer Institutes 2005, a brochure archived on the American University website at: http:// www. american.edu/ia/cnas/pdfs/si2005yearbook.pdf. The photograph of Senator John Cornyn addressing the students can be found on page 8 of the brochure and the photograph of the students holding up a sign above the stone inscription can be found on page 10.

Chapter Three

1. Herbert G. Grubel, "The Case for the Amero: The Economics and Politics of a North American Monetary Union," Fraser Institute, 1999. http:// oldfraser.lexi.net/publications/critical_issues/1999/amero/section_03.html.

2. Herbert G. Grubel, Brief Biography, http://www.sfu.ca/~grubel/.

3. "The Case for the Amero."

4. Ibid., "Executive Summary." http://oldfraser.lexi.net/publications/critical_ issues/1999/amero/section_02.html.

5. Ibid., "The Institutions of a North American Monetary Union." http:// oldfraser.lexi.net/publications/critical_issues/1999/amero/section_03.html.

6. "Building a North American Community."

7. "The Case for the Amero, Institutions of a North American Monetary Union."

8. Ibid., "Efficiency Gains from Monetary Union." http://oldfraser.lexi.net/ publications/critical_issues/1999/amero/section_05.html.

9. *Toward a North American Community*, 115.

10. Ibid.

11. Robert A. Pastor, "A North American Community: A Modest Proposal to the Trilateral Commission," delivered in Toronto, Ontario, Canada, on November 1–2, 2002. http://www.american.edu/ia/cnas/pdfs/PastorTrilateral.pdf.

12. Ibid.

13. Wanfeng Zhou, "Dollar loses 11% vs. euro in 2006 on rate differential," MarketWatch.com, December 29, 2006. http://www.marketwatch.com/news/story/dollar-loses-11-vs-euro/story.aspx?guid=%7B0B752618-C0C6-4A B2-9C93-FB03CF1F38F0%7D.

14. Federal Reserve Board, "Discontinuance of M3," a Federal Reserve Statistical Release, March 16, 2006. http://www.federalreserve.gov/releases/h6/20060316/.

15. John Williams's blog is titled: "Shadow Government Statistics: Analysis Behind and Beyond Government Economic Reporting." http://www.shadowstats.com/cgi-bin/sgs.

16. *Newshour's* Ask the Expert, Financial Sense Online, "John Williams, Consulting Economist & newsletter writer," July 23, 2005. http://www. financialsense.com/Experts/2005/Williams.html.

17. John Williams, Interview with Author, November 30, 2006.

18. Ibid.

19. Bureau of Economic Analysis, U.S. Department of Commerce, "News Release: Gross Domestic Product," January 31, 2007. http://www.bea.gov/bea/newsrel/gdpnewsrelease.htm.

20. John Williams, Interview with Author.

21. Bob Chapman's *The International Forecaster*, at: http://www.theinternationalforecaster.com. Chapman publishes a bi-weekly expanded version of his newsletter to a base of approximately 100,000 subscribers around the world.

22. Min Zeng and Daniel Kruger, "Dollar Little Changed Against Yen After Fed Says Growth Slowed," Bloomberg.com, December 13, 2006. http://www.bloomberg.com/apps/news?pid=20601101&sid=a.whVEFiRP_Q&refer=japan.

Chapter Four

1. "North American merger topic of secret confab: Meeting on integration of U.S., Mexico, Canada brings together top officials," *World Net Daily*, September 20, 2006. http://www. worldnetdaily.com/news/article.asp?ARTICLE_ID=52063.

2. Jerome R. Corsi, "North America confab 'undermines' democracy: Attendee of high-level meeting says officials wanted to hide it from public,"

World Net Daily, September 21, 2006. http://www.worldnetdaily.com/news/article.asp?ARTICLE_ID=52074.

3. Ibid.

4. Mel Hurtig, Interview with author, September 20, 2006.

5. The Internet home page of the Council of Canadians can be found at: http://www.canadians.org/index.html.

6. "North American confab."

7. The Internet home page of the Canada West Foundation can be found at: http://www.cwf.ca/.

8. The Internet home page of the Consejo Mexicano de Asuntos Internacionales can be found at: http://www.consejomexicano.org/.

9. The Internet home page of the Canadian Manufacturers & Exporters can be found at: http://www.cme-mec.ca/national/template_na.asp?p=1.

10. The attendee list for the Banff September 2006 meeting was published by *World Net Daily* at: "Attendance List North American Forum," WorldNetDaily.com, September 21, 2006. http://www.worldnetdaily.com/news/article.asp?ARTICLE_ID=52079. The author interviewed Perrin Beatty on September 20, 2006.

11. "North American confab."

12. Attendee list, Banff, September 2006.

13. The agenda for Banff September 2006 meeting was published by *World Net Daily* at: "North American Forum Agenda," *World Net Daily,* September 21, 2006. http://www.worldnetdaily.com/news/article.asp?ARTICLE_ID=52077.

14. Jerome R. Corsi, "Top U.S. Official Chaired North America-Confab Panel," *World Net Daily,* September 28, 2006. http://www.worldnetdaily.com/news/article.asp?ARTICLE_ID=52186.

15. U.S. Department of State, International Information Programs, "State Department's Shannon Addresses 'Why the Americas Matter,'" USInfo.state.gov, September 25, 2006. http://usinfo.state.gov/xarchives/display.html?p=washfile-english&y=2006&m=September&x=20060920153623 GL nesnoM0.1765406.

16. Eric Watnik, Interview with author, September 20, 2006.

17. This and all quotations and citations from the preceeding three paragraphs are all from Shannon's speech, "Why the Americas Matter."

18. Judicial Watch, press release, "Judicial Watch Releases Pentagon Records from 'North American Forum' Meetings," January 29, 2007. http://www. judicialwatch.org/6123.shtml.

19. *The Rapporteur* notes were included in the FOIA papers released by Deborah Bolton, NORTHCOM Political Advisor. http://www.judicialwatch. org/archive/2007/POLADBoltonNotesBanff.pdf.

20. Judicial Watch press release, January 29, 2007.

21. Robert Pastor, Center for North American Studies, American University, Washington, D.C., "A Vision of North America and Issues and Proposals for Discussion," presented to the North American Forum at Banff, Canada. Obtained among the papers submitted by attending NORTHCOM Plans, Policy & Strategy Director Major General Mark Volcheff. All quotations in this section referring to Dr. Pastor's paper come from this source. http://www.judicialwatch.org/archive/2007/MGVolcheffNotesBanff.pdf.

22. White House Press Release, "The Security and Prosperity Partnership of North America: Progress," March 31, 2006.http://www.whitehouse. gov/news/releases/2006/03/20060331.html.

23. Ibid.

24. Ibid.

25. International Trade Association, "North American Competitiveness Council Launched," Trade.gov, no date on the article, at: http://www.trade. gov/press/publications/newsletters/ita_0606/shorttakes_0606.asp.

26. This was initially reported on Mexidata.info, although the article has since been removed from the site.

27. U.S. Secretary of Commerce Carlos M. Gutierrez, "United States, Canada and Mexico Launch North American Competitive Council," U.S. Department of Commerce Press Release, June 15, 2006. http://www. commerce.gov/opa/press/Secretary_Gutierrez/2006_Releases/June/15_US_Ca nada_Mexico_ NACC_Launch_rls.htm.

28. Chairman's Welcome, on the website of the Council of the Americas, at: http://www.counciloftheamericas.org/coa/about/pres_report.html.

29. Council of the Americas, "NCAA Membership List," posted on CounciloftheAmericas.org   at: http://www.counciloftheamericas.org/coa/ NACC/NACC%20Members%20Updated.pdf.

30. See Robert Pastor's comments at the press conference reported by the Council on Foreign Relations, "Building a North American Community: Report of the Independent Task Force on the Future of North America," May 27, 2005. http://www.cfr.org/publication/8138/building_a_north_american_ community.html?breadcrumb=default.

31. White House, "President Bush, President Fox of Mexico, and Prime Minister Harper of Canada in Press Availability," March 2006, at: http://www. whitehouse.gov/news/releases/2006/03/images/20060331-4_f1g8582b-515h.html.

32. White House, Press Release , "President Bush, President Fox of Mexico, and Prime Minister Harper of Canada in Press Availability," Fiesta

Americana Condesa Cancun Hotel, Cancun, Mexico, March 31, 2006, at: http://www.whitehouse.gov/news/releases/2006/03/20060331-4.html.

33. White House, "Security and Prosperity Partnership: Next Steps," March 31, 2006, archived on SPP.gov at: http://www.spp.gov/pdf/ security_and_prosperity_partnership_of_north_america_fact_sheet.pdf.

34. NAFTA Secretariat, "Overview of the Dispute Settlement Provisions of the North American Free Trade Agreement (NAFTA). http://www.nafta-sec-alena.org/DefaultSite/index_e.aspx?DetailID=8#chap11.

35. Adam Ereli, Deputy Spokesman, U.S. Department of State, Press Statement, "NAFTA Tribunal Dismisses Methane Claim," August 10, 2005. http://www.state.gov/r/pa/prs/ps/2005/50964.htm.

36. Senator Kerry is quoted in: Adam Liptak, *New York Times*, "NAFTA Tribunals Stir US Worries," April 18, 2004, archived on Bilaterals.org, at http://www.bilaterals.org/article.php3?id_article=91.

37. Task Force Report, "Building a North American Community," Council on Foreign Relations, May 2005, 22. http://www.cfr.org/publication/8102/ building_ a_north_american_community.html.

38. Robert A. Pastor, Testimony before the Subcommittee on the Western Hemisphere, U.S. Senate Foreign Relations Committee.

39. http://www.spp.gov/report_to_leaders/index.asp?dName=report_to_leaders.

Chapter Five

1. Richard N. Gardner, "The Hard Road to World Order," *Foreign Affairs*, April 1974, Volume 52, Number 3, 563.

2. "2005 Report to Leaders," Security and Prosperity Partnership of North America, June 27, 2005, at: http://www.spp.gov/report_to_leaders/ index.asp?dName=report_to_leaders.

3. Security and Prosperity Partnership of North America, Foreign Affairs and International Trade Canada, at: http://geo.international.gc.ca/can-am/ main/front_page/security_prosperity-en.asp.

4. *Alianza para la Sequridad y la Prosperidad en América del Norte, Secretaria de Economia, Mexico*, at: http://www.economia.gob.mx/work/snci/negociaciones/ tlcan/htm/selec.htm.

5. "Myths vs. Facts," Security and Prosperity Partnership of North America, at: http://www.spp.gov/myths_vs_facts.asp.

6. George W. Bush, "The Security and Prosperity Partnership of North America: Progress," White House Press Release, March 31, 2006, at: http:// www.spp.gov/pdf/security_and_prosperity_partnership_of_north_ america_ statement.pdf.

7. David A. Sampson, Deputy Secretary of Commerce, speech to the Canadian-American Trade Alliance, September 13, 2005, at: http://www.commerce.gov/opa/speeches/Dep_Sec_Sampson/2005/Septembe r/13_ Canadian-American%20Border%20Trade%20Alliance.htm.

8. "Myths vs. Facts."

9. Les Kinsolving, "'No EU in US' Tony Snow responds to warnings about North American superstate," *World Net Daily*, July 12, 2006, at: http://www.worldnetdaily.com/news/article.asp?ARTICLE_ID=51029.

10. Les Kinsolving, "'No EU in US' Tony Snow responds to warnings about North American superstate," *World Net Daily*, July 12, 2006, at: http://www.worldnetdaily.com/news/article.asp?ARTICLE_ID=51029.

11. "Documents disclose 'shadow government,'" *World Net Daily*, September 26, 2006, at: http://www.worldnetdaily.com/news/article.asp? ARTICLE_ ID=52164.

12. "SPP FOIA Documents," on StopSpp.gov, a project of The Minuteman Project, at: http://stopspp.com/stopspp/?page_id=11.

13. Judicial Watch, "Newly Uncovered Commerce Department Documents Detail "Security and Prosperity Partnership of North America": U.S. Government Working Groups & Business Leaders Seek to "Harmonize" Regulations with Canada and Mexico," Press Release, September 26, 2006, at: http://www.judicialwatch.org/5979.shtml.

14. For a description of the Homeland Security Council, see: "Homeland Security Council," White House website, at: http://www.whitehouse.gov/hsc.

15. Government of Canada, SPP Working Groups, at: http://www. psp-spp.gc.ca/overview/working_groups-en.aspx.

16 "SPP Security High-Level Working Groups, a document obtained by Judicial Watch under a FOIA request, at: http://www.judicialwatch.org/ archive/2007/dhs06-978spp14mar07_001.pdf.

17. U.S. Department of Energy, Office of Policy and International Affairs, "North American Energy Working Group (NAEWG)." http://www.pi. energy.gov/naewg.html.

18. "North America—The Energy Picture II," prepared by North American Energy Working Group, Security and Prosperity Partnership, Energy Picture Experts Group, January 2006. http://www.pi.energy. gov/pdf/library/NorthAmericaEnergyPictureII.pdf.

19. Canada Border Services Agency (CBSA), "Become a part of NEXUS," on the official CBSA Canadian Government website, at: http://cbsa-asfc.gc. ca/travel/nexus/elig-admis-e.html.

20. U.S. Customs and Border Protection (CPB), "NEXUS Program Description," on the official CPB U.S. government website at: http://www.cbp.gov/xp/ cgov/travel/frequent_traveler/nexus_prog/nexus.xml.

21. U.S. Customs and Border Protection (CPS), Free and Secure Trade Program (FAST), on the official CPB U.S. government website at: at: http://www.cbp.gov/xp/cgov/import/commercial_enforcement/ctpat/fast/.

22. U.S. Customs and Border Protection (CBP), "Secure Electronic Network for Travelers Rapid Inspection (SENTRI)," on the official CPB U.S. government website at: http://www.cbp.gov/xp/cgov/travel/frequent_ traveler/ sentri/sentri.xml.

23. The discussion of Mahmoud Youssef Kourani is drawn directly from: Jim Gilchrist and Jerome R. Corsi, *Minutemen: The Battle to Secure America's Borders* (Los Angeles, CA: World Ahead Publishing, Inc., 2006), 162–163.

24. Associated Press, "Truck's secret hold hid 2 tons of drugs," March 30, 2007. http://www.chron.com/disp/story.mpl/metropolitan/4676545.html.

Chapter Six

1. Susan Segal, President and CEO, Council of the Americas, published greetings in the brochure for the North America Works II conference held in Kansas City, November 30–December 2, 2006. The conference was titled, "Building North American Competitiveness." http://www.kcmo.org/ international/agenda-web.pdf.

2. Jerome R. Corsi, "Feds threaten Texas over superhighway funds plan," *World Net Daily*, April 27, 2007 at: http://www.worldnetdaily.com/ news/article.asp? ARTICLE_ID=55420.

3. "Comprehensive Development Agreement: TTC High-Priority Corridor," by and between the Texas Department of Transportation and Cintra Zachry, LP, dated March 11, 2005, archived on the TxDOT website at http://www.keeptexasmoving.com/pdfs/projects/ttc35/TTC-35cda_ signed_version.pdf.

4. The website of Cintra Concesiones de Infraestructuras de Transporte, S.A. can be found at http://www.cintra.es/.

5. The website of Zachry Construction Corporation can be found at http://www.zachry.com.

6. Group Ferrovial's website can be found at: http://www.ferrovial.com.

7. "#84 Rafael del Pino & family," Forbes.com, billionaire net worth calculated on share prices and exchange rates as of February 13, 2006. http://www.forbes.com/lists/2006/10/L4FC.html. The report on Rafael del Pino is part of a larger *Forbes* report: Luisa Kroll and Allison Fass, editors, "Special Report: The World's Billionaires," Forbes.com, March 9, 2006. http://www.forbes.com/billionaires/.

8. The website of the Macquarie Group can be found at: http://www. macquarie.com/uk/about_macquarie/index.htm.

9. U.S. Department of Transportation, Federal Highway Administration (FHWA), Public Private Partnership (PPP) Case Studies, "Chicago Skyway," on the FHWA website at: http://www.fhwa.dot.gov/PPP/chicago_skyway.htm.

10. U.S. Department of Transportation, Federal Highway Administration (FHWA), Public Private Partnership (PPP) Case Studies, "Indiana Toll Road," on the FHWA website at: http://www.fhwa.dot.gov/ PPP/indiana_tollway.htm.

11. Comprehensive Development Agreement: Oklahoma to Mexico/Gulf Coast, TTC-35, "Overview," March 11, 2005. http://www.keeptexasmoving.com/pdfs/projects/ttc35/final%20cda%20overview.pdf.

12. U.S. Department of Transportation, Federal Highway Administration and the Texas Department of Transportation, "Trans-Texas Corridor-35 (TTC-35). Oklahoma to Mexico/Gulf Coast Element," a Tier One Draft Environmental Impact Statement submitted pursuant to the National Environmental Policy Act, dated April 4, 2006. The EIS document can be read on the TxDOT TTC website at: http://www.keeptexasmoving.com/pdfs/deis_05/document/ttc35_signature_page.pdf.

13. Executive Summary of the following document: U.S. Department of Transportation, Federal Highway Administration and the Texas Department of Transportation, "Trans-Texas Corridor – 35 (TTC-35). Oklahoma to Mexico/Gulf Coast Element," a Tier One Draft Environmental Impact Statement submitted pursuant to the National Environmental Policy Act, dated April 4, 2006. The EIS document can be read on the TxDOT TTC website at http://www.keeptexasmoving.com/pdfs/deis_05/document/ttc35_signature_page.pdf.

14. The artist's rendition of TTC-35 can also be seen in the following document: U.S. Department of Transportation, Federal Highway Administration, article authored by Antonio Palacios, "Public Roads: Trans-Texas Corridor," July/August 2005. http://www.tfhrc.gov/pubrds/05jul/07.htm.

15. "Master Development Plan: TTC-35 High Priority Trans-Texas Corridor," published on the TxDOT website at http://www.keeptexasmoving.org/pdfs/projects/ttc35/master_development_plan/Introduction.pdf. See also: TxDOT, "Crossroads of the Americas: Trans-Texas Corridor Plan," June 2005, published by Corridor Watch at http://www.corridorwatch.org/ttc/cw-plan 0206.htm.

16. From the website of Corridor Watch at http://www.corridorwatch.org/ttc/map2002junepriority.htm.

17. *Kelo v. City of New London*, 545 U.S. 469 (2005), http://www.supremecourtus.gov/opinions/04pdf/04-108.pdf.

18. "Myth vs. Reality," in the "Get the FAQs" section of the TxDOT TTC website. http://www.keeptexasmoving.com/faqs/myth_vs_reality.aspx.

19. U.S. Department of Transportation, Federal Highway Administration, "TTC 35 Early Development Agreement," published at http://www. fhwa.dot.gov/ppp/ttceda.htm.

20. The Kansas City resolution declaring the name of the inland Mexican customs facility to be built in the West Bottom area to be the Kansas City Customs Port can be viewed on the website of the Office of the City Clerk, Kansas City, Missouri, at http://cityclerk.kcmo.org/LiveWeb/Documents/ Document.aspx?q=%2bSOiLiH6CV0JIMnyTK6Jav6tMSRgrBqP1uJ3dfIFWX3kFlAN% 2bx9mJ7AQvJb3w%2bBs.

21. Kansas City SmartPort website, "Two Worlds...One Route," a brochure available at http://www.kcsmartport.com/pdf/ SmtPrtOneRoute.pdf.

22. Kansas City SmartPort website, http://www.kcsmartport. com.

23. Documented on the website of U.S. Congressman Sam Graves, November 30, 2004. http://www.house.gov/graves/newsroom/113004b.htm.

24. Documented on the NASCO website. "Along the Corridor— September, 2005. Kansas City SmartPort Receives Federal Funding." http:// www. nascocorridor.com/pages/about/along.htm.

25. The website of the Kansas City Southern is www.kcsi.com. Kansas City Southern is a public company that trades on the New York Stock Exchange under the symbol KSE.

26. The NASCO website can be found at www.nascocorridor.com.

27. Kansas City SmartPort website, http://www.kcsmartport. com.

28. Ibid.

29. "About NASCO," on the NASCO website at http://www. nascocorridor.com/pages/about/about.htm.

30. A biography of Jeffrey N. Shane, under secretary for policy, U.S. Department of Transportation, is available on the DOT website, at: http://www.dot.gov/bios/shane.htm.

31. Jerome R. Corsi, "Plan for superhighway ripped as 'urban legend,'" *World Net Daily*, January 26, 2007. http://www.worldnetdaily.com/news/ article.asp?ARTICLE_ID=53950.

32. Ibid.

33. The website of the Owner-Operator Independent Drivers Association (OOIDA) can be found on the Internet at: http://www.ooida.com/.

34. Office of Public Affairs, U.S. Department of Transportation, "Remarks for the Honorable Norman Y. Mineta, Secretary of Transportation, North America's Superhighway Coalition Transportation Forum, Fort Worth, TX," April 30, 2004. http://www.dot.gov/affairs/minetasp043004.htm.

NOTES

35. Jerome R. Corsi, "It's Official: Mexican trucks coming," *World Net Daily*, February 23, 2007. http://www.worldnetdaily.com/news/article.asp? ARTICLE_ID=54411.

36. "Mexican truckers to hit U.S. roadways next year," *World Net Daily*, Sept. 1, 2006. http://www.worldnetdaily.com/news/article.asp?ARTICLE_ID=51779.

Chapter Seven

1. "NASCO Frequently Asked Questions," on the website of NASCO (North America's SuperCorridor Coalition, Inc.), at: http://www.nascocorridor.com/NASCO_FAQs_072706.pdf.

2. Home page, the NAFTA Superhighway Coalition, at: http://www.ambassadorbridge.com/nafta_case.html. Today the Ambassador Bridge boasts that it was the first private sector entity to join NASCO.

3. Federal Highway Administration, "Future Interstates on the National Highway System Designated by Section 1105 of ISTEA as amended," last modified May 2, 2006. http://www.fhwa.dot.gov/hep10/nhs/hipricorridors/hpcfitext.htm.

4. "I-69/TTC (Northeast Texas to Mexico," Trans-Texas Corridor on Keep-TexasMoving.com, last updated April 10, 2006. http://www. keeptexasmoving.org/projects/i69/.

5. "I-69/TTC (Northeast Texas to Mexico) Project Milestones," Trans-Texas Corridor on KeepTexasMoving.com. http://www.keeptexasmoving.org/projects/i69/milestones.aspx.

6. "I-69/TTC (Northeast Texas to Mexico) Environmental Study Timeline," on KeepTexasMoving.com, at: http://www.keeptexasmoving.org/projects/i69/timeline.aspx.

7. Louisiana Department of Transportation and Development, "DOTD I-69, SIU 15 Project Site," Interstate 69, High Priority Corridor No. 18, at: http://www.i69dotd.com/.

8. Ibid.

9. Louisiana Department of Transportation and Development, "Announcing Public Hearings," Interstate 69, High Priority Corridor No. 18, at: http://www.i69dotd.com/ProjectNews/SIU15_Public_Hearing_Flyer_061005.pdf.

10. Arkansas Department of Transportation and Development and the Arkansas State Highway and Transportation Department, "Interstate 69: Shreveport to El Dorado," the I-69 Project Management Team, URS Corporation, at: http://www.i69arkla.com/default.asp.

11. Mississippi Department of Transportation, "The Road to Our Future. Interstate 69. Mississippi's Top Priority: Update," at: http://www.

msdoti69.net/pdf/I-69final.pdf#search=%22I-69%20in%20Mississippi%
20%2 B%20Mississippi% 20Department% 20of%20Transportation%22.

12. Tennessee Department of Transportation, "Tennessee and Mississippi Announce Preferred Alignments for I-69 in Memphis Area," November 30, 2004, at: http://www.tdot.state.tn.us/news/2004/113004.htm.

13. Press Release, "Governor Fletcher Unveils I-69 Corridor Designa-
tion," Kentucky Department of Transportation, May 15, 2005, at: http://
kytcnewsroom.ky.gov/News/5-16-06.htm.

14. "I-69 Evansville to Indianapolis Tier 2 Studies," Interstate 69, on the
website of the Indiana Department of Transportation at: http://www.i69
indyevn.org/.

15. "Interstate 69, Section 9—From Hernando, MS to Millington, TN,"
on the website of the Mississippi Department of Transportation, at: http://
www.mdot.state.ms.us/news/projects/section9.htm.

16. "NHS Priority Corridors Description. High Priority Corridors on
National Highway System," Federal Highway Administration, U.S. Department of Transportation, last modified on September 15, 2006.
http://www.fhwa.dot.gov/hep10/nhs/hipricorridors/hpcor.html#l18.

17. Antonio Palacios, "Trans-Texas Corridor," Federal Highway Administration, U.S. Department of Transportation, July/August 2005, at:
http://www.tfhrc.gov/pubrds/05jul/07.htm.

18. http://www.fhwa.dot.gov/PPP/.

19. http://www.keeptexasmoving.com/projects/i69/.

20. "President Nominates Mary Peters as Transportation Secretary,"
White House, September 5, 2006, at: http://www.whitehouse.gov/news/ re-
leases/2006/09/20060905-5.html.

21. The corridor map on the North American forum on Integration's
Internet home page can be found at: http://www.fina-nafi.org/
eng/integ/corridors.asp?langue=eng&menu=integ.

22. The copy quoted in this and the following paragraph come from the
NAFI website at: http://www.fina-nafi.org/eng/integ/corridors.asp?
langue=eng&menu=integ#ouest.

23. The home page of the International Mobility and Trade Corridor Project
(IMTC) can be found at: http://www.wcog.org/ DesktopDefault.aspx?tabid=22.

24. *"NHS Priority Corridors Description. High Priority Corridors on National Highway
System," Federal Highway Administration, U.S. Department of Transportation, last
modified on September 15, 2006. http://www.fhwa.
dot.gov/hep10/nhs/hipricorridors/hpcor.html#l18.*

25. "Coalition Connection," the official website of the I-95 Corridor Coalition, at: http://www.i95coalition.org/about.html.

26. Mercator Advisors, LLC and Alan E. Piraski, a study prepared by Cambridge Systematics, Inc. and the National Chamber Foundation of the U.S. Chamber of Commerce, "Executive Summary: Future Highway and Public Transportation Financing," 2005. http://www.a-t-m.org/NR/rdonlyres/emuy zvpzbm4qg7qbut4dh7wid6zfe5hygqxx2spxnor5cxqyvbwm5nnw5hzrq6zsrnb7 ucm7ucskkilbibkfvoj72za/ExecSummPhaseIITransportationFinance.pdf

27. The transportation industry publication "Innovation Briefs" can be found at www.infobriefs.com.

28. "The Carlyle Group Establishes Infrastructure Investment Team; Industry Veterans Robert Dove and Barry Gold to Co-Head Eight-Person Team that Will Purchase Public Purpose Projects," March 10, 2006, archived on the Carlyle Group website at http://www.carlyle.com/eng/industry/l3-topnews-article3323.html.

29. Oliver Burkeman and Julian Borger, "The Ex-Presidents' Club," *The Guardian,* October 31, 2001 http://www.guardian.co.uk/wtccrash/story/0, 1300,583869,00.html.

30. Dubai International Capital, a subsidiary of Dubai Holding, "Private Equity Funds & Co-Investments," at http://www.dubaiic.com/portfolio.htm.

31. The information in this paragraph is drawn from: Dan Briody, *The Iron Triangle: Inside the Secret World of the Carlyle Group* (Hoboken, NJ: John Wiley & Sons, 2003).

32. "Carlyle Group to Begin Investing in Mexico," December 15, 2003, archived on the Carlyle Group website at: http://www.thecarlylegroup. com/eng/news/l5-news2691.html.

33. "North American PPC:2006. The Infrastructure Finance Conference," September 19 and 20, 2006 at the Waldorf Astoria in New York City, archived on the website of Euromoney Seminars at: http://www.euromoneyseminars. com/default.asp?Page=102&eventid=ELE795&eventmenu=true&eventpassed= false=brochure. A multicolor conference brochure listing the scheduled speakers and complete conference agenda is available to download on the site as a PDF file.

34. Ibid.

35. Euromoney Seminars, "PPP: The North American Public Private Partnerships Intensive Seminar," to be held March 19–21, 2007, in Miami, Florida. http://www.euromoneyseminars.com/default.asp?Page=102&eventid= ELE838&eventmenu=true&eventpassed=false=brochure.

36. Federal Highway Administration, "PPP: Public Private Partnerships," dedicated website at: http://www.fhwa.dot.gov/PPP/.

37. Ibid., "What is a PPP?" at: http://www.fhwa.dot.gov/PPP/defined. htm#1.

38. Ibid., "SEP-15 Program," at: http://www.fhwa.dot.gov/PPP/sep15.htm.

39. Ibid., "PPP Resources," at: http://www.fhwa.dot.gov/PPP/resources.htm.

40. Ibid., "PPP Agreements," at: http://www.fhwa.dot.gov/PPP/agreements.htm.

41. Jerome R. Corsi, "Foreign ownership of U.S. airlines?" *World Net Daily*, July 18, 2006, at: http://www.worldnetdaily.com/news/article.asp?ARTICLE_ID=51113.

42. Bryan Bender, "Military considers recruiting foreigners," *Boston Globe*, December 26, 2006, at: http://www.boston.com/news/nation/washington/articles/2006/12/26/military_considers_recruiting_foreigners/.

43. William R. Hawkins, "U.S. Defense Industry Succumbs to Outsourcing National Security," AmericanEconomicAlert.org, December 27, 2006, at: http://www.americaneconomicalert.org/view_art.asp?Prod_ID=2649.

Chapter Eight

1. Edward Timberlake and William C. Triplett II, *Red Dragon Rising: Communist China's military threat to America* (Washington, D.C.: Regnery Publishing, Inc., 1999), 197.

2. Hutchison Whampoa Limited's website can be viewed at: http://www.hutchison-whampoa.com/eng/about/overview.htm.

3. The Hutchison Port Holdings (HPH) operations at Lázaro Cárdenas are reviewed on the company's website at: http://www.hph.com.hk/business/ports/america/mexico/lct.htm.

4. The Hutchison Port Holdings (HPH) operations at Manzanillo are reviewed on the company's website at: http://www.hph.com.hk/business/ports/america/mexico/timsa.htm.

5. Diane Linquist, "Mexico plans an alternative to the jammed docks in L.A., Long Beach," *San Diego Union-Tribune*, August 14, 2005, at: http://www.signonsandiego.com/news/mexico/20050814-9999-1n14port.html.

6. Judicial Watch, "Complaint Requesting an Investigation of Hutchison Whampoa, Ltd's Actions To Gain Controlling Interest in Global Crossing Ltd., and Former Defense Secretary William S. Cohen's Activities As A Director of Global Crossing, Ltd.," February 27, 2002, at: http://www.judicialwatch. org/cases/85/globalwhampoa.htm.

7. For a view of the current status of Global Crossing, see: John J. Legere, CEO, Global Crossing Limited, "Who We Are and What Makes Us Different," on the company's website at: http://www.globalcrossing.com/xml/news/2002/january/28.xml.

8. Todd Bullock and Katie Xiao, "Bush Administration Says Review of Chinese Unocal Bid Premature," archived on the U.S. State Department's website at: http://usinfo.state.gov/eap/Archive/2005/Jul/19-919521.html.

9. Phil Brennan, "Chinese Company Continues to Encircle the World," *NewsMax.com*, June 13, 2001, at: http://www.newsmax.com/archives/ articles/ 2001/6/12/210339.shtml.

10. Joseph Farah, "Long Beach won't give up on COSCO," *World Net Daily*, September 21, 1998, at: http://www.wnd.com/news/ article.asp? ARTICLE_ID=16720.

11. Ted Bridis and John Solomon, Associated Press, "U.S. Hiring Hong Kong Co. to Scan Nukes: Li Ka-Shin is pretty close to a lot of senior leaders of the Chinese government and the Chinese Communist Party," posted on InformationLiberation.com, March 24, 2006, at: http://www. informationliberation.com/?id=8499%22.

12. The website for the Port Authority of San Antonio can be found at: http://www.portsanantonio.us/.

13. The website for the Free Trade Alliance of San Antonio is: http:// www.freetradealliance.org/. The Free Trade Alliance of San Antonio is a public-private organization that was created in 1994 to lead the development of San Antonio as a competitive "inland port" and international trade center.

14. The website of the Maersk Line can be found at: http://www. maerskline.com/.

15. The website for CP Ships can be found at http://www.cpshipping.co.uk/.

16. Free Trade Alliance San Antonio, "Port Authority and Alliance to Promote Logistics Corridor in China," March 2006, at: http://www. freetradealliance.org/newsletter/admin/e_nternationaldetail.asp?id=795&pag eno=.

17. Rick Alm, "KC SmartPort leads way in boosting foreign trade," *The Kansas City Star*, October 25, 2005, archived on the website of KC SmartPort at: http://www.kcsmartport.com/sec_news/media/articles/ boostingforeigntrade.htm.

18. Free Trade Alliance San Antonio, press release, "Port San Antonio, Lázaro Cárdenas & Alliance conduct 2nd corridor Marketing Visit to China," October 30, 2006, at: http://www.freetradealliance.org/releasesdetail. asp?id=2333&pageno=.

19. Jesus Cañas, Roberto Coronado, and Robert W. Gilmer, "The Face of Texas: Jobs, People, Business, Change," Federal Reserve Bank of Dallas, October 2005, at http://www.dallasfed.org/research/pubs/fotexas/fotexas_canas.html.

20. William R. Hawkins, "NAFTA 'Superhighway' Spells the end of NAFTA Countries Manufacturing Alliance," *AmericanEconomicAlert.org*, July 18, 2006, at: http://www.americaneconomicalert.org/view_art.asp?Prod_ID= 2508.

21. For a container ship slideshow, see: "Unloading a post-Panamax container ship," at: http://www.speakeasy.org/~peterc/nicaragua/dryca-nal/containr/shipng02.htm.

22. Autoridad del Canal de Panamá, "Vessel Requirements," January 1, 2005, at: http://www.pancanal.com/eng/maritime/notices/n01-05.pdf.

23. Eloy O. Aguilar, Associated Press, "President backs expanded Panama Canal," from *The Miami Herald*, April 25, 2006, archived at: http://www.latinamericanstudies.org/panama/canal-06.htm.

24. Joseph Curl, "'Equal access' urged for Panama Canal," *The Washington Times*, November 8, 2005, at: http://washingtontimes.com/national/ 20051107-113120-6068r.htm.

25. Council on Hemispheric Affairs, press release, "Expanding the Panama Canal: A Wider Canal or More Governmental Payola?" August 8, 2006, at: http://www.coha.org/2006/08/08/expanding-the-panama-canal-a-wider-canal-or-more-government-payola/.

26. See: Panama Ports Company, on the website of Hutchison Port Holdings (HPH), at: http://www.hph.com/business/ports/america/ panama.htm.

27. Michael S. Bomba, Center for Transportation Research, University of Texas at Austin, "Shifting U.S.-China Maritime Logistical Patterns: The Potential Impacts on U.S. Gulf Coast Ports," August 1, 2004, at: http://www.trb.org/ Conferences/MTS/4C%20BombaPaper.pdf#search=%22percent%20of% 20Chinese%20imports%20headed%20for%20east%20coast%22.

28. Bill Geroux, "Smooth sailing ahead?" VirginiaBusiness.com, September 2005, at: http://www.gatewayva.com/biz/virginiabusiness/ magazine/yr2005/sep05/port.shtml.

29. Terence Smythe, Baltic World Ports, "Heavyweight Boxing," at: http://www.thebaltic.com/supplements/World%20Ports/heavy.htm.

30. Drewry Publications, "Post-Panamax Containerships: The Next Generation," published August 2001, described at: http://www.drewry.co.uk/www/ Main.nsf/CatByPrCode/R042!OpenDocument&Page=Description.

31. Hong Kong Trade Development Council, "Post Panamax vessels: How big can they go?" http://www.tdctrade.com/shippers/vol24_5/vol24_ 5_seafr03.htm#.

32. Port of Oakland, press release, "They've Landed!—Port of Oakland Successfully Moves its Two New Giant Container Cranes Ship to Shore," March 12, 2005, at: http://www.portofoakland.com/newsroom/pressrel/ pressrel_180.asp.

33. Ibid.

34. Cambridge Systematics, "Effects of the Panama Canal Expansion on Texas Ports and Highway Corridors," October 2006, prepared for the Texas Department of Transportation, Government and Business Enterprises Division. http://www.dot.state.tx.us/publications/government_business_ enterprises/panama_summary.pdf.

35. Ibid.

36. Lockheed Martin's home page can be seen on the Internet at: http://www.lockheedmartin.com/wms/findPage.do?dsp=fnec&ti=100.

37. "Global Transportation Network: An Intermodal Information System," archived on the Transportation Research Board archives at: http://pubsindex.trb.org/document/view/default.asp?lbid=488070.

38. Savi Technology, Inc., press release, "Savi Technology and Hutchison Port Holdings Establish New Company to Deploy RFID Network to Track and Manage Ocean Cargo Shipments," April 21, 2005. http://www.savi.com/news/2005/2005.04.21.shtml.

39. Ibid.

40. Security and Prosperity Partnership of North America, "2005 Report to Leaders," at: http://www.spp.gov/report_to_leaders/index.asp?dName=report_to_leaders.

41. William R. Hawkins, "NAFTA 'Superhighway' Spells the end of NAFTA Countries Manufacturing Alliance," loc. cit. 16.

Chapter Nine

1. Lou Dobbs, *War on the Middle Class: How the Government, Big Business, and Special Interest Groups Are Waging War on the American Dream and How to Fight Back* (New York, NY: Viking, 2006), 92.

2. *Minutemen.*

3. *War on the Middle Class.*

4. Financial Management Service, A Bureau of the United States Department of the Treasury, "2006 Financial Report of the United States Government," released December 15, 2006, at: http://www.fms.treas.gov/fr/.

5. Associated Press, "Federal deficit shrinks early in budget year," December 12, 2006, posted on the website of *USA Today*, at: http://www.usatoday.com/news/washington/2006-12-12-deficit_x.htm.

6. John Williams, "Shadow Government Statistics: Analysis Behind and Beyond Government Economic Reporting," home page at: http://www.shadowstats.com/cgi-bin/sgs. All quotes are from a telephone interview on December 16, 2006.

7. TREA Senior Citizens League, "Social Security Agreement with Mexico Released After 3-1/2 Year Freedom of Information Battle." http://www.tscl.org/NewContent/102800.asp.

8. The U.S.-Mexico Social Security Totalization Agreement was signed by the U.S. Social Security Administration and the Mexican Social Security Institute in Guadalajara, Mexico, on June 29, 2004. For a copy, see TREA's website: http://www.tscl.org/NewContent/Totalization_Agreement.pdf.

NOTES

9. U.S. General Accounting Office, "Proposed Social Security Totalization Agreement with Mexico," September 2003. GAO-03-993. http://www.gao.gov/new.items/d03993.pdf.

10. Wayne M. Morrison, Foreign Affairs, Defense, and Trade Division, "China-U.S. Trade Issues," Congressional Research Service, Updated May 16, 2006, page CRS-2, at: http://fpc.state.gov/documents/organization/67147.pdf.

11. "China's $1 trillion question," *Asia Times*, November 17, 2006, at: http://www.atimes.com/atimes/China_Business/HK17Cb02.html.

12. Democratic staffs of the Joint Economic Committee and the House Committee on Financial Services, "Relying on the Kindness of Strangers: Foreign Purchases of U.S. Treasury Debt," Economic Policy Brief, November 2006, at: http://jec.senate.gov/democrats/Documents/Reports/foreigndebtkindnessofstrangers.pdf.

13. Elizabeth Stanton and Daniel Kruger, "Treasuries Rise After Report Shows Wholesale Inflation Slowed," Bloomberg.com, August 15, 2006, at: http://www.bloomberg.com/apps/news?pid=20601103&sid=aBeq5x4GXl5Q&refer=us.

14. Stuart Larkin, "Managing China's forex reserves," TheStarOnLine.com, August 4, 2006, at: http://biz.thestar.com.my/news/story.asp?file=/2006/8/4/business/15032426&sec=business.

15. Edwin Hsiao, "Taipei to launch United Nations bid at 61st Session of General Assembly," Taipei Journal, August 18, 2006, at: http://taiwanjournal.nat.gov.tw/site/Tj/ct.asp?xItem=23035&CtNode=122.

16. Jerome R. Corsi, "2007 economic forecast: Dollar decline, recession," *World Net Daily*, January 2, 2007, at: http://www.worldnetdaily.com/news/article.asp?ARTICLE_ID=53587.

17. Douglas B. Weinberg, Bureau of Economic Analysis, U.S. Department of Commerce, press release, "U.S. International Transactions: Third Quarter 2006," December 18, 2006, at: http://bea.gov/bea/newsrel/transnewsrelease.htm.

18. William A. Ward, Professor of Applied Economics and Statistics & Director of the Center for International Trade, Clemson University, "Manufacturing Productivity and the Shifting U.S., China, and Global Job Scenes—1990 to 2005," Clemson University Center for International Trade Working Paper 052507, August 4, 2005, at: http://business.clemson.edu/cit/Documents/Mfg%20Employment%20Working%20Paper%20draft%208%202005.pdf#search=%22us%20manufacturing%20jobs%20lost%20to%20china%22.

19. Wayne M. Morrison, Foreign Affairs, Defense, and Trade Division, "China-U.S. Trade Issues," Congressional Research Service, Updated May 16, 2006, p. CRS-2, at: http://fpc.state.gov/documents/organization/ 67147.pdf.

20. Senator Charles E. Schumer, New York, press release, "Senators Announce Bipartisan Effort to Force China to Stop Currency Manipulation," September 9, 2003, at: http://www.senate.gov/~schumer/SchumerWebsite/ pressroom/press_releases/PR01993.html.

21. Senator Charles E. Schumer, New York, Press Release, "Schumer Details Plan to Get Tough on China in Wake of Mounting Manufacturing Job Losses," October 20, 2003, at: http://www.senate.gov/~schumer/ Schumer-Website/pressroom/press_releases/PR02116.html.

22. Senator Charles E. Schumer, New York, Press Release, "Schumer to Lead Bipartisan Senate Delegation Trip to China in Latest Effort to Address its Unfair Trade Practices," March 15, 2006, at: http:// www.senate.gov/~schumer/SchumerWebsite/schumer_around_ny/record.cf m?id=259493&.

23. See, for example: M. R. Kropko, Associated Press "Impact of plant closings on cities," December 23, 2006, archived on *The Philadelphia Inquirer* website, at: http://www.philly.com/mld/inquirer/business/ 16303237.htm.

24. *News Roundup*, "China Auto Exports Doubled During '06," *Wall Street Journal*, January 2, 2007. See also: Associated Press, "China's Auto Exports Double in 2006," December 31, 2006, posted on *Forbes.com* at: http://www.forbes.com/feeds/ap/2006/12/31/ap3290571.html.

25. Thomas Lum and Dick K. Nanto, Congressional Research Service "China's Trade with the United States and the World," March 14, 2006, page CRS-3. http://fpc.state.gov/documents/organization/64475.pdf.

26. Mark Magnier, *Times* staff writer, "A soft sell on China trade," *Los Angeles Times*, December 16, 2006, at: http://www.latimes.com/business/la-fi-chinaecon16dec16,1,6713476.story?coll=la-headlines-business.

27. Remarks by Chairman Ben S. Bernanke, at the Chinese Academy of Social Sciences, Beijing, China, December 15, 2006, posted on the website of the Federal Reserve Board, at: http://www.federalreserve.gov/boarddocs/speeches/ 2006/20061215/default.htm.

28. James T. Areddy, "Yuan's Ascent Begins to Pinch Chinese Exporters," *Wall Street Journal*, January 3, 2007.

29. "China Estimates Growth in 2006 Was Likely 10.5%," *Wall Street Journal*, December 29, 2006.

30. Bill Gertz, "Analysts missed Chinese buildup," *The Washington Times*, June 9, 2005, at: http://www.washingtontimes.com/national/2005060 9-120336-4092r.htm.

31. "Report: China has deployed missiles giving it second-strike capability against U.S.," *Insight on the News*, posted July 31, 2006, at: http://www. insightmag.com/Media/MediaManager/ChinaMissiles_0.htm.

32. Reuters, "China's Hu calls for powerful, combat-ready navy," Dec. 27, 2006. http://today.reuters.com/news/articlenews.aspx?type=worldNews&storyid=2006-1228T032301Z_01_PEK173323_RTRUKOC_0_US-CHINA-NAVY.xml&src=rss.

33. "Exclusive Interview: Hunter Eyes Presidential Campaign," *Human Events*, December 4, 2006. http://www.humanevents.com/article.php?id=18286&keywords=Duncan+Hunter.

34. Statement of Terence P. Stewart, Esq., "Executive Summary," testimony to the Subcommittee on Trade of the House Committee on Ways and Means, May 17, 2005. Archived on the Internet on the House Ways and Means Committee website at: http://waysandmeans.house.gov/hearings.asp?formmode=view&id=4093.

35. Home page of the American Manufacturing Trade Action Coalition is: http://www.amtacdc.org/. Quotes are from a telephone interview the author conducted with Auggie Tantillo on January 24, 2007.

Chapter Ten

1. Samuel P. Huntington, *Who Are We? The Challenges to America's National Identity* (New York: Simon & Schuster, 2004), 338.

2. Embassy of the People's Republic of China in the United States of America, "Chinese middle-class families defined" (02/06/04). http://www.china-embassy.org/eng/gyzg/t127568.htm.

3. CANAMEX Corridor Coalition, "Statistics," a separate tabbed section on the trade group's website, at: http://www.canamex.org/statistics.asp.

4. Ramin Pejan, "Laogai: 'Reform Through Labor' in China," Human Rights Brief, Volume 7, Issue 2, 2000, on the website of Washington College of Law, American University, at: http://www.wcl.american.edu/hrbrief/07/2laogai.cfm.

5. Ibid.

6. The Laogai Research Foundation, Laogai Handbook: 2003–2004, Washington, D.C., 2004.

7. The Laogai Research Foundation, Laogai Handbook: 2005–2006, Washington, D.C., 2004, at: http://www.laogai.org/news2/book/handbook05-06.pdf.

8. Ibid., 3.

9. Ibid., 1.

10. Ibid.

11. U.S.-China Security Review Commission Policy Paper on Prison Labor and Forced Labor in China, at: http://www.uscc.gov/researchpapers/2000_2003/pdfs/flabpol.pdf#search=%22laogai%20Chinese%20prison%20labor%20camps%22.

NOTES

12. Congressional-Executive Commission on China, 2005 Annual Report, at: http://www.cecc.gov/pages/annualRpt/annualRpt05/2005_3c_labor. php?PHPSESSID=21be998b2d569a64fc4248361284a374.

13. *Xinhua News Service,* "Seventy-five percent of world's toys made in China," in *People's Daily* Online, February 17, 2006, at http://english. people.com.cn/200602/17/eng20060217_243653.html.

14. Asia Human Rights Commission, "'Made in China': Toys for Children by Children, This Christmas," January 1, 2003, at: http://acr.hrschool. org/mainfile.php/0108/37/.

15. Also, see: Hong Kong Christian Industrial Committee, "How Hasbro, McDonald's, Mattel and Disney Manufacture Their Toys," December 2001, at: http://www.cic.org.hk/download/CIC%20Toy%20Report%20Web%20eng.pdf.

16. David Matas and David Kilgour, "Report into Allegations of Organ Harvesting of Falun Gong Practitioners in China," July 6, 2006, at: http:// investigation.go.saveinter.net/.

17. Ibid., the PDF version of the report is available at: http:// investigation.go.saveinter.net/Kilgour-Matas-organ-harvesting-rpt-July6-eng.pdf.

18. Photographs of Michael Wolf can be seen at: "China: factory of the world," on DesignBoom.com at: http://www.designboom.com/contemporary/ toys3.html.

19. The photographs of Lewis W. Hine can be seen on HistoryPlace.com at: http://www.historyplace.com/unitedstates/childlabor/index.html.

20. For Jacob Riis photographs, see: *College Street Journal,* "Rediscovering Jacob Riis: Photographer, Journalist, Social Reformer," at: http://www. mtholyoke.edu/offices/comm/csj/020901/riis.shtml.

21. A special joint report by the National Labor Committee and China Labor Watch, "New Balance Goes to China—A Rare Glimpse Inside the Emerging New Corporate Order," February 2006, published on the website of the National Labor Committee, at: http://www.nlcnet.org/live/reports. php?id=105#Production. All information in this section regarding the New Balance plant in China are drawn from this source.

22. The LaSalle Bank website for the 2006 Chicago Marathon can be viewed at: http://www.newbalance.com/chicagomarathon/? cm_re=Homepage_Bottom %20right%20promo-_-Chicagomarathon. The information in this section was initially published as: Jerome R. Corsi, "New Balance 'pays workers 32 cents an hour," *World Net Daily,* September 7, 2006, at: http://www.worldnetdaily. com/news/article.asp?ARTICLE_ID=51875. *World Net Daily* contacted the LaSalle Bank Chicago Marathon for comment prior to publishing the story and the La-Salle Bank Chicago Marathon declined comment.

NOTES

23. "Fact Sheet: New Balance Athletic Shoe, Inc." found on the New Balance website at: http://www.newbalance.com/cms-service/stream/pdf/?pdf_id=4642506.

24. The information in this paragraph is drawn from: Lawrence Mishel, "Globalization that works for working Americans," Testimony presented to the U.S. House of Representatives Committee on Ways and Means, January 30, 2007 at: http://www.epi.org/content.cfm/webfeatures_viewpoints_ globalization_works_4all.

25. Ibid.

26. *Minutemen.*

27. American Manufacturing Trade Action Coalition, "U.S. Jobs in the Manufacturing Sector: Fewer in 2005 than Since 1950," posted on the AMTAC website at: http://www.amtacdc.org/tradestats/charts/pdf/1c4.pdf.

28. Ernest Hollings & Charles McMillion, "China threatens America's lead in technology," *Financial Times*, January 14, 2007. https://registration.ft.com/registration/barrier?referer=http://www.mbginfosvcs.com/cgilocal/OtherLinks.pl&location=http%3A//www.ft.com/cms/s/b355aaee-a40e-11db-bec4-0000779e2340.html.

29. Reported by John Ydste, "Fed Chief Issues Warning on Income Gap," National Public Radio, February 7, 2007. http://www.npr.org/templates/story/story.php?storyId=7235086

30. Reported by Jeanne Sahadi, CNNMoney.com senior writer, "Mind the gap: Income inequality, state by state," January 27, 2006. http://money.cnn.com/2006/01/25/news/economy/income_gap/index.htm#table.

31. Remarks by Chairman Ben S. Bernanke, "The Level and Distribution of Economic Well-Being," Before the Greater Omaha Chamber of Commerce, Omaha, Nebraska, February 7, 2007. http://www.federalreserve.gov/BoarDocs/Speeches/2007/20070206/default.htm.

Conclusion

1. Jerome R. Corsi, "Mexico demanded U.S. prosecute sheriff, agents," *World Net Daily*, February 13, 2007. http://www.worldnetdaily.com/news/article.asp?ARTICLE_ID=54243.

2. Ibid.

3. Ibid.

4. David Wessel and Bob Davis, "Pain From Free Trade Spurs Second Thoughts. Mr. Blinder's Shift Spotlights Warnings of Deeper Downside," *Wall Street Journal*, March 28, 2007.

INDEX